For L. Bryce Boyer, M.D., and Harold F. Searles, M.D.,
two giants in the treatment of extremely regressed patients,
who directly and indirectly encouraged me
to spend a major part of my professional, clinical life
studying this type of patient.

The Infantile
Psychotic Self
and Its Fates

The Infantile Psychotic Self and Its Fates

Understanding and Treating Schizophrenics and Other Difficult Patients

Vamık D. Volkan, M.D.

JASON ARONSON INC.
Northvale, New Jersey
London

This book was set in 10 point Bookman by TechType of Upper Saddle River, New Jersey, and printed by Haddon Craftsmen in Scranton, Pennsylvania.

Library of Congress Cataloging-in-Publication Data

Volkan, Vamık D., 1932–
    The infantile psychotic self and its fates : understanding and
treating schizophrenics and other difficult patients / by Vamık D.
Volkan.
        p. cm.
    Includes bibliographical references and index.
    ISBN 1-56821-379-4
    1. Psychoses. 2. Regression (Psychology) 3. Psychodynamic
psychotherapy. I. Title.
    [DNLM: 1. Psychotic Disorders—psychology. 2. Psychotic
Disorders—therapy. 3. Psychoanalytic Therapy. 4. Schizophrenic
Psychology. 5. Regression (Psychology)   WM 200 V916i 1995]
RC512.V65   1995
616.89—dc20
DNLM/DLC
for Library of Congress   94-34516

Manufactured in the United States of America. Jason Aronson Inc. offers books and cassettes. For information and catalog write to Jason Aronson Inc., 230 Livingston Street, Northvale, New Jersey 07647.

Contents

Foreword

This new book by Dr. Vamık Volkan is a masterpiece that will doubtlessly become an essential text for psychiatrists, psychoanalysts, and other psychotherapists treating severely regressed patients. Dr. Volkan offers highly original clinical, theoretical, and technical proposals through his exploration of the inner worlds of those who are schizophrenic and those who have psychotic cores without being schizophrenic, and the psychoanalytic psychotherapies appropriate for the modification of their psychotic cores. His wide experience is clearly evident here, and I'm sure that every reader will be fascinated as he guides us through the mysterious labyrinths of the mind, where we discover how the psychotic self is formed, encapsulated, revisited, and transformed.

Writing from a metapsychological and technical point of view, Volkan demonstrates the importance of human interaction in the creation of the psychic structure; that is, human development is not only and absolutely determined by genetic or neurochemical factors. We also require human interaction, especially the experiences typically *channeled*, to use Volkan's metaphor, between mother and child, for the birth and subsequent development of a healthy psychic structure.

Researchers of infant–mother relationships agree (as noted in the Mother and Baby Observations Congress, September 1994, Toulouse, France) that the greatest part of the baby's mind is formed by, and thus depends on, what is in his or her environment—the roles of the mother, father, or other caregivers and the affects received. The latent biological and genetic factors within the baby can only be awakened by human stimulus—they are only *potentials*. When malignant or traumatic experiences are channeled to the child, unworkable early conflicts in object relations may result, thereby precluding the evolution of self- and object representations and the development of associated ego functions to more mature levels. Under these circumstances, a fragile psychic organization, which Volkan calls the *infantile psychotic self*, is created and is saturated with unnameable "bad" affects.

Volkan believes that several possibilities face the infantile psychotic self thereafter. In the child it may shrink and be replaced by a new core, or it may dominate, resulting in the likelihood of childhood schizophrenia. In the adult, the infantile psychotic self can be present in three different forms: it is encapsulated by a healthier self, but still exerts influence on the healthier self through "cracks," yet does not cause a generalized psychotic state; it is ineffectively and only partially encapsulated, and therefore significantly absorbed into the healthier self, causing a psychotic personality organization; or, encapsulation breaks down and the healthier self is replaced by a less effective one, resulting in prototypical adult schizophrenia.

Volkan believes that in prototypical adult schizophrenia, the shattering of the healthier self is accompanied by terror of this loss, and a new, weaker self is created in an attempt to overcome the infantile psychotic core once again. This new self, called the adult psychotic self, is *more* closely influenced by the infantile psychotic core, however, and is characterized by a break with reality associated with primitive perceptual-cognitive-motor processes and primitive defense mechanisms. The adult psychotic self does not exactly replicate the infantile psychotic self since it assimilates other and different processes, fantasies, identifications and primitive defense mechanisms. When Volkan describes the infantile and adult psychotic selves, they are not concrete, real entities lodged in a person's psychic organization, but psychodynamic entities that *change* according to the nature of the affects with which they are saturated. In my opinion, this theoretical approach to the description of the role of the psychotic mechanisms is important, not only in Volkan's theory, but in the technical field. In terms of treatment, all of us who work with severly disturbed and psychotic patients know that such structures can be changed if we work intensely with the patients and use intensive psychoanalytic and psychiatric treatment.

Volkan's book is *not* focused on phenomenology or clinical classification. It is a dynamic way of looking at severely disturbed and psychotic patients through clinical cases presented in their totality rather than as short vignettes. These clinical cases are explorations into the patients' inner worlds and psychic realities, and are the product of the detailed collection of data during numerous sessions and transference manifestations. I absolutely agree with Volkan that the presentation of clinical cases in depth, based in the transference, are the key to understanding effective psychoanalysis—a method completely distinct from the phenomenological and distant way of describing a case from the outside, as adopted by psychiatrists from the last century.

Important aspects of Volkan's theories came to life while he was the head of the Gender Identity Clinic at the University of Virginia, where he attended hundreds of individuals seeking sexual reassignment surgery. Researchers directed by the author concluded that the dominant cause of transsexual syndrome cannot be attributed to biological defect or malfunction. Instead, Volkan believes that transsexual patients' focalized desire to belong to the opposite sex represents a unique manifestation of their infantile psychotic selves; an attempt to modify the "bad" affects in the infantile psychotic self, and early mother–infant fusion that it contains, so that the new self is contaminated only with pleasurable "good" affects. Volkan returns to his metaphor of the *channel* to elaborate the cause of the syndrome. Early mother–infant experiences, especially depression in the mother as well as her unconscious fantasies that the infant is essential for her psychic and bodily existence, establish the true transsexual's infantile psychotic self. Actual trauma, usually at the oedipal age, later organizes the nature of the patient's clinical picture. Like Charles Socarides, who also wrote on this subject, Volkan believes that very few transsexuals seeking surgery are actually schizophrenic.

The reader will also find original theories in the beautifully detailed clinical cases presented in this book. Volkan does not purport to be a philosopher, but he is a master clinician precisely because he takes empirical data from the clinical practice and constructs his theories from it. The clinical description of the Attis case is an outstanding example in which we follow the fate of the infantile psychotic self over a lifetime. The young boy's finger was cut off by his older brother while chopping wood and preserved in a bottle by his mother. The patient's acute schizophrenic crisis at the age of 38 brought him to therapy, after which Volkan illustrates the patient's combination of psychotic personality organization and sporadic episodes of schizophrenia, as well as an evolution of a healthier self.

Another fascinating case is that of Carla/Carlos, a clinical case that will become indispensable reading for those studying true transsexuals. The Dogman is a case I had the privilege of consulting on during a visit to the United States, and is especially useful when studying psychopathologies. The final case is that of Jane, a young woman who sought treatment after being diagnosed as schizophrenic, but was eventually able to reach a psychoanalytic position with the analyst and ultimately termination.

Regarding the treatment of countertransference, the author develops his belief that the analyst should be better equipped to use his feelings in response to patients' primitive projections. Unfortunately, Volkan points out, not all psychoanalytic institutes provide the necessary training in the technical handling of countertransference. He agrees with Bryce Boyer, whose seminal papers on the subject have inspired psychoanalysts all over the world, that countertransference problems pose perhaps the greatest threat to the psychoanalytic treatment of regressed patients, and that the analyst needs to use his countertransference feelings as a signal for exploration of the therapeutic process and to recognize their use as a therapeutic tool.

I also agree that it is exceedingly important to write about our countertransference in a clinical description of a severely disturbed patient. Countertransference is a wonderful tool with which to discover the deepest structures and fantasies of such patients. Countertransference is today what dreams were for Freud—the best avenue to the unconscious and the deepest structures of the mind, and vital in transforming a patient's regression from chaotic to therapeutic.

In his special dedication to his great influences, Bryce Boyer and Harold Searles, Volkan hails them as "two giants in the treatment of severely regressed patients." This is typical of the warm, affectionate, and appreciative side of Volkan. To be a good psychoanalyst, it is also necessary to be a good person.

David Rosenfeld, M.D.
Buenos Aires, Argentina

Acknowledgments

During the last three decades Mrs. Virginia Kennan has edited the majority of the books I have written, collaborated on, or edited. She continues to challenge me intellectually and to help me sharpen my thinking. Once more I take great pleasure in thanking her for assisting me on this project. Bruce Edwards, editor at the Center for the Study of Mind and Human Interaction, and my former administrative assistant, Mrs. Lee Ann Fargo, worked on the manuscript beyond the call of duty, and I thank them also.

William Greer, Ph.D., of Hampton, Virginia, and As'ad Masri, M.D., of Petersburg, Virginia, collaborated with me in describing the cases of the Dogman and Carla/Carlos, respectively. The case of the female student, Arja, who had a habit of covering the mirrors and reflecting surfaces in her intimate environment, was provided by Margaretha Hupa, clinical psychologist and psychotherapist at the Finnish Student Health Service, Turku, Finland. The case of Mrs. L. was provided by James Stoeri, Ph.D., of New York City. I acknowledge the kindness of these colleagues with gratitude.

Introduction to Infantile and Adult Psychotic Selves

An estimated two million people in the United States have been diagnosed as schizophrenic, and there are, no doubt, many unidentified others who have psychotic cores and try, not always successfully, to control and hide them. According to epidemiological data, the occurrence of schizophrenia is roughly the same throughout the world, although there are certain regions for which reliable data are unavailable (Alanen 1993). This book explores the inner worlds of those who are schizophrenic and those who have psychotic cores but are not schizophrenic and discusses the psychoanalytic psychotherapy appropriate for the modification of their psychotic cores.

THE INFANTILE PSYCHOTIC SELF

To understand the clinical picture of those who go through life severely regressed without undergoing therapy and those who have deficient psychic organizations, we must consider genetic (biological) and physiological endowment along with nurture factors and the ways in which these individuals have internalized experience. Freud's (1914a) remark that "disposition and experience . . . are linked up in an indissoluble etiological unity" (p. 18) is even more applicable to regressed and undeveloped patients. Any discussion of nature/nurture should take into account the channeling of genetic (biological) and physiological factors in the mother–child interaction. Traumatic or growth-stimulating early experiences with the environment, culture, and education and their contribution to the child's founding of self- and object representations and the evolution of ego functions should also be considered. Furthermore, the developing child contributes to the mother–child experiences by modifying them with drive derivatives and unconscious fantasies. The mother and other caregivers also have unconscious fantasies for the infant, and they function as vessels for intergenerational transmission of psychological influences (Apprey 1993a,b, Rogers 1979, Volkan 1981a, 1987, Volkan and Ast 1992, 1994).

The term *channeling* serves to point out an analogy between a child's birth and the subsequent birth of a formed psychic structure. Activation of the species-specific mental function potentials (Tähkä 1993) of the infant depends on the relationships he has with crucial others in the environment. Once activated, these develop into mental phenomena.

The infant's environment is restricted to the mother and any of her surrogates who provide mothering functions. The environment expands slowly, and in some cases what passes through the channel is overlaid by genetically and physiologically flawed ingredients; in others, psychologically flawed ingredients dominate. In early life, ego deficiencies caused by genetic (biological), physiological, psychological, and environmental factors lead to conflict in object relations. Conversely, unworkable early conflicts in object relations preclude the evolution of self- and object representations and the development of associated ego functions to more mature levels. Under these circumstances a fragile psychic organization, which I call the *infantile psychotic self* (Volkan 1994a), is created and is saturated with unnamable "bad" affects. In our adult language we refer to these "bad" affects with terms such as *anaclitic depression, emptiness,* or *rage.* Tensions in object relations conflicts associated with the infantile psychotic self arise from difficulty in the ability to differentiate self-representations from object representations and one object representation from another. In contrast to a "normal" and ordinary infantile self-representation, the infantile psychotic self does not evolve and reach a more mature level at which the differentiation of self-representation from object representations and one object representation from another becomes stable, and at which unnamable "bad" affects are tamed.

The infantile psychotic self can also be formed through regression, which has to take place in the developmental years. The original psychic core may be "normal": it contains fused self- and object representations that are libidinally saturated. Such a core can begin to assimilate and sustain both "good" and "bad" self- and object representations and grow. It reaches as far as levels of differentiation of previously fused self- and object representations and maturation of associated ego functions. But an unbearable trauma (e.g., incest or object loss without suitable substitutes) can shatter the evolved psychic core and saturate it with "bad," aggressively determined affects. This causes the regressive appearance of an infantile psychotic self.

The ultimate fate of an infantile psychotic self, whether it is formed originally or appears regressively, is uncertain as a child grows and develops; it may virtually shrink and disappear as the child evolves a new core, or it may dominate personality development from infancy, in which case childhood schizophrenia may be anticipated. In other cases, other parts of the self evolve along with more mature ego mechanisms that surround the infantile psychotic self, which will persist in an encapsulated fashion (D. Rosenfeld 1992, H. Rosenfeld 1965, Volkan 1976) in the background and make the individual vulnerable to schizophrenia as a teenager or an adult. In other cases, the infantile psychotic self, which has existed as if it were a fossil, suddenly comes alive without causing schizophrenia.

Someone with a good reputation and seemingly well adapted to life, although possibly thought of as neurotic, will suddenly exhibit bizarre but focalized psychotic behavior, either transient or recurring in the absence of treatment.

In yet other cases, the infantile psychotic self is never turned into a fossil and is never totally encapsulated. Unlike schizophrenia, it does not cause a generalized psychotic state; however, it leads to the formation of a *psychotic personality organization* often associated with sexual or aggressive perversions and/or psychosomatic manifestations. The individual's primitive personality traits (e.g., paranoid attitudes, habitual and involuntary sexual or aggressive expressions, hypochondria, and psychosomatic conditions) deal with the influence of the infantile psychotic self along with his or her high-level compromise formations. People with such a personality organization seem "normal" in their day-to-day interactions with those around them, but they have secret lives in which they experience the unrepressed demands of and responses to their infantile psychotic selves. They are aware of inner forces not apparent to others, in effect leading double lives. They are not like the typical person with borderline personality organization, who uses a steady splitting mechanism supported by denial, devaluations, idealization, and projective identification to separate libidinally invested self- and object representations (and persons and things associated with them) from aggressively invested items. The individual with a psychotic personality organization lives a secret life dominated by self- and object fusions, paranoid fears, bizarre sexual and aggressive acts, and primitive defenses, along with a life reflecting a more mature, or seemingly more mature, self. The main task of the ego mechanisms associated with the mature part is to try to keep control, as though a disturbed, primitive, fantasy-ridden infant/child is living in the same skin with a protective adult.

SCHIZOPHRENIA AND THE ADULT PSYCHOTIC SELF

Schizophrenia in the teens and in adult life is caused not by simple regression but by the loss of the ego's maintenance mechanisms that mask the infantile psychotic self and support the existing adult sense of self, which may or may not reflect a psychotic personality organization. At some point it becomes no longer possible to contain the infantile psychotic self and keep it encapsulated due to some external situation such as loss, an internal situation such as the second individuation of the adolescent passage (Blos 1979), or a psychosomatic situation such as hormonal changes and the mental conflicts they engender. The individual will then experience terror caused by dread of losing his existing sense of self. A patient described this terror:

> It's like all my cells are exploded over the universe and I live in each of those millions and millions of nuclei, shooting in every direction. In the midst of all this, how could I possibly deal with the concrete, even tie my shoelaces, much less find my shoes? [Glass 1989, p. 37]

Pao (1977, 1979) called this terror *organismic panic*, reflecting Mahler's (1968) designation of *organismic distress*, which she defined as that psychological state of high tension experienced by an infant for whom no relief is possible without the mothering person. Such panic is of relatively short duration; the individual escapes from it by creating another self—a disturbed *adult psychotic self*.

James Stoeri (1992) reports that one of his patients developed a new sense of self after destroying the self that had existed earlier.

> Mrs. L. now told me that ever since what she referred to as her "breakdown" when she was 20, she accepted a kind of radical bifurcation in her identity as the norm for her; in her words, "*she* (her pre-breakdown self) died then and *I* am what is left." She was a senior at a prestigious music school, studying voice, when her breakdown occurred a few months before her senior recital. Significantly, it began when for several days she was *terrified* by a sensation that she was "falling forever": This was followed by her fear that she would destroy whatever had been in her field of vision when she blinked her eyes. She was hospitalized for two days, then dropped out of

school and eventually returned to her parents' home to live. She came to believe that her breakdown revealed her to be dangerous, unlike other people, an "other" for whom a mechanical, lifeless existence was a duty. To this end, and because it was a torment to feel her "throat needing to sing, the same as it needs to drink," she began to smoke cigarettes heavily in order to destroy her voice.

She stated that, in retrospect, the period in her parents' home after her breakdown was as bad or worse than the breakdown itself, because it was then that she felt utterly compelled to assume the mechanical, empty "otherness" as her means of adaptation.

The psychoanalytically oriented mental health worker should not diagnose adult schizophrenia without identifying a history of terror preceding the establishment of the adult psychotic self. Here I refer to what is *prototypical* of adult schizophrenia. When an individual's infantile psychotic self invades and dominates his personality from childhood on, the terror-adult psychotic self sequence is not expected to appear clearly or at all.

Although the adult's psychotic self is linked to his infantile psychotic self, it does not exactly replicate it because it assimilates unconscious fantasies, defenses, influences, and identifications from different phases of development (Volkan 1992a, 1994a,b). When the adult patient's psychotic self invades and dominates his or her personality, the schizophrenia has crystallized. There usually remains an uninvaded part (Bion 1957, Katan 1954, D. Rosenfeld 1992), the ego functions of which, in a typical adult schizophrenic individual, can observe and report on the nature of the psychotic self.

The adult psychotic self created to replace the self the patient had before undergoing organismic panic is structurally primitive, and its relationship to the patient's internal and external worlds is dominated by a break with reality associated with primitive perceptual-cognitive-motor processes and primitive defense mechanisms. The schizophrenic person is severely regressed and undeveloped because the previous self, which encapsulated the infantile self, is replaced by a more primitive version, which is directly linked with and reacts to the infantile self instead of enclosing it. The patient's symptoms (e.g., delusions, hallucinations, and strange language) arise from an attempt to protect a fragile self-continuity (Pao 1979) as well as the adult psychotic self (Volkan 1992a, 1994a).

Prototypical schizophrenic persons, in whom the adult psychotic self dominates the personality organization, exhibit thought disorders and gaps and shifts in the train of associations. Unable to test reality in a global way, they have hypochondriasis, experience hallucinations and delusions, interpret symbols in concrete fashion, become markedly different from their pre-schizophrenic selves, and are unable to form emotional, empathic relationships with others. They tend to neglect ordinary obligations and may behave brutally toward themselves and others. They may be either torpid or agitated. Their thoughts and behavior patterns cannot be understood from what is apparent on the surface; we must find ways to identify and deal with the meaning behind them.

Like Modell (1963), I believe that understanding the psychological factors of schizophrenia is more urgent than understanding the biological factors. Modell states, "the more inclusive, imprecise psychological observations must precede the less inconclusive, more precise biological observations. The psycho-analytic psychiatrist has first to sort things out in order that the biologist may know where to look" (p. 291).

OBJECTIVES

This book examines various fates of the infantile psychotic self. Part I is devoted to one of the fates, schizophrenia, reviewing psychoanalytic formulations, nature–nurture issues, and characteristics of infantile and adult psychotic selves. I do not consider infantile and adult psychotic selves as concrete and lodged in a person's psychic organization but as psychodynamic entities that change according to the nature of the affects with which they are saturated, the nature of the object representations with which they fuse, and the stories of unconscious fantasies with which they are associated. My focus is not on phenomenology and clinical classification. Rather, I attempt to shed light on the infantile psychotic self from a metapsychological point of view and to observe its operations and modification through psychoanalytic psychotherapy, pointing to mental mechanisms at work when the infantile self is encapsulated, when it is active in nonschizophrenic conditions, and when it leads to the formation of an adult psychotic self in schizophrenic conditions.

Schizophrenia is not a disease entity. As Jackson (1960) suggested, a variety of pathological conditions go through a final common pathway to produce a symptom complex. Modell (1963) agreed that in this sense "schizophrenia is comparable to the eighteenth-century diagnosis of dropsy" (p. 283). Common pathways are also seen in affective illnesses such as depression and manic depression. Hawkins (1985) reminds us that today diabetes mellitus is thought to result from a number of disorders, all of which cause ineffective functioning of carbohydrate metabolism: "So, too, in depression it seems almost certain that there may be a variety of pathways or abnormalities leading to the final common denominator which we term affective illness" (p. 375). The final common pathway notion allows for greater latitude in attributing to nature and/or nurture the cause of, or predisposition to, schizophrenia.

Part II is devoted to the fates of the infantile psychotic self other than schizophrenia, with special emphasis on psychotic personality organization. Part III deals with treatment issues. Much clinical material in this book supports the current theoretical and technical formulations. As a psychoanalyst, I believe that a detailed account of an individual case and its total treatment process is more illuminating than brief illustrative vignettes, and I suspect that most of my colleagues would agree, although most tend to refrain from giving in-depth studies of individual cases in fear of giving clues to a patient's identity. This is a realistic concern and one that may make discussion of certain cases impossible, but psychoanalysts do have cases that can be reported without threatening the patient's privacy.

Another difficulty in reporting in-depth studies of individual cases is that the analyst may reveal too much about himself or herself; I believe we can avoid this risk if we are cautious. If psychoanalysis is a means of understanding the human mind and the analyst–analysand relationship (transference–countertransference) in minute detail and offers a way to remove symptoms while initiating structural modification and new growth, we have no choice but to report what happens during the total process of treating representative patients. Because I am affiliated with a medical school and thus do not see as many patients daily as do most colleagues in private practice, I can keep extensive notes on each session with every patient and, in reviewing them, arrive at conclusions that can be published as individual and complete cases of neurotic, narcissistic, and borderline patients. In this book I refer to numerous clinical vignettes, but I also report three total case histories, which explore these patients' inner worlds and psychic realities as revealed by their transference manifestations, dreams, and the analyst's countertransferences.

The first case is that of a man I treated in psychoanalytic psychotherapy for 5 years and continued to see two to six times a year for 32 years thereafter. His case provides information about the lifelong adaptation and functioning of a man with psychotic personality organization who also had schizophrenic episodes and who, through psychotherapy, was enabled to modify his adult psychotic self. The second case, that of the Dogman, written with William Greer, Ph.D., illustrates the inner world of a person with a psychotic personality organization. The third case is that of a young woman who came to me in the middle of an acute schizophrenic episode, whom I treated four times a week for just over 6 years. Her first 18 months of treatment, which was conducted face-to-face, was punctuated by her brief periods as an inpatient, followed by 4½ years on the couch. She became a typical analytic patient, and after the successful termination of her analysis, I had collected 17 years of follow-up information on her.

This book, however, is designed to do more than present total case studies and other detailed clinical vignettes; it addresses the questions of whether there is a future for psychoanalytic psychotherapy for schizophrenic as well as chronically regressed and/or undeveloped patients, and if their infantile and adult psychotic selves can be modified. This issue is dealt with in an editorial in *Psychological Medicine*'s report of a study supported by the National Institute of Mental Health. Mueser and Berenbaum (1990) proposed "a moratorium on the use of psychodynamic treatment for schizophrenia . . . clinicians need to freeze their psychodynamic formulations and instead focus on building individual and family social competence, while decreasing ambient stress" (p. 260).

A response to this proposal is necessary, and this book provides one. Changes in the schizophrenic patient's infantile and adult psychotic selves and the development of healthier structures demonstrate some interesting aspects of psychoanalytic technique. Classic analysis removes neurotic symptoms mainly through transference interpretations and working through. The greater the patient's developmental impairment and early object-relations conflicts, the more his treatment should focus at first on the acquisition of more mature self- and object representations and new ego functions in order to benefit from the therapist's interpretations.

Developmental work during psychoanalysis, especially in the case of the developmentally impaired, depends on the patient's identifying with the analyst's various ego functions during the therapeutic experience. In treating schizophrenics and those who survive in regressed conditions, the analyst should focus on the patient's developmental processes and associated mechanisms of identification. Countertransference is critical. Once we understand the minds of those who are schizophrenic or have a psychotic personality organization, we will learn, just as we do when working with children, how to be better analysts with adults. If we can grasp how these minds work, our overall professional competence in dealing with all types of regressed persons is improved.

Part I

SCHIZOPHRENIA

2

The Schizophrenic Symptom Complex in Classic Formulation and Structural Theory

Before we examine the adult psychotic self—its origins, its relation to the infantile psychotic self, and my definition of *schizophrenia*—it is beneficial to review earlier psychoanalytic attempts to understand the symptom complex exhibited by schizophrenic persons. Many theoretical formulations have been offered. A truly comprehensive review of these formulations is beyond the scope of this book, but one may find discussion of the theories of Sigmund Freud, Otto Fenichel, Heinz Hartmann, Edith Jacobson, Melanie Klein, W. Ronald Fairbairn, Harry Stack Sullivan, and Paul Federn in the work of Pig-Nie Pao (1979). Nathaniel London (1973a,b) focused on Freud's contribution, pointing out that his ideas about schizophrenia can be classified under two incompatible headings: unitary theory and specific theory. The former deals with the intrapsychically motivated or purposive behavior arising from drives and defenses seen in both neurotic and schizophrenic individuals. Here Freud postulates continuity between schizophrenia and neurosis. Specific theory, on the other hand, focuses on a factor considered to be unique to schizophrenia: libidinal withdrawal from the object representation.

Psychoanalytic formulations about schizophrenia fall into four categories:

1. The classic category, according to which the schizophrenic's symptoms and behavior are a result of the withdrawal of libidinal cathexis (emotional investment) from the external world and its ensuing recathexis (in London's terminology, the specific theory of Freud).
2. A category based on the application of the structural theory to the complex interplay of id, ego, and superego and on ego psychology, which emphasizes the ego's functions.
3. A category that deals with object-relations theory (see Chapter 3).
4. A category referring to the concepts of the infantile psychotic self, the adult psychotic self, and their development (see Chapter 4).

The first two categories are discussed only in summary form, and much of my attention focuses on the third and fourth categories. My aim throughout is not the diagnosis of schizophrenia in accordance with phenomenology but the understanding of the symptom complex in a psychodynamic context.

CLASSIC FORMULATION

In his original conceptualization of schizophrenia, Freud (1911, 1914b) emphasized the economic factor—distribution of the schizophrenic individual's libidinal cathexis. He held that in schizophrenic psychosis one finds a break with reality as a result of a shift of available libido from object and a loss of interest in the outside world. He postulated that libido withdrawn from the external world is attached to the ego, resulting in megalomania and hypochondriasis. Such hypercathexis of the ego brings excessive interest in representations both mental and physical. Freud (1911) further postulated that the schizophrenic person establishes contact with the world outside after an initial period of withdrawal, but although this contact seems restitutional, it is pathological and characterized by delusions and hallucinations. London suggested that we call this Freud's specific theory. Freud compared the psychotic person to an infant because both are in a phase of libidinal development with little or no cathexis of object representation. His essay "On Narcissism" (Freud 1914b) explains that the psychotic individual has hypercathexis of the ego because he has withdrawn libidinal investment from object representations. Thus, he suggested, regression schizophrenia is a return to the stage of narcissism.

A year after publishing *The Ego and the Id* (Freud 1923), the cornerstone of structural theory, Freud (1924a) pointed to similarities between the psychic processes of neurosis and psychosis, applying to the latter his knowledge of the former (see London (1973a,b) on unitary theory). Freud saw ego prevailing over id in neurosis and relating to the external world, whereas in psychosis he saw ego overcome by id and separated from reality. He never abandoned his specific theory of schizophrenia, however, and never integrated it into his structural theory. He assumed that schizophrenia has a characteristic two-stage process, the first stage of which is regressive (from a break with reality to catatonia) and the second restitutive (from catatonia to partial recovery of the ability to test reality) (Freud 1911). Fenichel (1945) gives one of the best summaries of the two stages; although using the terminology of structural theory, he adheres to the concept of libidinal decathexis and recathexis. He maintains that schizophrenia is nosologically not a definite entity but a condition that includes many disorders with certain common features. Like Freud, he makes no judgment about the somatogenic or psychogenic origin of the regression seen in this group of diseases.

Symptoms of Regression

Symptoms in the regressive stage show a breakdown of the ego and an undoing of differentiations caused by mental development. Among symptoms of schizophrenic regression are *fanta-sies of world destruction* that represent an inner perception of the loss of object cathexis. Heightened hypochondriacal sensations that reflect narcissistic cathexis of the body are also evident. When this process evokes a defensive reaction, a sense of estrangement results. Withdrawal of object cathexis into mental ego can bring feelings of grandiosity, and if the individual defensively wards off his narcissistic enhancement, he will experience depersonalization. Schizophrenic thinking reflects primitivization, and catatonic symptoms reflect extreme regression. The catatonic patient experiences his own actions passively, as though being propelled into certain motions but not actually performing them. The patient does not believe that he is actually thinking but feels that thoughts are being put into his head; this indicates primitivization. Negativism and automatic obedience (echolalia and echopraxia) betray an indistinct apperception of objects, indistinct ego boundaries, and oral-level ambivalence toward objects in the outer world. Such manifestations pertain to the nursing stage. The absence of any restitutional attempt characterizes hebephrenia as the purely regressive type of schizophrenia.

Abse (1987) examined language peculiarities associated with schizophrenia, noting how, in schizophrenia, regression causes pronounced disturbances in metaphoric symbolism and allows "infiltration of that kind of symbolism that normally, after the repressive barrier has been established, is only evident in dreaming consciousness" (p. 318). He calls this infiltration *cryptophoric symbolism*, by which, for example, the male schizophrenic may speak of a snake or an airplane when having his phallus in mind.

Symptoms of Restitution

The symptoms of restitutive process directly express a tendency to restore what was lost by regression to pathogenic narcissism. Fenichel (1945) has suggested that a person hopeless about restitution will turn to some frightening prospect, whereas someone who does have hope will find some possibility that seems promising. *Fantasies of world reconstruction* are among the restitutional symptoms of schizophrenia. When the ability to test reality is lost or impaired, hallucinations substitute for perceptions, and when some accurate perceptions persist, they are mixed with hallucinations so as to bring about what we call *illusions*. Fenichel (1945) notes that delusions are formed by a process similar to that responsible for hallucinations, involving "condensed mixtures of perceptional elements, thoughts, and memories, symptomatically distorted according to indefinite tendencies that represent warded-off instinctual wishes as well as threats from the superego" (p. 436). They contain a "historical kernel" of truth (Freud 1938, Niederland 1974).

Fenichel's review deals with the way in which language peculiarities reflect restitutional phenomena. Abse (1987) elaborated further on language peculiarities as efforts at restitution (see also Abse and Wegener 1971). Focusing on attempts at forming new language "by naming objects for a constituent feature of the total situation in which the object so named participated" (p. 69), he gives the example of a catatonic woman, first described by Tuczek (1921), who "designated the object *bird* by the word 'song.' The word 'cellar' was changed to 'spider' and then to 'tearable' " (Abse and Wegener 1971, p. 69).

Fenichel (1945) says that a schizophrenic's object addictions reflect restitutional phenomena, a fear of losing the object, and a need to cling to everything and everyone. Certain catatonic symptoms indicate extreme regression, but others signal the start of restitutional phenomena. The patient will employ catatonic mimetic expressions to declare that he is not insane. In full-blown schizophrenia, regressive and restitutive expressions appear simultaneously or alternately, further confusing the clinical picture.

DISCUSSION

The original hypothesis of Freud, referred to by London (1973a,b) as his specific theory of schizophrenia, has its proponents even today. It is internally consistent, explains the meaning of certain symptoms very well, and is as tight and mechanically orderly as a theory in physics. Although it refers to transformation of energy—cathexis–decathexis—it fails to explain how and why each transformation occurs. Freud placed early emphasis on the libido and its adaptation to the inner world along with its attachment to or detachment from external objects. Neither the object nor the presence of aggression was considered then as important in the regulation of the inner environment as each is today.

In reviewing Freud's belief that a break with reality results from withdrawal of libidinal cathexis from the object representation, Pao (1979) points out that the break with reality "belongs to history" (p. 11) and advises the clinician not to rely on the patient's history but on an examination of him in arriving at a diagnosis. Pao considers Freud's specific theory incomplete, insisting that "it encompasses the genetic, economic, and dynamic points of view, but it fails to clarify the structural viewpoint" (p. 51). It is interesting that Fenichel also neglected consideration of the aggressive drive in examining the development of a schizophrenic's symptom complex.

STRUCTURAL THEORY, EGO PSYCHOLOGY, AND THE SYMPTOM COMPLEX OF SCHIZOPHRENIA

According to Freud's (1923) structural theory, libido accumulates in the id while a feeble ego is still in the process of forming.

> The id sends part of this libido out onto erotic object cathexis, whereupon the ego, now grown stronger, tries to get hold of this object-libido and to force itself on the id as a love object. The narcissism of the ego is thus a secondary one, which has been withdrawn from objects. [p. 46]

This suggests that the ego takes on the libido, turning it into narcissistic libido. It is hard to see how a feeble ego does this while simultaneously mediating and overseeing what is happening to the drive energy. How does the narcissistic libido taken from the object energize the ego to make it more mature while a similar process, according to his specific theory, accounts for such schizophrenic symptoms as hypochondriasis and megalomania? Further revision of the structural theory was needed and was later provided by Heinz Hartmann.

Hartmann's (1939) revision of Freud's structural theory assigns to the ego its own primary (libidinal and aggressive) energy and makes it a structure of the mind that has autonomous functions of its own, independent of the id. Moreover, focusing on adaptation to the external environment, Hartmann emphasizes the importance of studying object relations, pointing to their reciprocal interaction between internal and external worlds and the importance of the autonomous ego functions that may eventually evolve into other ego functions. When Hartmann (1953) applied his ego psychology to schizophrenia, he noted that we now think of schizophrenic symptoms from the point of view of the ego and its functions rather than from the viewpoint of libidinal cathexis-decathexis. He pointed out *selective* regression or progression of some ego functions. Hartmann's explanation offers a way to account

> for a lack of uniformity of schizophrenic symptoms that we witness in our clinical practice. When libidinal regression to the narcissistic stage of development was postulated as the cause of all symptoms, it was hard to imagine why there should be such a wide range of symptoms among schizophrenics. [Pao 1979, p. 67]

Hartmann also differentiated between the concepts of ego and self, pairing the object with the self rather than with the ego, which expresses itself as a bundle of functions (e.g., defensive, integrative, adaptive). Greenspan (1989) has given a precise definition of *ego*, declaring that this concept "designates the mental functions that perceive, organize, elaborate, differentiate, integrate, and transform experience" (p. vii). Greenspan's emphasis is on the ego's transformation of experience that includes drive-affect derivatives, self- and object organization at various levels, and relationships with objects perceived as close or as not so close to the subject. It is ego that organizes self- and object representations. Hartmann's formulations suggest that hypochondriasis and megalomania arise not from hypercathexis of ego functions but from hypercathexis of the self-representation. The ego as a psychic apparatus is known by its functions, but the term *self* is a layman's term referring to "I." It is thought that through ego functions (e.g., perception and memory) a mental image of the self is created. A durable collection of self-images as a mental phenomenon is referred to as the *self-representation.*

Arlow and Brenner (1964) suggested that the classic view of withdrawal of the libidinal cathexis is unwarranted and should be discarded as an integral factor in the psychoanalytic theory of psychosis. They held that Freud's later idea of structural theory, especially his notion of regression of ego functions, should replace his earlier ideas about libidinal cathexis and decathexis. They also tried to revise and expand his unitary theory of schizophrenia (London 1973a,b) as originally presented (Freud 1924a,b). They also referred to the drive regression that exists to a greater extent in psychosis than in neurosis and pointed out that understanding of aggressive drive (Bak 1954, Bion 1957, Gillespie 1971, Hartmann 1953, Klein 1946) places greater emphasis on its manifestation in psychosis and on the conflicts it causes. It is important when treating either a psychotic or neurotic patient to identify which ego and superego functions are disturbed, ascertain how they have been affected, and determine what the connection between evident disturbances and inner conflict may be. Arlow and Brenner (1964) focus on inner conflicts in schizophrenia and ask what anxiety is being awakened and what is being warded off:

> the great majority of the alterations in the ego and superego functions which characterize the psychoses are part of the individual's defensive efforts in situations of inner conflict and are motivated by a need to avoid the emergence of anxiety, just as is the case in normal and in neurotic conflicts. In the psychoses the defensive alterations in ego functions are

often so extensive as to disrupt the patient's relationship with the world about him to a serious degree. [p. 157]

In Arlow and Brenner's writing about psychoses it would seem more appropriate to refer to defensive disturbances in various ego functions than to consider a break with reality as the most precise differential aspect of the onset of these conditions. Departing from ascribing common classic features of schizophrenia to libidinal cathexis–decathexis, Arlow and Brenner tentatively conclude that fantasies of world destruction, for example, relate to the patient's violent anger and desire to destroy everything around him. They hold that his fantasy of a world destroyed through no fault of his own spares him the anxiety and guilt that would inevitably torment him were he to recognize his own anger and destructive intent. He may use defensive projection and blame the destruction he envisions on an outside agent—perhaps God. Because the patient's ego function in the service of an accurate assessment of reality is altered regressively, he sees his wish-fulfilling prophecy as real.

Applying further their emphasis on conflict, anxiety, and defense, Arlow and Brenner (1964) explain other schizophrenic symptoms, such as hypochondriacal preoccupation, which they see as being like hysterical conversion, giving bodily expression to a fantasy that permits compromise between an instinctual wish and the defenses against it. They consider megalomaniac ideas, delusions, and hallucinations as defense against anxiety effected by a complex interplay of id, ego, and superego.

The ego's ability to distinguish between external reality and the particular fantasy in question is impaired in order to avoid or minimize the development of anxiety. Thus the fantasy appears real to the patient. Instead of being experienced as a daydream, it is experienced as a delusion or a hallucination. What determines whether it is the one or the other is the presence or absence of sensory elements in the fantasy. If there are such elements, the result is a hallucination. If there are none, it is a delusion. [p. 175]

Pao's formulations about schizophrenia differ from Arlow and Brenner's in that Pao stresses a break in the ego function that maintains cohesion of the self and emphasizes integrative ego functions and their role in adaptation to internal as well as external reality. Despite Pao's reference to the state of the self, I examine here his ideas about structural theory because he (Pao 1973, 1977, 1979), not unlike Arlow and Brenner, bases his views on Freud's (1926) theory of anxiety and conflict and on Hartmann's (1939, 1950, 1953) ego psychology. Hartmann was not explicit as to whether schizophrenic symptom formation is caused by regression or by disturbance in what he described so well as the integrative function of the ego. Pao held that although regression may be accompanied by symptoms, it is not causative. He suggests that Freud may be responsible for the impression that regression does cause schizophrenia and that Fenichel reinforced this notion by emphasizing its role over that of the ego's other activities.

Pao describes five steps in the formation of schizophrenic symptoms:

1. A schizophrenia-prone person must deal with the same types of conflicts as others when some life event awakens repressed conflicts that involve erotic or aggressive impulses.

2. Conflict in such individuals leads to *organismic panic* rather than to ordinary anxiety. Pao deliberately used a term similar to Mahler's (1968) *organismic distress* for that physiological state of high tension experienced by an infant for which only the mothering person can provide relief. Pao stresses that organismic panic is of short duration.

3. Organismic panic evokes a reaction such as shock. The ego's integrating function is paralyzed, and most other ego functions are suspended. Pao and others have observed that once the patient is over this shock, he or she may recall the panic as a dreamlike experience. Giovacchini (1983) held that this phenomenon lacks psychic content, and Grotstein (1983) called it *nonpsychotic schizophrenia*, one dominated by a psychosomatic state of the central nervous system.

4. Integrative function is restored after the shock of organismic panic is over: "As it recovers, regression in perceptual-cognitive-motor processes makes its appearance. Along with

the reactivation of more primitive structures and defense mechanisms, self-experience will also be regressed" (Pao 1979, pp. 221–222). Pao declares that the drastic resultant personality change justifies a diagnosis of schizophrenia.

5. According to Sandler and Joffe (1969), symptoms of the illness crystallize according to a best possible solution, and Pao (1979) agrees that adaptation to the environment is but one aspect of adaptation, others being concerned with inner drives, wishes, and standards (superego). The nature of the best possible solution depends on the circumstances and resources. Such symptoms as delusions, hallucinations, ritual behavior, and strange language help buffer and protect the new self-continuity and retain hidden links to the past life. Pao tries to find a bridge between a structural understanding of manifest symptoms and the sense of self in schizophrenia. Referring to Hartmann's (1950) separation of the ideas of ego and self, Pao (1979) says that when one speaks of the self one has the object in mind. He agrees that the development of ego functions and the development of the sense of self-continuity are reciprocally influential.

Pao's clinical experience with schizophrenic patients indicated that in their childhood the mutual fit between mother and infant had been much reduced, either because of a deficit in the primary autonomous ego apparatus of the infant or because of the mother's emotional incapacity. Such factors bring organismic distress (Mahler 1968) to the child and, when persistent, cause libidinal-aggressive imbalance and a subsequent preponderance of organismic panic. Also, the absence of mutual cueing between mother and child causes developmental disturbance in ego functioning and in the establishment of self-continuity. The ego is burdened by having to maintain its precarious sense of self-continuity to avoid organismic panic. If it does occur, the patient may develop schizophrenia.

DISCUSSION

The appropriateness of applying structural theory to conflict in schizophrenia, as Arlow and Brenner have done, is problematical because psychotic persons, unlike neurotic ones, have no fully differentiated tripartite mental apparatus of id, ego, and superego. By their own admission, Arlow and Brenner presented their ideas without conducting actual intensive psychotherapeutic work with schizophrenic patients; thus, they did not see that such patients have types of conflicts and anxiety that are different from those of neurotic patients. Structural conflicts, such as those observed in the neurotic patient, cannot be considered the main problem of the schizophrenic. This individual's primitive anxiety floods him without leading to a signal, and conflicts arise from identity confusion, identity defusion, and the clashing of terrifying or idealized and fragmented self- and object images.

Although Pao departs from Freud's original notion about the symptom complex in schizophrenia, there are similarities between their views. According to Freeman (1983), "Both Pao and Freud base their theories of symptom formation on the hypothesis that a process of personality dissolution is followed by measures of reconstruction" (p. 82). Freeman notes that Pao makes little reference to "the multiple causes of mental pathology brought about by a disharmonious evolution of the drives and the ego, with failures in synchronization and integration. Instead, Pao seems to indicate the mother of the schizophrenic patient as 'rejecting' " (p. 79).

Issues of the self referred to by Pao need more systematic study. Although he takes into account their sense of self, he pays too little attention to the internalized object relations of his patients. The schizophrenic develops a new, pathological self and tries, through symptom formation, to avoid another experience with organismic panic; however, he is also involved in activity with objects and their mental representations. Pao (1977) called this process another maintenance mechanism to be used when experiencing or anticipating panic, but I think this view should be more focused (see Chapters 3 and 4).

3

Object Relations in Schizophrenia

In general, the many theories of object relations can be seen as offering

> a system of psychological explanation based on the premise that the mind is comprised of elements taken in from outside, primarily aspects of the functioning of other persons. This occurs by means of the processes of internalization. This model of the mind explains mental functions in terms of relations between the various elements internalized. [Moore and Fine 1990, p. 131]

Object-relations theories are not new to psychoanalysis. When Freud (1917) described a mourner's introjection of and identification with the representation of the one for whom he mourned, he was speaking of ego functions dealing with object relations. In his foreword to *Primitive Internalized Object Relations* (Volkan 1976), Kernberg (1976a) suggested that we can speak of at least three types of object relations; Modell (1990) classified four.

Kernberg's first—and broadest—category concerns the internalization of interpersonal experiences that remain inside the individual's mental structure. The quality of current interpersonal relationships can be best understood in reference to experiences the individual had early in life. Kernberg refers to the work of Klein and Fairbairn as representing a second set of views; these adhere to a rather restricted definition of theory and occupy the opposite end of the spectrum. He then offers a third schema, one representing a middle ground and stressing the formation of self- and object images and representations contaminated with affects that reflect the original infant–mother relationship as well as the subsequent development of more mature dyadic, triadic, and multiple internal and external relations in general.

According to Modell (1990), the first group of object relations theories is in the tradition of Balint and Winnicott. Kohut's self psychology comprises the second group; the third springs from the Kleinian-Bion theory of object relations, with some overlapping. The fourth group contains the theory of Kernberg, who followed the tradition of Klein and Fairbairn but modified it according to contemporary ego psychology, being especially influenced by Jacobson (1964) and Mahler (1968).

It is beyond the scope of this book to give the details of the various object-relations theories; thus, my focus is on what Kernberg referred to as being in the middle ground. It will be clear how I regard object relations as I apply this term to the understanding of the schizophrenic patient's inner world and/or that of persons who are not schizophrenic but who have an infantile psychotic self.

DRIVES AND THE ATTACHMENT TO OBJECTS

There was resistance to changing the classic Freudian idea of a baby being energized by instinctual drives and a mind that develops without crucial interaction with objects. This resistance was gradually overcome by observers such as Spitz, who in 1965 showed "The formative influences originating in the surround [i.e., in the mother]" (p. 122) and directed to the baby, indicating that a baby might actually die because he or she lacked necessary experience with a mothering person.

Mahler (1968) followed Hartmann's (1939) interest in the child's environment and narrowed this environment to reciprocal mother–child interaction (Mitchell and Greenberg 1983). Mahler showed how important the object and the child's relation to it, along with the influence of drives, are to the development of the child's mind. Unlike Kleinians, she focused on a slower evolution of the child's psychic structures, pointing out that self- and object representations must be differentiated slowly. The integration of differentiated "good" self-representations invested with libido and differentiated "bad" ones invested with aggression was also a gradual process. The same held true regarding the integration of "good" and "bad" object representations. Mahler's observations persuaded her that it takes 36 months or longer before "the child should increasingly become able to respond to the 'whole mother' and to realize that one and the same person can both satisfy and disturb" (Mahler and Gosliner 1955, p. 199). Thus ambivalence is reached.

Kernberg (1976b, 1984), who also relied on a slower evolution of the psychic structure, focused on the child's ability to use two ego functions in order to systematize the middle-ground object-relations theory and describe various levels of personality organization. These two ego functions are (1) differentiating the self-representation from the object representation, and (2) integrating self-representations that are libidinally invested with those invested with aggression and integrating object representations that are libidinally invested with aggressively invested ones. People such as schizophrenics, whose object relations are on the lowest level, cannot use both functions. Regardless of the genetic, biochemical, familial, psychosocial, and psychodynamic factors contributing to the etiology of their clinical state, their core object relations are on a level at which one cannot maintain a border between where he ends and where objects and their internalized representations start.

Anyone who can use the first ego function but not the integrative function is said to have a borderline or narcissistic personality organization. He can test reality to a considerable degree, because the representation of the self is differentiated from that of the object, but he will split his "good" self- and object representations from the "bad" ones. We say a person with both ego functions has a high-level (neurotic) personality organization; he has integrated and cohesive self- and object representations.

Kernberg (1966, 1972), following Mahler (1968) and Jacobson (1964), delineated the phases of the gradual process by which undifferentiated and unintegrated (split) "good" self- and object representations infused with libido and related pleasurable affects are differentiated from "bad" ones invested with aggression and related unpleasurable affects and integrated in a more realistic representation of the self and the world of objects. His theory reconciles the idea that object investment is secondary to the expression of libidinal and aggressive instinctual drives and the notion that stresses primacy of the infant's attachment to the object. Kernberg saw earliest expression of instinctual drives in the interaction of the infant with others in the *average expectable environment* and holds that instinctual drives are subsequently expressed in internalized object relations crucial to the organization of all other psychic structures.

STRUCTURAL CONFLICTS VERSUS OBJECT RELATIONS CONFLICTS

Psychoanalytic writings refer more and more to two types of conflicts: structural conflict and conflict involving object relations. Gedo and Goldberg (1973), Gedo (1979), Greenspan (1977), Volkan (1981b), Volkan and Akhtar (1979), and Volkan and Ast (1992, 1994) provide hierarchical models that suggest a tripartite model of id-ego-superego at the higher developmental level and a model of object relations at the lower. Classifiers of psychopathology and personality organizations have begun to see clinical entities as reflecting either structural or object-relations conflicts or both.

Persons such as schizophrenics or those with borderline or narcissistic personality organizations, who lack the ability to develop, to differentiate, and to integrate their self- and object relations, suffer from object relations conflicts, which differ from structural conflicts. The latter involve the differentiated id, ego, and superego and are experienced by neurotic individuals and by those with high-level personality organization. In object relations conflicts, the mind is full of split or even fragmented self-images and representations of *part objects*, all of which are contaminated by unneutralized, often opposing, affect dispositions. Conflicts and tension arise from the difficulties encountered in the natural, expected psychobiological evolution of mature (i.e., differentiated, integrated, and cohesive) self- and object representations. Opposing, fragmented, and split self- and object images or representations (and their opposing affective states) account for object-relations conflicts and result in anxiety that may be quantitatively different from that caused by structural (id-ego-superego) conflicts. In the latter, the anxiety has a signal function: heralding internal danger. In object relations conflicts, anxiety may be overwhelming and lose its signaling function. Anyone with object-relations conflict is preoccupied with developmental struggles and identity issues, and when he achieves integrated and cohesive self- and object representations, such conflicts, for practical purposes, disappear or are effectively repressed.

Dorpat (1976) notes that one caught up in object relations conflict experiences tension between his own desires and the values, prohibitions, and injunctions assigned to the representations of other people that he has internalized. It is different for one suffering from structural conflicts; he is aware—or can become aware by making the unconscious aspects of the conflict conscious—that all the opposing tendencies are his own. Dorpat adds that conflicts between being dependent and becoming independent—or between a desire to be close to an object (and its representation) and a desire to be distant—cannot be understood without applying a theory of object relations. Also, the schizophrenic symptom complex, which includes both need and dread in relating to objects and their images (Burnham 1969), cannot be understood without the application of object relations theory.

Greenspan (1977) offers a similar concept, pointing to the development of object constancy as the main criterion for determining whether a conflict concerns object relations or indicates structural disharmony. Following Mahler (1968), Greenspan defines object constancy as the ability to maintain a reasonably consistent internal representation of the self as well as of the object, with such constant representations being relatively independent of changes in drive tension and external stress.

CLINICAL MANIFESTATIONS

The following are certain clinical manifestations that are explained by the application of object relations theory.

Splitting

Unable to integrate opposing self- and object representations and their accompanying affects, the child experiences *developmental* splitting at first but, when developing normally, achieves gradual integration, which peaks at 36 months. Influences such as a constitutional biological predisposition, trauma, and experience with multiple mothers may interfere with integrative ability. Clinical experience demonstrates the importance of the contamination of self- and object representations by derivatives of the aggressive drive. Inability to tame aggression may be a result of *constitutional factors*—to use a general term that includes physiological and biochemical determinants—or of excessive early frustration in the child–mother interaction. When, however, aggression excessively overloads "bad" self-object images, it is impossible for some individuals to integrate them with opposing "good" units because they defend against the establishment of better, integrated inner structures as though the excessive "badness" makes it impossible to retain what was "good."

A schizophrenic person always has an undifferentiated psychotic core but uses splitting for differentiated, but unintegrated, self- and object images or representations. In schizophrenics, splitting, unlike that seen in borderline patients, is not an effective defense because it fails to protect against the tensions of object-relations conflicts for very long. The schizophrenic's unintegrated self- and object images and representations (a) shift rapidly from being invested with libido to being invested with aggression, and vice versa, and (b) move rapidly within an introjective-projective cycle. Therefore, what is experienced as "good" may suddenly be "bad," and vice versa, and something experienced as outside may suddenly be thought of as inside, and vice versa. The rejection of unwanted units from the self-representation, and their quick subsequent retrieval, constitutes an introjective-projective cycle usually associated with unconscious fantasies of incorporation and ejection of the love object.

The Introjective-Projective Cycle and Fusion

The terms *introjective-projective cycle* and *introjective-projective relatedness* (Volkan 1994a,b) are used here in a general sense to include all the inner and outer flow through the self-representation. These terms cover different types of introjections and projections, including projective identification; therefore, it is necessary in each instance to describe just what is being introjected or projected. For example, we introject and project various self- and object representations, and, on a higher level, we do this also with thought processes. Moreover, it is important to know how a patient differentiates his or her self-representation from that of another when introjection or projection is taking place.

When self- and object representations fuse, introjective-projective relatedness is at its most primitive level in combining inner and outer flow. Imagine a schizophrenic person holding on to a chair and answering "chair" when asked his name. We would conclude that he had fused his image with that of the external object. When the boundary separating the image of the self from that of an external object is tenuous, what is projected onto the external object or its representation can easily boomerang. The greater the differentiation between self- and object representations, the greater the possibility of stable projections.

The analyst should heed these psychic activities and see where they lead. For example, we should see if introjection leads to identification or to a quick turnaround and a new projection. We should pay attention to how an introjection or a projection affects the sense of self. We must observe the derivatives of unconscious fantasies associated with each introjection and projection. Functions of the mouth, anus, and nostrils may represent in fantasy the orifices through which the inner and outer flow passes (Volkan 1982a). Suslick (1963) compared the constant and various introjections and projections of schizophrenics to the product of earthworms, which throughout their lives continually take in and eject material. In schizophrenics, introjections do not usually lead to new identifications, and projections may quickly return.

Ricky, a teenage schizophrenic patient of mine, made sucking sounds and kept licking his lips as he sat before me. He had concluded that the name on my door was German, and in his delusional life he was Joseph Goebbels, Hitler's right-hand man. Born with a deformed hand, Ricky fantasized that his mother was Hitler, and he submitted to her. If he were her extension, she could, he supposed, repair his deformity. He explained that his sucking represented his drinking German wine (his mother's representation). He had projected my image onto her representation, fused the two, and proceeded to introject what resulted through his mouth. Learning that I am not German but Turkish, he asked if Turkish wine is sweet or sour (Volkan 1976).

Inner–outer flow is observable in a gross and exaggerated way by means of the patient's associated fantasies. Introjective-projective movement may also disclose itself in the patient–therapist interaction. The patient repeatedly puts aspects of his or her inner world into the therapist, and then withdraws them. Through this process the therapist can come to know the patient's inner world.

Frances, a young patient I have described elsewhere (Volkan 1981a), claimed that she communicated with "good" and "bad" spirits from another world and felt herself to be half-woman, half-man and half-alive, half-dead. A believer in reincarnation, she was convinced of having had a previous existence. At the age of 4 days, she had been adopted to replace her adoptive mother's brother, a pilot shot down in combat, and her adoptive mother's dead fetus (this woman had an abortion a few days before adopting Frances). Frances was regarded by important others in her early environment as a living link to the dead man and the fetus. The unconscious fantasies of others were passed into the little girl's self-concept when her self-image as a child could not be integrated with the concept of the dead man and the fetus. When she was in her half-dead state she behaved in treatment like a zombie. I sometimes felt uncomfortable, as though I were dead myself, but realized that she was projecting her half-dead aspect onto me. I slowly came to understand what half-dead, half-alive and half-man, half-woman meant to her. I sensed this first within the introjective-projective cycle without using thought processes on the subject; information about the patient's background, thoughts, and words to explain what I sensed came to me only gradually.

What I call an *introjective-projective cycle* reflects what Federn (1952) observed: close attention to a schizophrenic's facial expression yields clues to many changes of what he called *ego states*. Ricky's face might reflect comfort as he took in "good" wine, but it reflected fear as he took in "bad" wine. In a similar situation, an attentive therapist may see self-object-affect units changing place in an uncommonly open way.

Splitting and Introjective-Projective Cycle in Delusions and Hallucinations

A patient's involvement in splitting and an introjective-projective cycle may reveal the meaning of some delusions and hallucinations and novel language. Michael, a 24-year-old schizophrenic patient, believed that his head was a ball with which he could play a game he called *spindamomsis*. He would ask me to watch him play it and did not seem to realize that I saw no game. As time went on, he was able to explain that word images of his father (*da*), mother (*mom*), and sister (*sis*) would appear in his head, on the left side at first and then on the right. They were not stabilized but moved from one side to the other, alternating faster and faster. They would spin, turning his head into a ball. Spindamomsis was the spinning of word images; it meant spin(ning) of da(d), mom, and sis. As Michael played, some images would escape from his head (ball) and continue to spin; others would return and spin. The game involved object images that constantly shifted from one side to the other side of splitting and introjective-projective processes. The movement of symbolic object representations was rapid in Michael's case, but some schizophrenics experience the same process at a slower pace; the location of the representations is seldom fixed. In paranoid schizophrenia, projections seem to last longer, indicating that in such cases some stability in the use of projection is possible, although complete stability is not ensured.

Projective Identification

Schizophrenics project aspects of self- and object representations to make the process of splitting more effective. Novick and Kelly (1970) apply the term *externalization* to this type of projection. For them, the term *projection* refers to higher-level projection of thoughts, affects, and other mental content. Having used externalization, the patient gains greater comfort about what he or she retains within as a self-representation. The effectiveness of externalization differs from one patient to another and according to whether the illness is acute or chronic (Volkan and Akhtar 1979).

Externalization enhances splitting and self-continuity at least temporarily; feared units are attributed to someone else on the outside, but this fails to bring relief because a schizophrenic can readily fuse and identify with whatever he or she has externalized or projected. Such identification occurs by means of a process usually called *projective identification*. This term was introduced by Melanie Klein (1946) as a process of the paranoid-schizoid position. Hanna Segal (1973), a follower and "interpreter" of Klein, describes projective identification as follows: "Parts of the self and internal objects are split off and projected into the external object, which then becomes possessed by, controlled and identified with the projected parts" (p. 27).

In the present-day psychoanalytic literature there is confusion about the use of the term *projective identification* (Goldstein 1991). This confusion relates to the existence or nonexistence of boundaries between self- and object representations when the self-representation assimilates the object representation. I use the term when there is a blurring of the boundaries between the self- and object representations. Because projections and introjections are not stable at the early phase of life as well as in many schizophrenic conditions, however, I prefer to use the terms *fusion-defusion cycle* and *introjective-projective cycle* and describe what is involved in a specific cycle in each instance and how quickly or slowly the cycle completes itself. *Projective identification* often is *not* a good term to be used in relation to schizophrenic processes, especially in acute cases. When what was projected boomerangs back into the patient's self-representation, it seldom leads to a stable identification, but it is quickly projected or externalized once again. In chronic schizophrenia, however, some clinical manifestations can be best described by this term.

The following vignette illustrates projective identification. A schizophrenic patient thought of me as Father Time. This identity, which he projected onto me, reflected the seemingly endless humiliation he had received from his father as a child. After accusing me of being Father Time, a creature who tormented him endlessly, he would suddenly start saying "ticktock" and move his arms like the hands of a clock for hours, demonstrating his identification with Father Time.

Fragmentation

The schizophrenic's clinical picture is further complicated when fragmentation occurs within "good" and "bad" self-object-affect representations, making for tension on both sides of the split. The borderline individual seems able to gather "good" representations together without conflict and to place them on a continuum, following the same process with "bad" representations. With schizophrenics, however, fragmentation within the representational units makes it possible, for example, to feel tension between a "good" mother image and a "good" aunt image, or the "bad" penis representation and a "bad" breast representation. Like Michael, a patient I called Mrs. F. (Volkan 1964, 1976) spoke of being sometimes dominated by one side of her mind and then by the other. She sensed a bar between them, evidence of splitting. Therapy uncovered multiple frames of mind on either side and showed that one was sometimes in conflict with another on the same side. Her different frames of mind reflected different self- and object images with their associated affects.

Bleuler (1911) described split, and perhaps fragmented, self- and object representations without modern terminology. He saw that affects attached to the fragmented units determined their nature.

> A woman patient may be "switched from a virgin to a married woman." Another woman is "a man named Bauman, and then again myself." For the most part, the different conceptions are mixed up in an irregular way, occasionally even in the very same sentence. [p. 144]

Personalities may differ in speech and voice, and one personality may completely ignore an argument while another interprets it correctly at some later time (Bleuler 1911).

World Destruction, World Construction, and Terror

Experiences of world destruction or reconstruction can be considered in connection with object relations; the patient perceives the merging of self- and object representations as a loss of both the outside world and sense of self. The patient then tries to find a new identity and to be differentiated from the objects and people around him. This is why a schizophrenic young woman (Volkan and Akhtar 1979) was obsessed in naming everything, saying, "This is me; that is you. This is the chair, the bed, . . ." and so on.

A prototypical schizophrenic in adulthood starts with an organismic panic (Pao 1979), and the world destruction fantasy reflects the loss of self-representation. We can imagine that there may be many beginnings of the illness of a typical schizophrenic succumbing as a teenager or young adult. Fantasies of world destruction may surface again and again as the self is lost, only to be followed by the formation of new ones. Each acute feeling of losing the self, either through sudden fusion with, or introjection of, an aggression-laden object representation or by explosive diffusion of self- and object representations, brings terror of annihilation.

A study from the Sheppard and Enoch Pratt Mental Hospital (Glass 1985, 1989) gives poignant descriptions of psychological breakdown of the inner world in schizophrenics and its subsequent reconstruction. Glass, a professor of political theory, sought to demonstrate that events in a mental hospital might serve as a frame of reference to enlarge our understanding of politics; he spent 7 years observing patients and published his findings. One of the patients described slipping into psychosis and told of the terror he experienced.

> Psychosis is like being cornered and I just let myself go. . . . It explodes and the whole world begins to shatter and you see yourself lit up like a thousand-watt light bulb traveling a million miles an hour. . . . It's no longer a problem of whether to wear a shirt or wash your jeans. . . . You fly into your world and all else diminishes in importance. [Glass 1989, p. 35]

I believe that often the experience of losing one's sense of self and the ego functions that support it, however primitive they may be, is more horrible than fear of actual physical death.

The unexpected death of a loved one brings acute grief, and although we theorize about metapsychological consequences in the inner world of those who mourn, there is nothing theoretical about the reality of grief. It is experienced, and it is observable (Volkan 1981a, Volkan and Zintl 1993). A neurotic patient in analysis leaves behind—loses—aspects of his old self and related ego functions in order to gain better structures, but the schizophrenic loses so much of his self-representation and related ego functions that he cannot simply grieve over his loss as would a neurotic individual; he experiences horror and, to fill the void, creates a new self that is psychotic, choosing the better of two evils. One of Glass' subjects illustrated the validity of comparing this experience to the loss of a loved one when he said that "to rebuild identity is a task as monumental as weaving a million disconnected pieces of thread" (Glass 1989, p. 37). Arlow and Brenner (1964) suggest that fantasies of world destruction reflect the patient's defensive projection of aggression into external reality. I observe, however, that while defensive projection of aggression occurs, fantasies of world destruction refer primarily to the perception and intolerable affect of the destruction of one's self-representation and internalized object representations, which may be projected into the external world.

The Role of Libido and Aggression

The schizophrenic's main way of relating to the world involves a fusion-defusion cycle and an introjective-projective cycle. These processes, however, also reflect primitive defenses against the tension of object-relations conflicts. Some fusions are libidinally determined; the patient fuses his "good" representations with "good" or idealized object representations to arrive at an ecstatic condition. In a sense, self is surrendered to fusion in order to make it a part of a larger support system or to protect its fragile cohesion against threatening objects.

When the patient invests the "other" with rather raw aggressive drive derivatives as well as libidinal derivatives, he wants alternately to fuse or identify with and distance himself from that "other," which by then includes elements of which the patient is the source. Freud's explanation that the source of schizophrenic symptom formation is object decathexis and recathexis can be better understood in reference to object relations conflicts by considering the role of the aggressive drive (Volkan and Akhtar 1979). Some fusions or identification may be directed according to aggression; the patient then fuses or identifies with a terrifying object representation in order to destroy it and banish the terror. The terror is felt within, however, because of the fusion or identification, and there is no satisfactory remedy. If externalization of the terrifying representational units then occurs, the cycle begins again, unless the patient becomes a chronic schizophrenic, with his adult psychotic self, and such supporting ego mechanisms as externalization and projection, becoming stable.

The Need-Fear Dilemma

A schizophrenic person seems unable to do without those others who are contaminated by externalization but is equally unable to tolerate them. Fenichel (1945) described object decathexis and simultaneous or alternating *object addiction*. Burnham, Gladstone, and Gibson (1969) examined this phenomenon from the point of view of object relations, referring to it as the *need-fear dilemma*. The schizophrenic needs an external structure because he lacks an internal one that provides autonomous control of impulses and object relations. Because this need for others is excessive, the mental images of others have great power over him, and others are accordingly dangerous. So the schizophrenic defends himself either by clinging to them or by avoiding them altogether. In their extreme form the two tendencies sometimes manifest themselves in echolalia, echopraxia, and automatic obedience or in autistic withdrawal, mutism, and stupor. The patient may even exhibit such manifestations alternately. Such alternation accounted for the incessant blinking of one of Akhtar's patients (Volkan and

Akhtar 1979), who said he tended to "take too many cues from other people" and often mimicked their words and gestures. He wanted to be struck blind so he could be himself and not a replica of someone else.

Burnham and his colleagues (1969) have written of another resolution of the need-fear dilemma that also defends against the lack of object constancy that is so characteristic of the schizophrenic's reality. In this maneuver, a pseudoconstancy of objects is achieved by redefining them through primitive ideal-ization, an extreme example of which is erotomanic delusions. Another type of object redefinition is the division of the whole object field into "all good" and "all bad" objects, accompanied by cognitive scotoma and intolerance of ambiguity. Although Burnham (1969) sees such splitting of the object as a reaction to the schizophrenic's need-fear dilemma, I believe that it is a basic defensive maneuver arising from the inability to integrate internalized self- and object representations tinged with libido and aggression, respectively, and that these, in turn, produce a need-fear dilemma.

Nonhuman Objects

The schizophrenic's customary investment in nonhuman ob-jects should be mentioned here. Searles (1960, 1965) wrote on the mother-directed aspect of the nonhuman environment, and Fenichel (1945) and Burnham and colleagues (1969) observed the attempt of schizophrenic patients to regain a semblance of object contact by using substitute nonhuman objects and their mental images. Like human objects, these may convey feelings of fear or security and may be clung to, avoided, or broken to pieces. Sometimes the object is literally devoured: a schizo-phrenic patient whose therapist took a week-long vacation ate a newspaper photo of his therapist that he kept in his room. Through this act the patient kept the therapist within himself.

One often sees the affective investment in nonhuman ob-jects shift quickly. Akhtar (Volkan and Akhtar 1979) describes a patient who picked up a little frog he thought must be lonely and took it home, devoting himself to its comfort and feeding it bread crumbs. Angered by the frog's failure to respond, he chased it around the room, damaging furniture in the process. When he caught it he dashed it against the wall with all his might, until the thought that he was committing murder stopped him. Picking it up, he struggled with the temptation to squeeze it to death but took it to the door and gently let it out.

Modell (1963) wrote of ego arrest in schizophrenia at the level of transitional objects (Winnicott 1953). Many adult borderline patients of mine, as well as those who were schizophrenic, turned to "magical" inanimate and nonhuman objects (Volkan 1976, Volkan and Kavanaugh 1978, Volkan and Luttrell 1971) in response to conflict in object relations. These objects were carefully selected with unconscious motivation, much as a child chooses a transitional object from among many possibilities. Such objects are Janus-like (Volkan 1976), providing a choice between being attached to their representation or being distanced from it. The illusion of control over a transitional object seems to guarantee the illusion of absolute control over all external objects and their representations.

DISCUSSION

It is very useful to recognize in the clinical setting the role of early object-relations conflicts in the formation of a schizophrenic symptom complex. Not all symptoms in schizophrenia can be explained by object-relations theory, however. We must always integrate data that can be well illuminated by object-relations theory with that illustrating disturbance in different ego functions. Furthermore, we need to keep the following questions in mind: How can we overcome the tendency to use object relations theory by referring to self- and object representational units as if they are mechanical constructs? How can we encourage the introjective-projective cycle to be thought of as a complicated and affect-laden ego experience, and not as a wholesale movement of self- and object representation? How can we avoid isolating object relations theory from the wealth of other psychodynamic processes (e.g., important unconscious fantasies, traumas, and influential psychosexual symbolism), as well as from biological potentials when we try to understand a schizophrenic's symptom complex?

Some clinicians who apply object relations theory to schizophrenia often fail to describe the more mature object relations of the healthier part of the personality and how the healthier part and the psychotic part relate to each other. According to object relations theory, the core object relations in schizophrenia are on the level at which self- and object representations are not differentiated. This core, however, is not the same in every schizophrenic, as I will describe in Chapter 5.

The type of object relations theory I use involves the drives attached to different representations of self and object and their affective expression. The adoption of a point of view concerned with object relations should not divert us from examining the disturbances as well as the primitivization of ego functions. A reciprocal influence is at work between the theoretical structures of self- and object representations and the theoretical structures of id, ego, and superego (Greenspan 1977, 1989, Volkan 1981b). Initiation of the former set is helped by autonomous ego functions, while the development of the self-system and its differentiation from the internalized object world brings about full separation of the ego from other related structures. We notice in treatment the interplay between the two sets of theoretical structures—between object relations theory and structural theory—especially as the patient improves. A detailed study of both a borderline and a narcissistic patient (Volkan and Ast 1992, 1994) shows the continuous interplay of phenomena best explained from the standpoint of object relations and phenomena best understood from that of structural theory. An understanding of the symptom complex in schizophrenia may require a similar approach.

Recent research on infants has challenged as well as enriched object relations theory. We know now that the infant's mind is more active than formerly believed, and Mahler's idea of an autistic phase must be abandoned. In personal communications written before her death, Mahler herself questioned the existence of a truly autistic phase. We know now from documented research that the infant is capable of accomplishing many organizing experiences in an adaptive fashion. For example, at birth or soon thereafter, a baby responds to pleasure and displeasure (Lipsitt 1966), forms intimate bonds, and makes visual discriminations (Klaus and Kennell 1976, Meltzoff and Moore 1977). The neonate experiences and tolerates in a stable way a range of stimuli, including those involved in social interaction (Brazelton, et al., 1974, Emde 1988a,b, Escalona 1968, Stern 1985). Between the ages of 7 and 12 months, an infant can show surprise (Charlesworth 1969) and fear (Ainsworth et al., 1974, Sroufe and Waters 1977). By the middle of his second year he will exhibit behavior that suggests functional understanding of objects (Werner and Kaplan 1963), and later in the same year, symbolic capabilities emerge (Bell 1970, Piaget 1962).

Overgeneralization from focused experimental findings in infant research challenged object relations theory. Greenspan (1989) opposes the overgeneralization and questions Stern's (1985) suggestion that the child's ego structure is differentiated when he demonstrates the ability to discriminate between visual designs and sounds. Greenspan studied how individually different biological and experimental family patterns join to determine either adaptation or psychopathology. His findings are based on his and his colleagues' systematic observation of at-risk infants and their families, findings that have not yet been tested experimentally. Greenspan postulated that the infant is *pre-wired* and that from early weeks or months he can organize experiences and progress to higher levels. According to Greenspan, the infant's first task is to regulate himself and at the same time take an interest in the world; he uses each sensory pathway and a range of sensory modalities to deal with phase-specific challenges.

Not all infants are alike; some may be hyperarousable and others hypoarousable. Some may have difficulty integrating different sensory pathways, such as vision and hearing. Meanwhile, a fit between the infant and caregiver is important; the mother may be soothing, hyperactive, or hypoactive. Under

optimal conditions, the use of early sensory and affective processing, discrimination, and integration permits the gradual
organization of experience. Under unfavorable conditions, however, such organization cannot be fully achieved, and the infant
may be unable to discriminate and integrate all or some of the
sensory-affective-motor pathways; some somatic and behavioral experiences do not constitute a pattern that is abstracted
and reflected in mental representations.

The object-relations theory systematized by Kernberg focuses on object-relations conflicts but says little about deficiency. How do deficiencies in the mind's developing structures
influence object-relations conflicts? Because in schizophrenia
we are dealing with most primitive self- and object relations, we
should establish what is "normal" in these very early stages.
Object-relations theory should be studied developmentally; the
adult psychotic self of the schizophrenic that dominates the rest
of the personality does not suddenly appear, but is built on
predisposing developmental factors—both deficiencies and conflicts—in combination with others, such as genetic (biological)
influences.

4

The Infantile and the Adult Psychotic Selves: A Developmental Approach

All the theories about the schizophrenic symptom complex and behavior described in the previous chapters fall short in one degree or another in accounting for all relevant clinical findings. I include Freud's specific and unified theories (London 1973a,b), structural theory, the application of ego psychology, and object relations. I do not dwell on restricted object-relations theories, especially Kleinian theory, which is problematic when applied to schizophrenia. Klein holds that the strength of the death instinct and weak tolerance of paranoid-schizoid anxiety determines the development of the schizophrenic's symptom complex. The mother/environment may provide good experiences, but as Pao (1979) states, Kleinian theory fails to explain the development of schizophrenia when the infant is normal but the mother/environment is extremely pathological.

It is no wonder that psychoanalytic writers continue applying various theories to primitive clinical conditions in accordance with their own orientation. The developmental approach described in this chapter represents an attempt to link compatible aspects of these theories. By means of a clinical illustration, I focus first on the adult psychotic self and then examine its foundation, which has been formed in the infant's development.

The adult psychotic self dominates the personality in schizophrenia and is the seat of the schizophrenic symptom complex and behavior. As Bleuler (1911) noted, and Katan (1954) and Bion (1957) demonstrated, part of the personality escapes its influence and remains intact. Katan basically followed Freud's specific theory but modified it. He believed that schizophrenia arises from a bisexual conflict that leads to relinquishing the heterosexual position and then regression. I cannot support this theory, but Katan remains an important contributor to psychoanalysis with his description of the prepsychotic period and the nonpsychotic part of the personality in schizophrenia. He says, "we must conclude that a part of the personality continues to behave as if the prepsychotic personality structure still existed" (1954, p. 125). He states that the nonpsychotic part does not remain constant in size but changes all the time, and that the defenses of the nonpsychotic and psychotic parts of the personality are different. He advises the therapist to secure a foothold in nonpsychotic territory. The therapist can hold a "normal" conversation with the sound part of a patient's personality, although this may fall under the influence of the adult psychotic self in time, only to free itself again. Accordingly, one cannot consider wholesale regression in schizophrenia. A different consideration is proposed here, one that does not focus on regression—total or partial—but explains the psychotic and healthier parts of the patient.

I offer here the case of Saint Sam, whom I consider to be prototypical of the adult schizophrenic individual inasmuch as he was able to verbalize, in his own way, the workings of his inner world and had an observable and understandable history. I focus metapsychologically rather than phenomenologically on the nature of the adult psychotic self, the infantile psychotic self, and what is common to the inner worlds of all schizophrenic persons.

SAINT SAM

Sam, whose case I have described in detail elsewhere (Volkan 1992a, 1994a), was a socially shy college student who fancied himself in love with a woman he once saw passionately kissing another man. The sight greatly disturbed him despite the fact that he had admired her only from a distance. This situation seems to be a classic triangle, but in speaking about it in treatment he saw it as a dyad. It was rejection by the object of his affections rather than jealousy of and/or competition with the man who kissed her that made an impression on him. He soon began dreaming of Soviet planes bombing the town where he and the woman attended the university. While driving home from a nearby farm, he was horrified to see something he perceived as a mushroom cloud rising into the sky. Stopping his car, he took refuge in a ditch, screaming with terror. When taken to the hospital, he looked like a frightened animal. Later, when he managed to speak of his experience, he recalled that although he knew the atomic bomb had exploded over the city, he felt that it had also exploded within himself. The loud internal explosion he had experienced in the destruction of the city reminded me of another schizophrenic patient, who felt great pain from the roar of a passing train, as though it had passed through his own body. Like the patient reported by Glass (1989), Sam felt that his cells had exploded all over the universe, and he said he sometimes felt like a monster. What Sam and other prototypical schizophrenics describe is the fragmentation and loss of their dominant self-representation, which is experienced in both inside and outside worlds.

Sam was admitted to the hospital as an acute schizophrenic but was discharged after a month when he showed some understanding of the connection between his symptoms and the sight of his "girlfriend" kissing another man. Although discharged into the care of his family and a special nurse, he returned to the hospital within 2 months, referring to himself as Saint Sam and claiming a new, religious identity. He said he was in touch with God, who had appointed him to do good on Earth. Saint Sam, his adult psychotic self, was to repair the world that had been destroyed. Sam had been clean-shaven and had a baby face, but Saint Sam wore a beard. Sam had been shy and gentle, but Saint

Sam was loud and irrepressible. Sam had enjoyed classical music, but all music bothered Saint Sam.

In his walks around the hospital, Saint Sam flicked his tongue like a snake, explaining that with it he could taste and sense the world around him. He tried to lick the faces of other patients to see whether or not they were evil. He hoped to find "the angel of God," whom he could taste and consume so they could be together forever. When people resisted being licked or when he found someone "evil," he would distort his face, roll his eyeballs, and turn purple.

It is likely that some members of his extremely wealthy family were mentally ill, perhaps schizophrenic. He recalled hearing as a child about a "crazy" maternal grandfather who died young, perhaps a victim of suicide. While Sam was growing up, an often-hospitalized uncle lived on the horse farm owned by Sam's parents, in a house behind their mansion. This uncle, who had a beard and clung to a religious delusion of being called on to save mankind, sometimes brutalized the family's black servants. Sam's mother, whom I interviewed many times, was the uncle's elder and only sister, and she "protected" him. I concluded that this shallow and narcissistic woman always wanted to be the only one or the best one in any situation, and her preoccupation with her brother arose from reaction formation based on sibling rivalry, of which she had been well aware as a girl.

Sam's father, though rich and handsome, felt inferior in status in comparison to his wife's wealthy family, who treated him as a second-class citizen. The management of his wife's farm, where they had lived after their marriage, was his only appropriate role. He had become obese, cynical, and alcoholic and paid little attention to the solitary child who appeared in the seventh year of his parents' union and who had been sired by another man, according to his mother, who kept the matter secret. I sensed that her husband was aware of her infidelity. By the time Sam fell ill, his legal father was in very poor health, drank heavily, and seemed confused and uncaring about Sam's well-being.

Sam's mother had refused to breast-feed her baby and, indeed, played with him only when he was "clean and happy." He was given into the care of a black woman in her early twenties, who was considered "primitive but loyal." She was in the habit of licking the baby dry after bathing him, and Sam's mother paid no attention to this until Sam was 2, when she made an issue of it and dismissed the girl. Shortly before this, Sam's biological father was hurt in a bar fight by a man he had cuckolded. Sam's mother lost interest in the father after he became crippled, and he left for an unknown destination. Sam was unaware of all this on a conscious level but did recall his mother's endless talk during her alcoholic bouts about "the good old days" and her accompanying preoccupation with the man who had disappeared.

A series of black women became Sam's mother substitutes; all "loved" him but turned "bad" (in his mother's mind) and were dismissed. He had many experiences of being seduced and then abandoned, being overstimulated and then isolated. His real mother treated him, at best, with ambivalence, often dressing him elaborately and showing him off in company. She thought he resembled his uncle, who died when Sam was 6 and who had predicted that the boy would be a savior one day and treated him as "Baby Jesus."

After the death of his uncle, Sam underwent his first personality change and withdrew to his room, where he became preoccupied with making puppets of devils and angels. He lived in a private world with them, talking to them in a language of his own invention. He ignored real people, played with matches, and showed cruelty toward animals on the farm. Upset by his "nasty stubbornness," his mother found a middle-aged white woman, a widow with two children of her own, to care for Sam when he was 8 years old. Dedicating herself to her small charge, this woman helped Sam to emerge from his private world and often read to him. When Sam was about 11 he clung to his mother substitute, but when he was 14 she moved away and he never saw her again. More than ever he turned to reading and listened endlessly to classical music, as though it were God's soothing voice. His performance in school, however, was no more than average.

Only after entering the university and feeling rejected by the object of his affections did he become openly schizophrenic. One of my able assistants treated him during both stays in the hospital and, after his departure for the second time, gave him intensive outpatient treatment under my supervision. Sam had enough ability in reality testing to keep his appointments and developed a transference psychosis (Searles 1965) that I considered very lively and workable. In his sessions he fused with various representations of his therapist or related to them in an introjective-projective way, and he continued to do so between sessions, remaining withdrawn from day-to-day involvement with other people. We felt that the widow who had come into his life when he was 8, and who had been able to enter his private world and tame his aggression, had staved off schizophrenia in his childhood. In his transference psychosis he tried mainly to recapture his experience with her.

In his second year of treatment Sam began testing his therapist with a quickly shifting transference, relating to him as though he sometimes perceived him as altogether "good" but at other times totally "bad." He identified him with his crazy uncle, and we began to grasp the meaning of his experiences with this man, with whom he had had an important relationship. He may have been afraid of the older man, but he drew from him a sense of continuity despite a lack of reality-testing experience. He was overstimulated or rejected by the women with whom he came in contact.

I was pleased with Sam's progress. However, when his legal father died and his mother promptly remarried, she sent Sam to a private institution, where he was heavily medicated. It seemed clear that she wanted to be rid of him in order to travel with her new husband. On a deeper level, she wanted to "kill" him; she had transferred her murderous rage toward her father and Sam's biological father to her son. Six months later, while home on a visit, Saint Sam came to see me, looking like a zombie. I had seen him during his diagnostic workup, and while my assistant was treating him, he occasionally chatted with me. Now he seemed lifeless and claimed that the excessive medication had so killed his soul that he had no possibility of being "a savior." I was very sad at the sight of him. I never saw him again but later learned that he was wasting away in a state hospital as a chronic schizophrenic.

THE FORMATION OF THE ADULT PSYCHOTIC SELF

Sam clearly illustrates world destruction and world construction experiences. In accordance with Freud's specific theory, I would explain these experiences as a shift of libido from the external world to the ego; this causes a break with reality, and the patient develops hallucinations and delusions when he attempts restitution. This theory does not address the issue of aggression in Sam, nor does it explain his pre-psychotic period and the influence of interaction with his early environment. It does, however, emphasize libidinal regression to the narcissistic stage of development. According to the structural theory, Sam's symptoms arose from his altering the functions of his ego and superego by way of defense, from his relationship to the environment, and from his breaking with reality. In this view, Sam's rage at seeing the girl he fancied kiss another man, and his wish to destroy everything about him, can be associated with defensive displacement and projection; he blamed the destruction of the city on an outside agency—the Soviets. Because his ego function in the service of accurate reality testing was regressively altered, he saw his wish-fulfilling prophecy as real.

The structural theory, with its emphasis on id-ego-superego conflict, signal anxiety, and defense, offers a problematic explanation of Sam's inner world. Schizophrenics, unlike neurotics, do not have a fully differentiated tripartite mental apparatus of id, ego, and superego. Also, the structural theory does not offer an adequate explanation for certain aspects of Sam's behavior: his perception of an inner explosion, his sense of being both destroyer and destroyed, his change of identity to Saint Sam, and his constant object-seeking and object-rejecting behavior.

Explaining the world destruction experience as the reflection of a threat to Sam's sense of self-continuity may help us to understand a wide range of symptoms. Sam was terrified by the experience of being fragmented and without a sense of self. There was no differentiation between what was his and what belonged to the outside world, so he felt the destruction of both and confused the destroyer and the destroyed. It should be recalled that when he saw the mushroom cloud and felt terror, he also perceived himself to be a monster.

Sam experienced terror, lost his personality, and created an adult psychotic self (Saint Sam) that dominated most of his personality. According to Pao's (1979) theory, the adult psychotic self was formed after an external event (perceived rejection by his "girlfriend") mobilized aggressive and sexual conflicts and caused organismic panic. Existent ego adaptation and defenses were shocked, and Sam, in accordance with a best possible solution (Sandler and Joffe 1969), mobilized for recovery. As a result he developed an adult psychotic self. Pao (1979) described the loss of self-continuity as a marker for the diagnosis of schizophrenia. A patient like Sam cannot maintain a sense of self and its representation because the ego functions are paralyzed when anxiety about a conflict becomes organismic panic rather than simply signaling internal danger.

My explanation of the adult psychotic self parallels the ideas of Pao, drastically modifying some and suggesting further considerations, including those that involve the role of object relations.

Differences between Pao's Descriptions and My Formulations, and Modifications of Pao's Ideas

(1) Pao stresses the fact that schizophrenic persons experience the same types of conflict that others do, and the schizophrenic symptom complex is not determined by the contents of the conflict but rather by the way the ego responds to it. He writes, for example, of a patient who had undergone two drastic personality changes before he became bewildered when a go-go girl wearing provocative perfume sat next to him in a bar. According to Pao (1979), "the go-go girl incident reactivated [his] oedipal conflicts and forced an alteration in his sense of self" (p. 215). A closer look, however, does not indicate oedipal conflict and unbalanced loving–critical functioning of the superego. I do not believe that those likely to become schizophrenic are burdened by the same types of core conflicts as neurotics, nor do they have formed superegos; they are predominantly burdened by object relations conflicts. When Sam saw his "girlfriend" kissing another man, it did not bring about a genuinely oedipal conflict; he was preoccupied with dyadic issues. Those who do experience oedipal conflict *reach up* (Boyer 1961, 1983, Volkan 1976) to oedipal constellations (which are not genuine) to defend against anxiety arising from the interplay of self- and object representations, some of which are primarily laden with aggression and others with libido.

Classic analysts like Katan (1954) were quite correct in observing that an unrepressed Oedipus complex was the outstanding characteristic in the pre-psychotic period of schizophrenic patients. They explained this situation as an end result of regression. Katan stressed that in such patients "the Oedipus complex has lost its cathexis" (p. 120). Boyer and I consider the appearance of the unrepressed oedipal material a defense; the patient reaches up to the oedipal issues in order to flee "hot" pre-oedipal object relations conflicts.

(2) Organismic panic is not altogether an exaggerated, paralyzing anxiety initiated by any conflict. Anxiety over conflict in object relations that can precipitate schizophrenia disturbs the maintenance and protection of the existing sense of self and leads to terror (organismic panic) over the loss, or threatened loss, of existing self-representation. I have found that the future schizophrenic's core representation includes psychotic tissue (the infantile psychotic self) that becomes the foundation of the adult psychotic self (the new identity replacing the existing pre-terror identity) in order to end the terror.

(3) I am uncertain why, in a vulnerable person, one object relations conflict leads only to signal anxiety, while in another it precipitates schizophrenia and leads to organismic panic (terror) without signaling function. I can only agree with Greenspan (1989) that "one must consider three possible precipitants" (p. 89) when the signal anxiety is lost: cognitive changes, psychosocial challenges, and neuroanatomical and neurochemical shifts. These precipitants may be interrelated.

(4) Organismic panic is usually accompanied by diffused motor activity, such as the autoaggressive or autoerotic activities of psychotic children. This is "probably . . . an attempt on the child's part at defining the body-self boundaries, an attempt to feel alive even if at the price of enduring pain" (Mahler 1968, p. 215). I have seen adult patients slap their faces while experiencing terror (Volkan 1976). I have also noted that these seemingly different motor activities may have primitive symbolic meaning; through them the patient makes a last-minute effort to reactivate his childhood object representations or

images that could say "No!" It is usually through a child's identification with the representation of the mother/protector who says "no" that the child learns to say "no" as well as "yes" (Spitz 1957). By utilizing and temporarily identifying with the"no"-saying protector, the patient wants to say "No!" and stop the terrifying fragmentation and loss of his sense of self-continuity. At this point we often hear patients repeatedly saying "no" or shaking their heads as if saying the word.

(5) A new sense of self, the adult psychotic self, emerges as it is first sensed by the patient, in accordance with the aggressive or libidinal affect that saturated it; the patient will refer to himself as a monster or an angel. Soon after being taken to the emergency room, Saint Sam, experiencing terror, declared that he was a monster. At first the adult psychotic is made of saturated affect; its cognitive intentional aspects evolve gradually.

(6) The adult psychotic self is established more firmly when the patient attaches ideas to it and defines it. Thus, the initial experience of it, essentially reflecting only the nature of affect, gives way to a more experiential description of a new sense of self. Although I agree with Pao that the adult psychotic self develops in accordance with the principle of the best possible solution (Sandler and Joffe 1969), I believe that its nature is predetermined according to the nature of the infantile psychotic self and that the two are always related.

THE INFANTILE PSYCHOTIC SELF

As indicated, genetic (biological), physiological, psychological, cultural, and environmental factors, combined with what comes from the inner world of the child and the mothering person (i.e., derivatives of instinctual drives and unconscious fantasies), are channeled through the child–mother experiences in order to provide the developing child with ego functions and a foundation of self- and object images. Sometimes what emerges contains much that is biologically disturbed, and, in some cases, psychological disturbance may dominate. Fragile psychic tissue is thus laid down in the infantile psychotic self, which is saturated by unnamable "bad" affects.

The first psychobiological (Jacobson 1964) self is at the mercy of ever-changing internal and external influences, but as it evolves, it becomes a matrix that can begin to resist the assaults from both within and without. A stable matrix is necessary for absorbing both the "good" and the "bad" self- and object images, for the development of ego function to differentiate such images, and for providing a "glue" to integrate them with their associated drive derivatives (i.e., affects). Repeated pleasurable fusions with the mothering person through skin contact, eye contact, and mouth-nipple contact (Lehtonen 1991) are necessary for the establishment of a "normal" matrix. "Good" affects must characterize early contact between infant and mother and saturate psychic tissue if the core is to strengthen and evolve and to manage self- and object images laden with both "good" and "bad" affects. Stability depends on what has been channeled through experience with the mother. The matrix is vulnerable to many factors; if it never becomes strong and stable but stays fragile because of stimuli from within or without, it will become what I describe as an infantile psychotic self. When structure-building identifications depend on such a self, they sink in the matrix and become fragmented, being held in pieces by existing stresses. Thus, in clinical practice we see patients who describe their infantile psychotic selves as having been full of so-called part-objects. In such circumstances, the infantile psychotic self reaches for more identifications in order to respond to a psychobiological need for a more mature psychic structure. It is, however, unable to attain this because each new identification becomes fragmented in turn and either sinks or floats in the matrix. Moreover, when not fused or defused, fragmented self- and object images become involved in an exaggerated introjective-projective cycle that blocks the evolution of more mature structures.

Some infantile psychotic selves are formed regressively. First a "normal" core develops and evolves. But if there is a devastating blow in infancy or childhood (e.g., an unbearable surgical procedure, prolonged hunger, incest, or identification with psychotic or murderous adults), and when necessary environmental safety is lacking, the child's psychic tissue can be torn apart, resulting in a regressively created infantile psychotic self.

My experience with the infantile psychotic selves of a number of patients, described in Part III, led me to conclude that their salient characteristic is saturation with unbearable aggressive affects. They contain some self- and object images (part-objects) that are libidinally invested. Unlike a "normal" and evolving self, however, the psychotic self is dominated by "bad" affects attached to early undifferentiated—or barely differentiated—and unintegrated self- and object images. Primitive defenses (e.g., an introjective-projective cycle) are set in motion to protect the infant from experiencing "bad" affects. We name such affects *anaclitic depression, emptiness, helplessness,* or *rage,* but what infants experience is really unnamable.

Affects can be conceptualized as unconscious feelings. Lacking a good psychoanalytic theory about affects, we conclude that initially the infant's affects, as well as unconscious fantasies and thoughts, are without form and differentiation. We wonder about the initiation of affects; are they simply derivatives of instinctual drives? Is infantile rage a simple manifestation of the aggressive drive? Do affects arise from interaction with caregivers? For example, is a frustrating experience at the breast necessary in order for infantile rage to occur? If we believe that affects result from the earliest object relations, do we need to hold on to the concept of instinctual drives? These are difficult questions to answer. My position is that in early infancy the organism's drives dovetail with experiences with the outside. I maintain the concept of drives in my metapsychological thinking because they make many clinical phenomena easier to explain. For example, using the concept of drives can help us to better describe the differences in reactions of two or more infants who have similar experiences with the external world.

In Sam's case we should consider the possibility of genetic (biological) factors because some family members seem to have had similar mental disorders, probably schizophrenia. We should also consider *psychological genes*, which were included in his initial self-representation and which were coded with self-destructive potentials. His psychological genes were like time bombs set to explode in the future.

Shapiro and colleagues (1977), Grotstein (1986), and Volkan (1987) have described how family members "choose" the future borderline or schizophrenic as a reservoir for their shortcomings. In fact, Grotstein suggested that the schizophrenic "is selected as the 'human sacrifice' by the family system" (p. 61). Apprey (1994) states that in a schizophrenic there exists (1) an injunction, received from an anterior other (e.g., parent, grandparent), to hasten the subject's death; (2) the subject's submission to this injunction; and (3) complicity between other and subject to feign restoration.

When I interviewed Sam's mother on various occasions, she unknowingly described her infanticidal fantasies about Sam, her only child. Her fantasies were basically reflected in a symptom she developed when Sam was a small baby. Despite repeated assurances from a pediatrician that her infant was healthy, Sam's mother was obsessed with the idea that he would die. She was conscious of seeing aspects of her father and brother in the baby but was not aware of transferring her murderous rage toward them onto the infant. Her brother, by being a boy and being ill, had taken her parents' attention away from her. When she was at the oedipal age, she felt that her depressed father did not respond to her wish to be loved by him. She developed a narcissistic personality organization and felt paralyzed once her psychobiological motherly functions were activated. She could not breast-feed Sam and he was exiled to the care of others. She was aware of her death wishes toward her psychotic brother but also felt obliged to "love and protect" him and behaved the same way toward Sam.

Sam was a child of secrecy. He was not supposed to be born and serve as evidence of an illicit affair. But simultaneously he was to serve as a secret tool of aggression against her devalued husband, a man who also stood for her brother and father, whom she hated. Since his conception, Sam had a confused, false, secret, unreal identity in his mother's mind that was primarily invested with aggression. The mother's object representation of Sam was the psychological gene that was passed on to the initial self-representation of the boy. Sam's other childhood traumas and experiences (e.g., his identification with his psychotic uncle) were absorbed into his original psychic tissue.

Furthermore, Sam's experience with multiple mothers may have taxed the integrative function of his ego as it developed (Cambor 1969, Kramer 1986, Volkan 1979, 1987).

> The child to whom more than one mothering figure is available may move from one who frustrates him to another and thus need not experience pressing frustration from any one individual. Thus it is hard for him to see any "mother" as a total individual; if his caretakers differ significantly from one another or are inconsistent, integration becomes even more of a problem. [Volkan 1987, p. 38]

HIERARCHY

A look at Sam's early life and his early biological and physical environment gives us a clue to the multiple factors that play a role in the establishment of an infantile psychotic self. Sam's most likely existed in his infancy, but even if he were able to develop an initial "normal" self-representation, it would eventually be shattered and an infantile psychotic self would be established regressively. Determining when Sam's infantile psychotic self was crystallized is really a moot point.

Ego deficiencies caused by genetic (biological), physiological, psychological, environmental, and drive-oriented factors lead to object relations conflicts, which in turn lead to the maintenance of defects. As Greenspan (1989) noted, it is "a chicken or egg question" (p. 44) as to which comes first. Pao (1979) described three types of schizophrenia, and in doing so depended on the maturity of the patient's family system. These three types also reflect the fate of the infantile psychotic self.

Type 1. This type of patient appears able, at least on the surface, to function adequately until the late teens, when he becomes floridly psychotic, although aware of what is going on around him. One does not expect to learn that the patient's mother had shown schizoid tendencies during his childhood; with successful therapeutic intervention he may recover socially within months, but without long-term treatment he will be vulnerable to recurrence of the symptom complex.

Type 2. The parents of Type 2 patients, unlike those of Type 1, seem to have been troubled when the patient was a child. Despite a disturbed infancy and childhood, he does rather well during latency but becomes schizophrenic in mid-adolescence while loosening ties to parental representations.

Type 3. The family members of this type of patient are quite disturbed, and defective ego functioning is exhibited from childhood on, with the patient responding badly to the slightest drive intensification. He becomes insidiously schizophrenic at the dawn of puberty, and his prognosis is poor.

Pao holds that any one of the three types can become chronic with no hope for recovery. I believe that in Type 3 patients, the infantile psychotic self becomes globalized early in life, causing childhood schizophrenia—or, at least, extreme vulnerability to the development of full-blown schizophrenia at puberty. In Type 1 and 2 patients, the infantile psychotic self is pushed into the background while ego mechanisms that are associated with areas uninvaded by the infantile psychotic self surround and control the fragile tissue and its saturation with "bad" affects.

As noted earlier, it is not simple regression that causes prototypical schizophrenia in the adult but the loss of maintenance mechanisms that previously supported the self that encapsulated the infantile psychotic self and compensated for or concealed its fragility. Failure to keep fragile infantile material in the background and maintain the existing self-representation brings terror, so the individual develops an adult psychotic self with associated primitive ego functions on the foundations of his fragile, infantile psychotic self. A schizophrenic is regressed because of the reappearance and reactivation of already existent, previously covered over, early, fragile psychic material. In schizophrenia, it is not the previous healthier self that surrounds the infantile psychotic core but the adult psychotic self, which is linked to and absorbs the infantile psychotic self. It seems that a healthier part always remains in some degree, however.

Salonen (1979) reported on a patient whose infantile psychotic self was at the level of "the primal representative matrix" (p. 80) without cathexis of drive representations. In other cases, the infantile psychotic self is at a higher level but still lacks clearly differentiated self- and object images. As reported in Chapter 3, the core of the infantile psychotic self, and accordingly the core of the adult psychotic self, is not the same for every schizophrenic. Therefore, we should think of mixed levels. I believe that David Rosenfeld (1992) and Kernberg (1992) expressed a similar opinion but using slightly different terminology. In his foreword to David Rosenfeld's *The Psychotic: Aspects of the Personality,* Kernberg states that in the most severe cases we see a "dismantling of internalized object relations" (p. ix). Earlier, I referred to this level of severity as the crumbling and sinking of such relations (identifications), through wear and tear, into the psychobiological matrix. In slightly less severe conditions, there is "the autistic encapsulation of early object relations under conditions of extreme trauma," and toward the middle spectrum of severity "we find the dominance of symbiotic, fused, or undifferentiated relations between self and object" (p. ix). Kernberg continues, stating that "At the less pathological pole of psychosis, we find the differentiation proceeds, and more sophisticated splits between idealized and persecutory relationships are played out in the context of improved reality testing" (p. ix).

The infantile psychotic self may not remain static but grow—assimilating influences and unconscious fantasies related to self- and object images from different phases of childhood—and come to include identifications with early part-objects while reality testing remains ineffective. As far as my experience indicates, at whatever level the infantile psychotic self always remains saturated with "bad" affects.

THE LINK BETWEEN INFANTILE AND ADULT
PSYCHOTIC SELVES

The adult psychotic self is established more firmly when ego functions are recovered after being paralyzed. I believe this stage of the illness is predetermined according to the nature of the infantile psychotic self. Saint Sam exhibited traits that echoed those of Sam the child; the early fragile psychotic self partly identified with the nursemaid who had licked his body after bathing it, and Sam used licking as an expression of introjective attempts. Sam's mother thought of him as an extension of her "crazy" brother, with whom Sam also partly identified, especially after his death. Saint Sam, the repairer of the world, was also modeled after his uncle, whose representation was fused into the boy's infantile psychotic self.

Sam's infantile psychotic self became dominant when he was a very disturbed child, but when he went through the psychologically determined second individuation of adolescence (Blos 1979) as well as hormonal changes, he changed identity again with the help of his nurturing caretaker of that period. His personality traits at this time included his identification with the functions of this "good caretaker." When the book-loving woman left, Sam crystallized the self-representation of a shy bookworm. He lost his existing self-representation (which kept his infantile psychotic self in the shadows) when he became Saint Sam and had fantasies of world destruction and reconstruction. Saint Sam was his adult psychotic self, in which his experiences as an infant and child and as an adult schizophrenic were connected. His metamorphosis into Saint Sam was tied to an infantile psychotic self and a predisposition to schizophrenia. No adult psychotic self appears without prior connection to an original infantile psychotic self that was created by multiple psychobiological factors.

5

A Reexamination of the Issue of Nature versus Nurture

A look at how the infantile psychotic self develops suggests a new discussion of nature (genetic/biological factors) versus nurture (the internalization of experience with the environment) in the etiology of schizophrenia and related conditions. Studies of twins (Gottesman and Shields 1972, Kendler 1983) offer an interesting measure of the major etiological role of genetic factors.

Gottesman and Shields (1972) felt that neither genetic nor environmental factors alone are sufficient to cause schizophrenia. They state:

> it is the data showing that identical twins are as often discordant as concordant for schizophrenia that provide the most impressive evidence for the important role of environmental factors in schizophrenia, whatever they may be. [p. 319]

Tienari and his co-workers' research in Finland on the interaction between genetic vulnerability and family environment is impressive (Tienari 1991, Tienari et al. 1985). They state that schizophrenia runs in families but do not specify whether this relates to genetic (biological) or psychosocial (environmental) transmission. According to Tienari, it is meaningless to ask which of these two factors is more important. We need to examine their combined effect. Research so far has failed to identify exactly how this joint influence operates. Even after nine major twin studies between 1928 and 1993, we cannot say that genes directly code for schizophrenia.

Biological research into the mysteries of schizophrenia has increased and, through the use of technological advances, has also become highly sophisticated. Biological theories of schizophrenia, however, are "devoid of psychological content" and "increasingly suffer from reductionism" (Cancro 1986, p. 106). Nonetheless, we cannot say that our psychological theories give a true and complex insight into the way schizophrenia develops, although those with a purely biological point of view fare worse than psychoanalysts in theorizing about the causes of its onset.

I will not review the biological findings here but emphasize that at present there is no unified biological theory explaining how schizophrenia or its symptom complexes occur. Scholars and researchers seem to be looking everywhere. Some topics have been made popular by biological researchers and epidemiologists, causing the literature to become saturated with claims and disclamations. The result is what I call *scientific obsessionalism* and in the long run sheds no light on what schizophrenia is and especially on what its symptoms mean. I think that the seasonality of schizophrenic births has been one of these scientifically popular preoccupations (see, e.g., Dalen 1990, Franzek and Beckmann 1992, O'Callaghan 1991, Pulver 1990, Pulver et al. 1992, Sacchetti et al. 1992, Torrey and Bowler 1990, Watson 1990). We really do not know the significance of the statistics such studies have produced. Others have focused on viral infections during pregnancy (influenza epidemics; see Crow and Done 1992, O'Callaghan et al. 1991) or noted the similarity between several aspects of schizophrenia and autoimmune illnesses, and still others (Eagles 1991, Harrison

1990, Kendell 1989) refer to the migration between countries as an environmental risk factor.

The prefrontal cortex in the brain of some schizophrenics does appear to have atrophied or developed abnormally, but this is not the case for all schizophrenic patients. Discovering eye movement dysfunction (EMD) in schizophrenics and their first-degree relatives, Bartfai and his associates (1989) suggested that EMD may be a genetic marker for vulnerability to schizophrenia. For a while it looked as if hyperdopaminergia was the primary or sole event in either the cause or the pathogenesis of schizophrenia.

Additional examples show how biological researchers are groping to find and evolve theories to explain schizophrenia. Davis and colleagues (1991) provided a good review of all published studies regarding dopamine and schizophrenia. This review focused on postmortem studies, positron emission tomography, neuroleptic drug actions, plasma levels of the dopamine metabolite homovanillic acid, and cerebral blood flow. It showed compelling evidence that hyperdopaminergic transmission alone cannot explain the etiology or pathogenesis of schizophrenia. Thus, these reviewers suggested the "possible co-occurrence of high and low level dopamine activity in schizophrenia" (p. 1474). According to them, it is possible that low prefrontal dopamine activity causes deficit symptoms of schizophrenia, such as passivity, isolation tendencies, and impoverishment of speech. Meanwhile, high dopamine activity in mesolimbic dopamine neurons causes positive symptoms, such as thought disorders, delusions, and hallucinations. They concluded, however, that many of the notions their review suggested "will prove overly simplistic, but the gathering of more data will, by further reformulations, inevitably bring us closer to an understanding of the pathophysiology of schizophrenia" (p. 1483).

Weinberger (1987) reviewed a neurodevelopmental account of various aspects of schizophrenia, which, according to him, does not result from the onset of a neurodegenerative disorder in adulthood. Instead, his model focused on a silent brain lesion that becomes unmasked by neuromaturational changes during late adolescence, especially by the activation of sex hormones. This unmasked lesion then renders the mesocortical dopamine function underactive and, in time, results in secondary meso-limbic dopamine overactivity.

Although Weinberger's theory has been the subject of considerable discussion among his colleagues in biological research, it falls short of providing a unifying explanation. My discussions with biological psychiatrists lead me to believe that there is no biological formulation that can do so. We must hope that the difficult search for a connection between the mind and the body will attract more attention and lead to better theories about the development of schizophrenia. Meanwhile, psychoan-alytic observation of patients remains a primary source of information about the meaning of the schizophrenic's inner world. We know as much about psychological genes as we do biological ones.

Let me return to the channel metaphor and focus on the mother's unconscious fantasies, as well as on those of the other caregivers that enter into this channel, and on the child's own unconscious fantasies as they eventually develop (Apprey 1984, 1993a,b, 1994, Volkan 1981a, 1987). An understanding of these unconscious fantasies from both sides of the child–mother dyad is possible only by a psychoanalytic approach. Thus, this ap-proach is a necessity in the examination of the schizophrenic's inner world. Unconscious fantasies, first coming from the mother/caretaker and then from the child himself, color the nature of the latter's experiences with the environment and the self. The mother may have unconscious homicidal fantasies about the baby (I suggest this was true with Sam's mother). Unconscious fantasies, some more devastating than others, play a role in the development of symptoms, including schizophrenic symptoms, as well as of adaptations.

The family members may also unconsciously deposit within the baby's developing self-representation a fully formed mental representation of another person, perhaps that of someone who died before the baby's birth. In 1987 I gave examples of what I called *deposited representations*. The de-veloping child experiences himself consciously but also, more importantly, unconsciously, as a depository of a representation of someone else that existed in the mind of his parents. The woman whose delusion was that she was half-dead, half-alive and half-woman, half-man was recreating a representation of her mother's dead sibling and lost fetus that the mother and grandmother had deposited into the child's developing self (Volkan 1981a). Later (Volkan 1987) I compared

> the transmission of anxiety from mother to child with the transmission of germs that cause infection; and the passage of unassimilated self- and object representations and their affect dispositions from parent to child, with the inheritance of genes. [p. 43]

Most psychoanalysts agree with Mahler (1968), who suggested that both nature and nurture play a role in the etiology of schizophrenia, and that the issue of dominance is moot. This is not a new attitude in psychoanalysis. At present we can speak of the nature–nurture issue in rather general terms: If a child has a biological weakness disturbing the ego functions that organize and integrate experiences, develops self- and object representations, forms memories, maintains thoughts, tames unbearable and unnamable affects, and represses unacceptable conflicts, he may be prone to schizophrenia. On the other hand, clinical observations demonstrate that if a constitutionally sturdy child experiences devastating and repeated trauma during his developmental years without a background of safety (Sandler 1960), he, too, may be prone to develop schizophrenia. How a child, with a given biological state, experiences interaction with the environment, and how he assimilates such experiences into his developing mind, determines the juncture at which disposition and environmental influence meet. The child's ability to introject and identify properly with the functions of others may depend on his constitutional potentials. On the other hand, he has no choice but to take in experiences available in the environment. Some children with "bad" environmental influences do well as adults, and only longitudinal studies of their lives as a psychodynamic process can disclose what makes certain individuals more creatively adaptable than others. Although studies attempting to combine biological and psychological factors are becoming more sophisticated, we obviously should continue relevant research.

Lichtenberg (1983) reported that some infants, when approached by the mother or mothering person, appear uncoordinated rather than alert and physically coordinated as usual. His explanation of this unexpected response is that some neonates cannot use stimuli to learn about the environment because they overtax the immature nervous system. Lichtenberg's data, which depend on 24-hour observation of split-screen photography of infant–mother interactions, show that if the neonate responds negatively to the approaching caregiver (i.e., the mother), the effect on the mother may be profound.

> Rather than feeling the competence of their babies and their accomplishments with them, they become confused and frustrated. Here we have a biological factor turning into an environmental trauma, affecting the concrete experience of both partners. [1983, p. 91]

A more systematic look at the meeting of biology and psychology is provided by Emde (1988a,b) and Greenspan (1989). Emde shows an intricate biological preparation for the beginning of social relationships as the mother paces her own stimulation of the infant (e.g., she speaks to the infant in baby-talk). Thus stimulated, the infant begins to consolidate the affective core of his infantile self-representation and his relationships and experiences. According to Greenspan (1989), the interaction between age-specific experience and the state of the central nervous system determines how the ego organizes itself. He developed a most interesting hypothesis regarding the foundation of affective disorders and thought disorders, one based on early sensory and affective experiences and specific processing difficulties. He states that while there is an overlap between a number of sensory and motor patterns, "the auditory and visual spatial pathways seemed specific for different types of disorders" (p. 70). The affective disorders arise from an underlying constitutional-maturational vulnerability in visual-spatial processing and integration. In Greenspan's model, the intensity of affect is communicated through the visual-spatial pathway, while the meaning of affect is communicated predominantly through the auditory-vocal-verbal channel. Thought disorders emanate from difficulty in processing auditory-vocal-verbal information in an environment that tends to confuse the meanings of communication.

Greenspan reminds us that Jackson (1960), Lidz (1973), and Wynne, Matthysse, and Cromwell (1978) reported on the confusing pattern of communication in so-called schizophrenic families. He adds, however, that difficulty may also come from the child who confuses family members because he processes their verbal or gestural cues poorly, thus encouraging them to try harder, and thereby confusing the child even more.

Using the term *mutual cueing*, Mahler (1968) spoke of the necessity of a fit between the infant and mother (or the mothering person). Mutual cueing is the essential psychological ingredient for the development of a feeling of safety and of a solid psychic foundation. Because the infant is more stimulus seeking than we had supposed (Lichtenberg 1983, Stern 1985), he reaches the stimulus barrier from his side; because he has the innate equipment to regulate stimuli, mutual cueing is influenced by both infant and mother.

THEORETICAL CONSIDERATIONS ON THE BEGINNING OF THE MIND

While some child analysts/researchers began showing how genetic (biological) and psychological factors influence each other in the development of ego functions (as well as self- and object representations), others see the beginning of mind from a theoretical or metapsychological perspective. Some of these theoreticians' views are useful in conceptualizing the development of the infantile psychotic self.

At present, combined clinical and theoretical work on schizophrenia in Finland surpasses that being conducted elsewhere. Examples are Pekka Tienari's work (1991) in Oulu; the need-adapted treatment approach of Yrjö Alanen (1993) in Turku; the metapsychological and therapeutic approach of Simo Salonen (1979), also in Turku; the psychosomatic approach of Johannes Lehtonen (1991) in Kuopio; and the theoretical and therapeutic approach of Veikko Tähkä (1984a, 1993) in Helsinki.

Tähkä speaks of the infants' species-specific mental function potentials that depend on the relationships they have with others in their environment and which, once activated, develop into mental phenomena. He states that some of these mental function potentials (e.g., perception and memory) are fundamental, and that their activation is almost certain to occur in an average environment (e.g., the simple nursing activity of the mother). The other potentials are activated only with more complicated relationships and thus are more vulnerable to deficiencies and complications in the child-environment interaction (e.g., the evolution of certain mental function potentials requires ego and superego identifications).

Consider the particular interplay between nature and nurture that makes an individual schizophrenia-prone and circumstances in which the infantile psychotic self is likely to appear. I propose the following two possibilities.

(a) If there is a genetic (biological) disturbance influencing the infant's fundamental mental function potentials, a foundation for the infantile psychotic self is laid down with little psychological (nurture) content. Lehtonen (1991) has researched the beginnings of mental function and reminds us that for Freud (1940), the psychical and the physical were end points of our knowledge; everything in-between was unknown. Because psychosomatic research deals with the connection between the two, investigation of the interdependence between mind and body is difficult, if not impossible. Lehtonen proposes that the psychophysiological connection originally comes into being when the body ego—the first ego—forms. He holds that during the first months after birth, a body ego evolves out of the fusion of the infant's pleasurable experiences and vital satisfactions with sensory impressions coming from the mother, especially from her breast. Referring to Isakower's phenomenon (Isakower 1938) and Lewin's (1948) dream screen, Lehtonen (1991) attempts to find clinical manifestations of a primordial matrix of psychic organization consequent to this psychophysical fusion and states that the nascent body ego is " 'bilingual' and sensitive to both physical and psychic factors" (p. 489). I believe that disturbances at this level comprise the foundation of the infantile psychotic self and thus initiate a truly psychosomatic disturbance that causes the child to develop schizophrenia at some stage of his life.

(b) Other mental function potentials that require complicated relationships with the environment have psychological content and may also be influenced by biological-constitutional factors; the crucial effect of human interaction on the child's developing psychic world cannot be dismissed. This different type of infantile psychotic self may or may not involve childhood schizophrenia, but persons in this category will remain schizophrenia-prone. They are likely to benefit more from a psychotherapeutic approach; their relationship with a therapist, and identification with his functions, may activate processes to correct initial deficiencies with their accompanying object relations conflicts.

6

Characteristics of the Adult Psychotic and Uninvaded Selves in Schizophrenia

I have noted that an adult is schizophrenic when his adult psychotic self invades his personality; however, an uninvaded part always remains. Certain key aspects of the psychotic and uninvaded selves therefore need consideration.

THE ADULT PSYCHOTIC SELF'S REALITY: THE OUTER BOUNDARY

The concept of *ego boundary* and its loss was first formulated by Tausk (1919). Federn (1952) later referred to an outer ego boundary that was the ego's sense organ; it did not enclose the ego like a rigid band but shifted from time to time. For example, a lecturer's ego boundary embraces his audience. It might be better, in current terminology, to speak of the boundary of the self-representation rather than that of the ego. Nevertheless, it is the ego's function to establish a boundary for the self-representation and to act as a sense organ. We can say that the self-representation is surrounded by ego functions, especially those that test reality, and, hence, has a border. Federn believed that if the external ego boundary expands, earlier ego boundaries are not lost but repressed. I think in cases of low levels of personality organization (e.g., narcissistic, borderline, and psychotic personality organizations), and in schizophrenia, it is better to speak of the splitting, fragmenting off, or denying of the experience of the earlier ego boundary from the current one than to speak of its repression.

The outer boundary deals with reality testing. The adult psychotic self's boundary is weak and permeable. The ego becomes unable to differentiate between what belongs inside the self and what belongs outside, and reality testing is lost or at least confused. One of Harry Stack Sullivan's (1962) patients, while watching a game of billiards, ejaculated when he saw a particular ball dropped into a pocket; he could not differentiate a symbolically sexual occurrence in the environment from the sexuality of his own body. Burnham (1970) describes the interpenetration of inner and outer in one of his patients who said, "When the light went on, I could feel it in my bowels," and "I shouldn't think that thought; as soon as I did the sun went back behind the clouds" (p. 200).

Another way of reconstructing reality involves the weakening or breaking of the outer boundary that causes a shift from one symbolic level to another. Burnham (1970) tells of a patient who, struggling to control her aggressive and sexual impulses, displaced this struggle onto a ritual of turning on hot and cold water faucets alternately in order to get warm water. As noted, the schizophrenic also uses splitting mechanisms, but not in the stable way a borderline patient does. I believe that Burnham's patient was unsuccessfully trying to integrate. Hot and cold aspects were involved not only in the splitting but also in the introjective-projective process.

> She explained that if she did not exert great care the "hot water man," who she thought was downstairs holding the pipe, might be burned. This woman's family had first become convinced of the seriousness of her illness when they discov-

ered her pouring water into the furnace. It is noteworthy that she displaced her struggle for control not only from one symbolic level to another, but also from the inner to the outer realm of events. [p. 209]

Still another type of confusion about reality testing can be seen in the operations of an adult psychotic self when a representation of one external object is fused with that of another. This is why Saint Sam called a bearded hospital attendant "uncle."

The same types of confusion appear in the schizophrenic as a deficiency in logical thinking. Abse (1987) explains how such patients abandon Aristotelian logic (as expressed in *The Organon*) when anything beyond the intersection of two or more realities is ignored, as illustrated by von Domarus (1944). Thus, a schizophrenic's observation that "certain Indians are swift" and "stags are swift" leads to the conclusion that "certain Indians are stags."

THE INNER BOUNDARY AND AFFECTS

Another type of confusion about reality is still more intriguing. It is caused by the permeability of an inner boundary of the adult psychotic self that surrounds the infantile psychotic self. Using current terminology, I suggest that the outer ego boundary comes into existence primarily because of the ego's reality testing function; the inner boundary is the result of the ego's function that tames the affects. Federn (1952) suggested that in schizophrenia mere thought becomes reality; I believe that this is secondary to affects becoming reality. When the adult psychotic self is first formed, the nature of the affect that saturates it defines it; thoughts are attached to it later. This formulation is similar to Werner's (1948) observation that "affect actually forms the world itself" (p. 81) in schizophrenia, especially when this world is felt within, but even when it is projected outward. I should note here that the infantile psychotic self is originally made of affects or precursors of affects. Self- and object images and representations are later built on this matrix saturated with affects. If this matrix remains an infantile psychotic self and is permeated with unbearable affects, self- and object representations do not follow a path to maturity. In being saturated with affects, especially negative affects, the adult psychotic self is linked to the infantile psychotic self.

Overwhelming emotionality and accompanying fragments of self- and object images that pertain to the adult psychotic self often become associated with bodily functions and, as Arlow (1963) suggested, may unconsciously represent the loss of control over urinary and anal sphincters. Thus, a schizophrenic whose adult psychotic self is saturated with an aggressive wish may experience himself as an uncontrolled urinary tract or anus. Aggressive feelings are then experienced as "bad" urine or feces. In my experience, however, multiple meanings are condensed in a schizophrenic's identification of the adult psychotic self with body waste.

A patient named Feriha had been born in a conservative Muslim country, from which her parents emigrated when she was less than 1 year old. Although both parents were highly educated professionals, they found it difficult to adjust at first. The young wife regressed and so offered her child less than adequate mothering. The couple prospered later, but their already damaged daughter stayed emotionally dependent on them despite academic achievement, always feeling different from American-born girls. In her last year of high school she fell in love with an American boy and experienced sexual conflict. Should she stay a virgin, as her Middle Eastern parents had taught her? Or should she behave like her classmates? Was she an American or from the Middle East? In her unconscious, she had object relations (identity) conflicts and faced a separation crisis; should she remain a child or become a woman? Her separation anxiety, heightened by higher-level concerns about sex, paralyzed her ego functions in day-to-day activity. When she had been less than 1 year old, her mother experienced separation and adaptation anxieties, and these were passed on to Feriha's infantile self as "bad" affects, due to repeated fusions between mother's self-representation and the child's developing self-representation. Furthermore, the mother could not convey effective ego functions to a daughter now dealing with such worries. The girl's separation anxiety peaked and evolved into terror, and she developed an adult psychotic self that dominated her personality, which she called "the shit woman." She would defecate in her hospital room and, whenever her therapist or other caretakers entered, would scoop up a piece of fecal material and smear it on the walls, crying "Shit! Shit!" and saying nothing else. The therapist visited her daily for about a month and sat with her as she went through this routine; the hospital administration had consented to this filthy activity and arranged for the mess to be cleaned. After a month Feriha began speaking to her therapist and stopped smearing the walls. The symbolism involved in her behavior eventually became clear.

Feriha's adult psychotic self—the shit woman—had many layers of symbolism, including identification with the anal self that belonged to the time when sphincter control had given her a sense of mastery. The anality originally included in her infantile psychotic self was now in the service of making order out of her confused life. Object searching and object rejecting also motivated her to smear feces in her hospital room, as did an expression of anal rage toward internalized parental images and their representations. She was seeking a caregiver who would be forced to "clean" her by removing her "dirty" (sexualized) feelings. At a lower level, she used the fecal material as a transitional object; she played with it, abused it, and used it to soothe her anxiety. The illusion of control over her feces, like a child's illusion of control over a transitional object, allowed her to feel that she controlled all external objects and their representations as well as the saturation of her adult psychotic self with unpleasant affects.

MAINTENANCE ACTIVITIES IN THE INNER WORLD

The involuntary activity associated with the adult psychotic and uninvaded parts of schizophrenic patients reveals much about their characteristics. One should look for meaning in the schizophrenic's hallucinations, rituals, and disordered thoughts, considering them in light of his life experiences and unconscious fantasies. Leaving aside symptoms or behavior patterns specific to one individual case, I shall focus on the involuntary inner-world activities and object relations common to all schizophrenics.

The seriousness of a schizophrenic's clinical condition does not depend on the surface picture, no matter how bizarre that may be, but on the degree to which the adult psychotic self has invaded the whole personality and crystallized. Because the adult psychotic self has been created in response to terror, the patient tries to maintain it in order to avoid reexperiencing that terror. The adult psychotic self is maintained through its own operations or from the support it receives from the nonpsychotic (uninvaded) part. I now report on some areas discussed earlier, this time illustrating their role in the maintenance of the adult psychotic self.

Fusion-Defusion and Introjective-Projective Cycles

Relations with the external world hinge on the status of the adult psychotic self, whether it relates to the environment in a fusion-defusion or an introjective-projective mode. Without a sense of a border between the adult self and an object representation, they fuse into temporary identification and are quickly separated and differentiated repeatedly in a cyclical pattern. When a boundary between self- and object representations is experienced, we see an introjective flow from the outer into the inner world, followed by a projected return to the outer. Saint Sam (see Chapter 4) illustrated this graphically when he tried to "eat" (introject) others and then "spit them out" (project them) while thinking himself a snake. He was never able to find "God's angel" because every "good" object or its representation quickly turned "bad." He seemed doomed in his introjective-projective relatedness to regulate and control relationships between the adult psychotic self and external objects and their representations in order to protect his psychotic self.

Transitional Objects and Phenomena

The adult psychotic self creates a new version of transitional objects and phenomena in order to maintain itself by managing and controlling the influences of external objects and their representations (Volkan 1976). In childhood, a transitional object or phenomenon causes an infant to respond to the ministrations of the "good enough" mother with "the illusion that there is an external reality that corresponds to [his] own capacity to create" (Winnicott 1953, p. 95). The transitional object is like a lantern with one opaque side and one transparent side, and only the latter side is able to illuminate the outside world. In the moment of this illumination, the child links not-me with mother-me (or object-me) (Greenacre 1970) and has the illusion of control over their relatedness. If the child feels psychophysiological tension, he or she can turn the opaque side toward the world and, thus, blot it out.

When reality testing is uncertain, the adult psychotic self returns to the re-creation of transitional objects or phenomena in an effort to regulate and protect itself. The transitional object or phenomenon of an adult psychotic self is not in the service of growth and creativity; only with treatment does the schizophrenic show evolution in the utilization of transitional objects and phenomena and use them to get well.

Volkan and Luttrell (1971) reported how an 18-year-old schizophrenic patient used a tape recorder as a transitional object, holding it between himself and his therapist, hospital staff members, and other patients. He could communicate with others only through this device, which, by the same token, enabled him to admit or exclude the outside world and its representation in an omnipotent way. Feinsilver (1980) implies that relatedness based on a transitional object or phenomenon protects the psychotic self. Saint Sam used copies of a certain religious publication as transitional objects.

Delusions, Hallucinations, Language Peculiarities, and Other Common Symptoms

Although one may attach specific meaning to such schizo-phrenic symptoms as delusions and hallucinations, my focus here is on their role in protecting the adult psychotic self from the recurrence of terror and maintaining the status quo. Pao (1979) describes how the patient experiencing organismic panic in the acute phase of illness *is* the delusion or hallucination. (Again, I believe that this follows a state in which the patient is the affect.) In the subacute phase, the patient experiences unfamiliarity with his new adult psychotic self and may search for the old one, asking questions such as "Where is he?" Once the delusion is fixated, it ensures the patient of safety. This accounts for the stubborn way in which patients cling to their symptoms, especially delusions, hallucinations, and other common features. I think that delusions and hallucinations originate in the adult psychotic self rather than in the patient's uninvaded parts, because they are associated with a break with reality. At times, however, it may be difficult to locate the part from which they originate. The difficulty is that the precursor of some of these symptoms can be found in the patient's pre-psychotic period. For example, some delusions can be traced back to fantasies present in the pre-psychotic period. Lichten-berg and Pao (1974) give clinical examples that illustrate that the material of the past on which a delusion can be built might be a persistent fantasy. A fantasy is notably associated with pleasurable feelings—even if the content of the fantasy is being beaten. Lichtenberg and Pao state that when a delusion is built on a persistent fantasy, it becomes unpleasurable.

Another reason for the difficulty in locating the origin of delusions is that some crystallized delusions are based on identifications that may be in the infantile psychotic self or in the healthier part of a past self-representation. Sam's religious delusions supported his adult psychotic self's continuous quest to restore what he had lost. It also let him maintain contact with his "crazy" uncle's identification. As his therapist learned during Sam's treatment, this uncle had given the young Sam a certain degree of stability. I believe that the uncle's representation was included in both his infantile psychotic self and his healthier part.

MECHANISMS OF THE UNINVADED PART OF THE PERSONALITY

Some mechanisms that protect the adult psychotic self clearly come from the patient's uninvaded parts. Mechanisms such as avoidance, ritualization, intellectualization, and higher-level projections and displacements support the adult psychotic self and help the patient to avoid another terror. On a clinical level, these mechanisms may appear as phobias, rituals, obsessions, compulsions, or suspicions. Saint Sam ritualistically called on a religious institution as if to refuel his adult psychotic self; at the same time, he avoided student gatherings, where external reality would bring into question his fantasies of being an omnipotent savior. It is ironic that a schizophrenic's most stubborn resistance against modifying the adult psychotic self may sometimes come from uninvaded parts.

Part II

OTHER FATES

7

The Fates of the Infantile Psychotic Self

Every adult who becomes schizophrenic has an infantile psychotic self, but not everyone with an infantile psychotic self becomes schizophrenic. This self may remain encapsulated for life when the developing infant creates from life experiences another core. The second self evolves from this core, and ego functions associated with it effect encapsulation of the infantile psychotic self, as noted by S. Klein (1980), Tustin (1986), H. Rosenfeld (1965), and D. Rosenfeld (1992). If encapsulation of the infantile psychotic self holds throughout the individual's life, we have no evidence of encapsulation's existence. We have clues to this type of encapsulation, however, when we examine persons who are to all intents and purposes "healthy" or, at worst, neurotic, but who, as adults, suddenly have focalized breaks with reality, delusions, hallucinations, and other symptoms of psychosis. Following P. Kramer (1955) and Niederland (1956), I have described (Volkan 1965, 1976) the appearance of a previously encapsulated aspect of personality in a young woman who demonstrated the *little man phenomenon*. Whenever she looked in a mirror she saw herself reflected as a tiny figure that represented her encapsulated baby self. We note that in such cases the encapsulated infantile self emerges only partly alive; it does not invade the personality. Therefore, the individual does not have full-blown schizophrenia but continues to be neurotic or "healthy," except when entering the arena where the previously fossilized psychotic self erupts with vitality. Because such cases are rare, and because psychoanalytic data from longitudinal studies are not readily available, I cannot say with certainty what makes a seemingly fossilized infantile psychotic egg hatch. My experience with such individuals suggests that hatching occurs when the patient regresses and experiences the environment as it was during the crucial development of the infantile psychotic self.

It is more common for the infantile psychotic self to stay only partly encapsulated and, from childhood on, drastically influence the personality. If a healthier infantile self develops in addition to the psychotic one, the ego functions of the healthier unit react and adapt to the effects of the other, even if the healthier part stays under the spell of the infantile psychotic self. The mode of relationships and primitive defenses associated with the infantile psychotic self (e.g., the introjective-projective cycle) are absorbed by the healthier part of the personality. Thus, the person freely uses them daily, as if such relationships and defenses were dominant in adult life, and appears as a healthy individual in other relationships, especially those that do not require intimacy (e.g., work-related relationships). Under these conditions, we say that the individual has organized a *psychotic personality*; he is not a schizophrenic because he can test reality better than a schizophrenic can.

The individual's main behavioral pattern is to reenact the infantile environment in endless ways so that the reality of the infantile psychotic self finds an echo in the external world. He can change the environment to fit the primitive demands of his infantile psychotic self—or change primitive defensive operations to fit the infantile psychotic self in a new environment—and to gain support for the efforts of the healthier part. People with psychotic personality organization are constantly involved in various actions that should not be called the *acting out* of wishes (and defenses against them); they are reenactments of the relationship with the early environment to maintain a sense of reality. Also, the person is constantly involved in psychic activity to replace the infantile psychotic self, saturated with "bad" affects, with a new core saturated with libido; however, he is doomed to fail, and the activity is therefore repeated. These reenactments and activities are the key to the diagnosis of psychotic personality organization above and beyond the abundance of primitive defense mechanisms associated with it.

Individuals with a psychotic personality organization use avoidance to preclude intimacy with others and stay in relationships without emotional stress. One woman with a psychotic personality organization read books she carried with her to avoid relating to the world around her. Even when stopped at a stoplight she would quickly open a book and begin to read. Thus she created her own objects and/or transitional objects, which buffered her from the environment. Such persons can hold jobs and organize their healthier parts to deal logically with their obligations, but a close look at their everyday lives reveals obligatory reenactment of the relationship between their infantile psychotic self and the environment, accomplished by an introjective-projective cycle and a search for support for the healthier part so that it can deal with the influence of the sicker part. When such people undergo treatment, the therapist sees them using any behavior pattern to deal with their infantile psychotic selves and recognizes that although they seem to have healthy object relations, their minds are full of fragmented self- and object images (part objects) that are involved in fusion–defusion and/or introjective-projective cycles and associated conflicts in object relations.

Earlier I noted a third possibility—the invasion and domination of the personality by an infantile psychotic self early in life. In this case the individual becomes schizophrenic in childhood or at least during the early teens. The subsequent crystallized adult psychotic self is a result of its gradual evolution and expansion of the infantile psychotic self; the terror occurring in the formation of the prototypical adult psychotic self is missing. In typical adult schizophrenia, terror is experienced and an adult psychotic self develops which is linked to the infantile psychotic self and reflects its influence. The effects of various fantasies and traumas from every level of psychosexual development change the nature of the link between the infantile and adult psychotic selves.

Psychiatric literature that emphasizes phenomenology points to three subgroups of adult schizophrenia: hebephrenic, catatonic, and paranoid. From a metapsychological point of view, hebephrenic schizophrenia reflects a gradual expansion throughout life of the infantile psychotic self. Catatonic and paranoid types are more typical of the adult psychotic self. It may be impossible to distinguish among phenomenological subgroups in the event of chronicity.

Under certain circumstances a person with a psychotic personality organization may become schizophrenic, whereas in other circumstances an individual with a similar organization has many episodes of adult psychosis but does not develop full-blown schizophrenia. The more crystallized and stabilized the psychotic personality organization, and the more effectively the patient uses a variety of ego functions that deal with the infantile psychotic self, the more capable the individual is of maintaining the psychotic personality organization without psychotic breaks and/or developing schizophrenia.

A SCHEMA

The following is a schema summarizing the various fates of the infantile psychotic self:

1. *Effective encapsulation.* If the infantile psychotic self, whether regressively formed or not, is effectively encapsulated throughout the individual's life, the situation is like having a calcified initial tubercular lesion. We will not know of its existence; however, we theorize that this happens. For example, a patient who previously exhibits an infantile psychotic self

never manifests it again after treatment that does not modify the core self-representation (see the case of Attis, Chapters 9 and 10).

2. *Hatching*. This occurs when a previously and effectively encapsulated but "live" infantile psychotic self suddenly erupts through the patient's healthy self-representation (see the case of Mr. President, this chapter).

3. *Partial encapsulation and absorption into the healthier part of the personality*. The individual's healthier self-representation attempts to split off the partially encapsulated infantile psychotic self. This splitting is not stable or effective. Therefore, the healthier self-representation absorbs aspects of the infantile psychotic self and becomes the spokesperson for it. It is involved in reenactments and actions to promote a fit between the external reality and the infantile psychotic self in order to maintain a sense of reality and replace the "bad" affects of the core with "good" ones. Meanwhile, the individual presents a "normal" front. This leads to a psychotic personality organization (see the case of Arja, this chapter, and Dogman, Chapter 12).

4. *Nonencapsulation*. The infantile psychotic self—originally formed in early infancy or regressively formed in childhood—dominates and removes any effectiveness of the healthier self-representation from childhood on. This leads to childhood schizophrenia. (Because I am not a child analyst, no detailed case of childhood schizophrenia is presented in this book; however, see the case of Sam, Chapter 4, and the case of Attis, Chapters 9 and 10.)

5. *Being put under a new but primitive self-representation in adulthood*. This takes place in adulthood when the existing healthier self-representation that surrounds the infantile psychotic self and maintains and controls it is lost. The individual experiences terror but creates a new self-representation, albeit a primitive one (the adult psychotic self), to surround the infantile psychotic self. This time, however, the adult and infantile psychotic selves are linked more strongly. They form an alliance and dominate whatever healthy self-representation re-

mains. When this situation crystallizes, prototypical adult schizophrenia is established (see the case of Sam, Chapter 4, and the case of Jane, Chapter 14).

OBSERVATIONS ON THE INFANTILE PSYCHOTIC SELF IN NONSCHIZOPHRENIC INDIVIDUALS

This chapter examines the inner worlds of two nonschizophrenic individuals. The first patient, a man in his mid-forties, suddenly behaved in a focalized psychotic way that indicated the presence of an infantile psychotic self that never previously dominated the rest of his personality. Its influence, however, was strong enough to cause the man's downfall in a milieu in which he had previously enjoyed considerable success. The second patient was an average female postgraduate student who had a secret personality that reflected the activities of her infantile psychotic self and the constant efforts of her healthier part to deal with its influence and primitive object relations.

These two patients exemplify the clinical appearance in nonschizophrenic patients of the infantile psychotic self and its expanded adult version. I did an extensive diagnostic workup of the first patient, consulting extensively with his second analyst, and briefly supervised the treatment of the second patient. Accordingly, certain details of their progress were not available to me.

The Fall of Mr. President

Dr. Martinez, a married man with three children, was so well regarded that he was elected to the presidency of a prestigious mental health professional organization, which he held for two consecutive terms. His colleagues continued calling him "Mr. President" even after he was succeeded by another man. He was a Catholic Hispanic who followed the rituals of his church without religious commitment. He was considered a solid citizen and family man, and his children were a credit to him, two becoming respected professionals. His youngest was still a graduate student when I first knew him. He had a flourishing clinical practice, and his wife was prominent in charitable organizations.

In his early forties he had undertaken analysis with a psychologist-analyst about whose training and professional affiliations I know nothing. The analysis was initiated to promote Martinez's standing in a department that was psychoanalytically oriented; however, I learned that he had a special reason for welcoming analysis. His first child had been born about 20 years before he started analysis, and as a new father he had experienced obsessional thoughts about the child's possible death. Once, while walking near a cliff with the baby in his arms, the thought of tossing it into the sea below came to him. This led him to consult a psychiatrist, whom he saw once a week for 6 months. His symptoms disappeared, and he did not realize until much later that this was not because of insights gained in treatment but because he had used his charismatic therapist as an external superego. He told none of his colleagues about his symptoms and his psychotherapy, and throughout the following years he remained symptom free. Just before starting work with his psychologist-analyst, a visit to a relative with a newborn baby awakened the fear of obsession with the infant's death, and he was relieved to start psychoanalysis. His analysis went well, but he began to sense that his analyst, who was presumably inexperienced at the time, became anxious whenever his analysand expressed angry feelings. It is difficult to tell whether Martinez's impression was correct, but he did recall that on many occasions, whenever he sensed his patient's anger, the analyst said, "Let's be sure that we are just talking."

During the fifth year of treatment, which took place in the analyst's home office, the analyst's wife fell terminally ill and later died after a long struggle. The analyst never referred to this personal sorrow, maintaining a professional detachment, nor did his analysand, who was well aware of what was taking place. The analyst never questioned his patient's silence, and soon after losing his wife he suggested that Martinez's analysis was complete. They parted on friendly terms.

A week after leaving treatment, Martinez developed a delusion that the only way to cure one of his female patients, an obese and unattractive widow, was to make love to her during her sessions. He began rubbing her thighs and engaging in oral sex with her, believing that his new method of treating depression was rational; he was not aware of having a delusion. He treated his other patients with conventional methods and enjoyed his unblemished reputation, assuming greater teaching responsibility and promoting the techniques of conventional therapy. He later said that when the widow with whom he was having sex left him 6 weeks after the initiation of his unorthodox treatment method, her condition was greatly improved and she expressed gratitude (this seems to have indeed been the case). Because she had made no complaint, his focalized delusion crystallized further, and he began using his new technique on other unattractive and obese women. From oral sex he slowly generalized his approach and eventually had sexual intercourse with certain patients, continuing at the same time to use conventional psychotherapeutic methods with others. He sometimes thought of himself as "crazy" and thought he should abandon his unorthodox method, but as soon as an obese woman entered his office, such doubts disappeared. Eventually, a patient complained to the authorities, and an investigation was undertaken. Martinez resolved this by buying off the complainant. After a decade of sexually abusing some of his patients, he was nevertheless sufficiently alarmed to return to analysis.

His second analyst was older and more experienced, and four years of work with him gave Martinez much insight. Slowly and most painfully he came to realize that his sexual technique had been based on a delusion, and he allowed himself to experience some remorse and grief. Even then it was difficult for him to describe completely actions, feelings, and perceptions pertaining to his sexual involvement with his patients. The meaning of what he did with his patients emerged slowly: while engaging in oral sex and rubbing their thighs, he would lose his sense of where he ended and where the women began. Sexual activity served to fuse his self-representation with the external object and her representation and saturated this fusion with pleasurable affects. Accordingly, he would lose his reality testing and his customary identity. He had often ejaculated on a woman's abdomen, not understanding until much later that the ejaculate symbolized bullets meant to "kill" the fantasized mother–child unit in the woman's belly. It is clear that aggression in the long run dominated and ruined the fused Dr. Martinez–patient representation that was saturated with pleasurable affects. With each sexual involvement, he would once more seek to obtain a libidinally saturated, fused representation. This cycle would then be repeated.

Martinez's past caught up with him when an ex-patient brought charges against him. This, coupled with the temporary illness of his second analyst, prompted the analyst to ask that I consult with them both. It was too late for Martinez, however; he, who had been so admired and envied, lost his license to practice, along with his reputation.

Martinez's delusion can be traced to his infantile psychotic self. His mother's family had emigrated from South America and settled in a rural area of the United States where his grandfather obtained work on a farm. His mother worked in a restaurant as a teenage girl and married a Hispanic man she met there. She had three children in a short time, and when her youngest was 5 she became pregnant with the child who would become Martinez. Severely depressed during this pregnancy, she had wanted an abortion (according to an aunt) but did not pursue the matter because of her Catholic upbringing. For the first 8 months of his life Martinez was in the care of a depressed mother who had unconscious thoughts of murdering her infant (Apprey 1994). She finally committed suicide with carbon monoxide, and her baby was taken into the home of his maternal grandmother, an obese woman who reared him as her own. His father disappeared. The child first learned that his grandparents were not his biological parents when he entered elementary school and was questioned about the difference between his surname and that of his grandparents.

My assumption is that Martinez developed an infantile psychotic self during the 8 months he spent in the inadequate care of his depressed and murderous mother, and that his repeated fusion with her initiated a self that was filled with unbearable and unnamable affects. This initial psychotic self could not support formed and differentiated images that could evolve into more mature self- and object representations with their more mature ego functions. As an adult Martinez had been told that his mother had sometimes forgotten to feed him, and that he would drift off to sleep hungry. I assume that later, through experiences with his grandmother, he developed another nucleus of the self, which was healthier and split off from the infantile psychotic self. This healthier self surrounded and encapsulated the infantile psychotic self.

Martinez did not seem to consciously pay attention to his mother's real story, but after he married he visited her grave "by accident" when visiting a cemetery to pay his respects to other dead relatives. Looking at his mother's grave for the first time, he felt empty but became aware of "something horrible" lodged in his body; he could only name it an emptiness.

His second analysis revealed that throughout his life he had made certain assumptions but had never heretofore clearly defined or verbalized them. One was that there was "something horrible" deep within his being, and he realized that this was the reason for his inability to enjoy the many successes in his life; it accounted for his chronic problem with self-esteem. Although he knew this, he hid it from his family. He fantasized that this core was so evil that his mother had been unable to tolerate it and so had killed herself. He learned that it was not guilt over his mother's death that made this core so horrible, but that it was composed of horrifying affects. Through early mother–child experiences his mother had played a key role in his developing an infantile psychotic self filled with depression and murderous impulses.

An uncle of Martinez's had died in adolescence, and his death had complicated the grandmother's relationship with Martinez's mother, who named Martinez after him. During his second analysis, Martinez revealed an unconscious fantasy—that his mother had killed herself so that the infant son she had named after her brother would be a gift to her parents; they would rear him as a replacement for their dead son. It is clear that although Martinez's infantile psychotic self was encapsulated, it absorbed certain unconscious fantasies and was modified accordingly.

Martinez's focalized psychosis occurred when his first psychoanalytic environment seemed to him to be identical with the environment in which his original infantile psychotic self had evolved. He became therapeutically regressed and reacted to his analyst with marked transference distortions that were not analyzed. When the analyst's wife died, causing the analyst to become depressed, Martinez's infantile psychotic self reemerged. The wife represented the analyst/mother in the mind of the patient, who was prematurely discharged from the analyst's home. He then identified the unit composed of himself as patient and his grieving and depressed (dead) analyst with that of the depressed, murderous, and dead mother and himself as infant. A week after losing his analyst, he developed his delusion.

On the surface, the female patients that Martinez tried to save (and "kill" or hurt, because his sexual acts also included aggression) were the obese grandmother. His delusion seemed to include responses to oedipal elements with which his uninvaded part had been originally obliged to deal. As a child he had slept in a crib in his grandparents' bedroom. In the oedipal period of the boy's life his grandfather died, and he began sleeping in the bed with the obese grandmother. It must have been difficult to handle this oedipal triumph. He had to express aggression and distance his grandmother in order to handle the incestuous stimulation. He recalled masturbating excessively as a child and displacing his aggression from his grandmother to an obese teacher in his elementary school. In her class he called out loud, "There is the blimp; where is the rest of the parade?" and was punished. The Catholic school he attended made his developing superego (that of his uninvaded part) rather rigid and harsh. He adapted to it later, living a clean and orderly life, using it to keep his encapsulated infantile psychotic self in check.

His sexual relationships with obese female patients can be seen as an expression of oedipal triumph as well as an effort to make his grieving grandmother happy; his unconscious fantasy suggested that he was a gift to his grandmother, but his second analyst and I were impressed with the secondary meaning of his delusion: behind the obese widow/grandmother stood the mental representation of his depressed mother and his infantile experience with her. He had seen the obese widow and many others he had sex with as lifeless, like his mother. His impulse was to bring them back to life and turn depression into pleasure. In turn, his own existence would be worthy, and the unit of mother/child/depression that was the core of his first self-representation could then go through its psychobiological evolution. Because his semen was perceived as bullets, however, he could not maintain the pleasurable fusion with his women.

At first the patients Martinez included in his delusion had to be unattractive and unlovable, but much later he seduced a slender young woman who was suicidal and looked like his mother in the only photograph he had of her. It was this "mother" that ruined his life by bringing charges against him. Because of repetition compulsion he unconsciously sought to destroy the early mother/infant/unbearable depression unit and, consequently, the patient–therapist unit. Because the disturbed early mother representational unit was the matrix of his infantile psychotic self, he was acting to maintain or reestablish it while trying to change its accompanying affects. This main aim of his unconscious lurked behind activities that, on the surface, were in the service of oedipal issues and/or "saving" the women.

With the birth of Martinez's first child the early mother/child/depressive affect (the infantile psychotic self) was stimulated, and he had obsessional thoughts about his baby's death without developing a delusion. Still, I believe it was his regressive state at the end of his first analysis, in an environment that fit well with his infantile environment, that awakened his infantile psychotic self.

Martinez had appeared to be a psychologically sound man until his mid-forties, when his focalized psychotic behavior appeared. If an individual has a psychotic personality organization, the infantile psychotic self is to a great extent absorbed by the healthier one. Furthermore, the ego defenses of the latter defend against the influence of the infantile psychotic self and militate against an open schizophrenic episode while allowing expression (fusion, introjective-projective relatedness) of the infantile psychotic self. When these defenses are overcome, the individual appears to be psychotic until the defenses are once more reconstituted. I have described psychosis-prone borderline patients (Volkan 1987) and believe that the terms *psychotic personality organization* and *psychosis-prone borderline personality organization* can be used interchangeably, although in the latter, the defensive splitting of the differentiated self- and object representations according to their libidinal and aggressive investments is more noticeable and stable.

All of us use various adaptations and defenses in our daily lives to protect our sense of self. If we are "normal" or have a high-level neurotic organization, we use sophisticated mechanisms and do so silently, unaware of it most of the time. When a person has a psychotic personality organization, protection of the healthy part and his attempted control of his infantile psychotic self is not silent; the defenses, which mostly appear as various actions, are aimed at (a) establishing a fit between the infantile psychotic self and the healthier one; (b) establishing a fit between the infantile psychotic self and the external world; (c) maintaining a certain level of self-continuity and reality testing; (d) splitting off the infantile psychotic self from the healthier one and thus slowing down expressions of the infantile psychotic self; and (e) changing the nature of affects—from "bad" to "good"—that saturate the infantile psychotic self.

A Young Woman Who Covered Mirrors

Arja, a Finnish woman, was able to maintain her reality testing well enough to become a graduate student in a good university; there was little wrong with her intellectual abilities, but from childhood on she had had an infantile psychotic self with which she constantly had to deal. According to one account, she had heard from an aunt that her maternal grandmother had killed a baby born out of wedlock before she married Arja's grandfather. This was known to her children, including Arja's mother, but had been kept as a family secret. One of her mother's eyes had been injured in childhood when her brother pierced it with a fork; it had been operated on many times, but it was always "ugly." The mutilated woman was incapable of adequate mothering and aggressively tickled the baby Arja or "drowned her in kisses." Arja's infantile psychotic self appeared soon after she learned to speak and think; she kept asking such questions as "When does never end?" She also had fears and, perhaps, delusions that her *pissapully* (Finnish baby-talk for genitalia) would be torn by a wolf. This probably reflected her identification with the mother whose eye had been injured, as well as her assimilation of "bad" affects.

As a graduate student she became the patient of Margaretha Hupa of Turku, Finland, who distinguished two types of chronic defenses or adaptations by which Arja was able to keep her infantile psychotic self in check.

(1) By changing her external environment and her relationship to it, Arja could find a fit between her infantile psychotic self and the outside world, thus maintaining a type of reality and self-continuity. For example, even as a young woman she dressed in an infantile way in dresses with nursery prints. She had no friends. She covered every mirror or other reflecting surface in her home to avoid her reflection, which represented something ter-

rible she had externalized onto the outside world but feared might boomerang. By avoiding her reflection she was changing her intimate environment, making her externalizations stable—or, at least, slowing down her introjective-projective cycle. In her apartment she refused to talk on the telephone to anyone except her mother. This behavior, and her use of the telephone as a transitional object or buffer, altered her external world so that she could control what went out and what came in (introjective-projective relatedness). When talking to her mother, who lived elsewhere, she used her as an external ego. Her infantile psychotic self could not maintain identifications with the mothering functions, so she had to be temporarily refilled with such identifications whenever she needed them. Arja's object constancy (Hartmann 1952, Mahler 1968) was deficient. She listened daily to her mother, who reminded her when to eat, when to sleep, and when to do other tasks. As long as an external ego took care of her psychobiological functions, Arja could study and function as a university student.

(2) Arja's healthy part also dealt internally with her infantile psychotic self and its influence. At any time of the day she could stop relating to the external world, populate her mind with the images of celebrities, dead or alive, and be preoccupied with them. These celebrities ranged from Franz Kafka to modern thinkers, but Sigmund Freud was her dominant image. She had started reading Freud in her early teens and had a fantasy of lying on his couch. She could reactivate his image at will and thus the great psychoanalyst could take care of her dysfunctional core. If what she saw, heard, or read damaged her image of Freud, she would busy herself reconstituting it. For example, when she read a book by Jeffrey Masson, who she considered was attacking Freud, she stopped everything, especially her relationship with the external world, until Freud's image was "saved."

8

True Transsexuals

True transsexuals, both male and female, are excellent cases for illustrating the individual's attempt—and failure—to replace the existing infantile psychotic self saturated with "bad," aggressive affects with a new core that is saturated with "good," libidinal affects. For 5 years in the 1970s I was head of the Gender Identity Clinic at the University of Virginia Medical Center, where my colleagues and I saw hundreds of individuals seeking so-called sexual reassignment surgery. We studied many of them through various psychotherapies and psychological tests. Throughout the years, my colleagues and I published our findings (Volkan 1974, 1976, 1980, Volkan and Berent 1976). This chapter is not a review of what we previously reported about these troubled individuals but an examination of their focalized delusion of belonging to the opposite sex as representing a special fate of their infantile psychotic selves.

Despite the possibility of fetal hormonal influences or other intrauterine events, at the present time we await proof of biological defect or malfunction as the cause of the transsexual

syndrome. There is clearer and more definitive evidence supporting the channeling (see Chapter 1) of psychological ingredients as a cause of transsexual syndrome rather than the role
played by inherited biological factors. It is fascinating to note
the key role played by the mother's unconscious fantasies in
determining whether a baby becomes a true transsexual (Apprey 1993a, Volkan and Greer 1994, Volkan and Masri 1989).

Socarides (1970) has identified four characteristics of those
suffering from transsexual syndrome: (1) an intense, insistent,
and overriding desire to be transformed bodily into a person of
the opposite sex; (2) a conviction of being trapped in a body of
the wrong sex; (3) concomitant imitation of the behavior of the
opposite sex; and (4) an insistent search for sexual transformation by means of surgery and endocrinological supplements. It
is evident, not only on the basis of clinical evaluation but also on
that of psychological tests, that men and women demanding
sex change show considerable variety in personality organization. The wish to have sexual reassignment surgery coexists
with schizophrenia only in a few. Socarides diagnosed this
group as schizotranssexuals. It, thus, becomes necessary to
ask: Who among the many people seeking surgical sex change
are the true transsexuals?

In my previous writings I have described the true transsexuals as those who possess a special version of borderline
personality organization. I now add that these individuals possess infantile psychotic selves. The transsexual syndrome responds and corresponds to wishes and defenses against them at
many levels of their developmental years, but at the lowest
level, the syndrome serves to keep their infantile psychotic
selves in check so that they do not develop more generalized
psychotic conditions. In their infantile psychotic selves, the
mother–infant body selves are fused and saturated with "bad"
affects (e.g., anaclitic depression, emptiness, rage). The deepest
meaning of the transsexual syndrome implies an attempt to
change or modify the "bad" affects in the infantile psychotic
self and to make the earliest fused mother–infant representational unit within it contaminated only with pleasurable "good"
affects. The true transsexual, then, repeats his or her effort,

through the characteristics described above (and another characteristic that will be described shortly), to strengthen the fragile matrix and to give it hope for evolution. The hope is to evolve and maintain a "good" matrix capable of supporting more mature self-representations and internalized object representations. The patient, however, keeps failing in these attempts.

Although the person with borderline personality organization has risen to the level at which self- and object representations are differentiated, "bad" and "good" representations are still split apart. Persons with borderline personality organization use primitive splitting as their main defense and actively dissociate mutually contradictory self- and object representations as well as drive derivatives (i.e., affects) connected with such representations. Thus, the neutralization of most of their drive derivatives has failed to take place (Kernberg 1975).

Although this formulation requires painstaking scrutiny of the transsexual, even the surface picture presented by the true transsexual provides clues to the existence of unintegrated self- and object images. One male transsexual had undergone repeated traumatic separations from his prostitute mother early in his life and had experienced many other traumas. As a child, he had a fantasy that the men who came to enjoy her favors were like bees coming to a hive. Later he learned that male bees die after mating with the queen. As an adult, he became a bee keeper and developed a ritual of separating the queen bees into "good" and "bad" ones, painting them different colors, and ceremoniously killing the "bad" ones. It became evident that his separating one queen from another symbolically represented the split of his mother's representation.

My reason for referring to a *special version* of borderline personality organization in true transsexuals is that they can differentiate between the images and/or representations of the self and those of the object, except in regard to the genitalia. Their genitalia remain fused with the genital body representations of their mothers. Thus, true transsexuals, above and beyond their typical borderline expressions, exhibit a psychotic aspect of their personality.

Let me explain with a vignette what I mean by fused genital representation. A male transsexual I treated on the couch was preoccupied with thoughts of Hawaii, especially its volcanic landscape. This had a transference reference because my last name, Volkan, means "volcano." He had spent some time on the islands before coming to analysis, however, and his fixation on Hawaii predated our association. I came to understand, as the analytic process unfolded, that his fascination was related to his inability to differentiate the image of his genitalia from that of his mother's despite his intellectual awareness that they were not alike. The changing volcanic terrain, altered by eruptions and the hardening of flowing lava, attracted him by its plasticity and shifting; he saw in the concept of such physical fluidity a way of dealing with the uncertainty (Bak 1968) of genital outline. As he lay on the couch, I noticed a bulge between his legs and in due time found out that he had extended his trouser pocket so that a wallet placed in it lodged between his legs, creating the bulge. On one level, this bulge represented his mother's genitals—was a vagina or a penis there?

What is interesting here is the clinical observation that although this patient had no difficulty in differentiating himself from the mother's representation, once the analysis focused on the bulge, he began making frequent slips of the tongue in which he referred to himself and his mother interchangeably. He could separate himself from his mother's representation in most areas, but in the genital area, differentiation was not possible for him.

Socarides (1988) has produced a unitary theory of perversion that our investigation indicates also fits our understanding of true transsexualism. It holds that the pre-oedipal period, especially that between 18 months and 3 years of age, is crucial to the genesis of sexual perversion because it is in this period that a primary pre-oedipal fixation occurs. This fixation includes not only the desire to fuse with the representation of the mother—to reinstate the primitive mother–child unit—but also an equally strong dread of such fusion.

Expanding this formulation, I stated in my earlier writings that the true transsexual seeks to unite only with the "good" mother representation, to expand the existing genital fusion to fusion of the total "good" representation, while at the same time dreading the fusion of his own "bad" self-representation with the "bad" mother representation.

A SEARCH FOR PERFECTION

Now, let me return to my main focus: the existence of an infantile psychotic self in the true transsexual. The existing fusion of the genital representations points to this psychotic core. A fifth characteristic that my co-worker and I added to the four characteristics described by Socarides (1970) tells a great deal about how the transsexual patient handles his infantile psychotic self. I call this fifth characteristic *a search for perfection*. It involves a kind of insatiability: the man who before surgery is preoccupied with his penis and wants to be rid of it is no less preoccupied with the vagina that is surgically constructed for him. He wants it to be perfect and is no less concerned with the perfection of secondary feminine sexual characteristics and will, in due course, seek more surgery, this time to reduce a prominent Adam's apple, thick legs, or whatever. One of our patients who had genital surgery 18 years prior to seeing us came to our attention for the first time when "she" was about to undergo a seventh surgical procedure designed to make "her" into a more perfect woman. We had another male transsexual patient who, at great cost, employed an artist to paint a picture of an idealized woman, which he took to the surgeon to indicate the way he wanted to look once his treatment was completed. The biologically male transsexual is not only engaged in a search for physical change but is psychologically committed to an effort to become a perfect woman; as one patient put it, he wanted to be "virgin white." Similarly, the biologically female transsexual desires perfection when she seeks to become masculine by means of surgery and endocrinological supplement; she wants to be not just a man but a he-man, powerful and strong—a type of man created within her own idealizing imagination.

Clinical investigation has identified that an attempt to get rid of derivatives of the aggressive drive and "bad" affects is behind such a search for perfection. I observed that the basic surgical change does not end the search, and that unless the transsexual undergoes a change of psychological structure, he or she continues to seek perfection and keeps arranging for more surgery. Because the transsexual's main aim is to be rid of unwanted aggression, I have proposed the term *aggression reassignment surgery*, instead of *sex reassignment surgery*, for the procedures involved.

The battery of psychological tests given to true transsexuals, especially the Rorschach test, gave us further proof that these patients are actually more concerned about aggression than about sexual matters (Volkan and Berent 1976). The Rorschachs demonstrated that men who want to be "virgin-white" females viewed the penis as a symbol of evil condensed with the symbolic feature of masculinity. They wanted to be rid of it in order to deal with anxiety of panic proportions induced in them by the possession of this weapon of aggression. The same tests indicated that the true transsexual woman, on the other hand, views maleness as wholeness and all that is feminine as unwholesome. She feels a need for a perfect penis with which to protect herself from the aggression she sees threatening her in the world around her. She sees the acquisition of a penis as not only completing her but providing her with such completeness and perfection that she will never again need to exhibit her own aggression or be flooded with unbearable and unnamable affects.

The true transsexual makes a continued effort to make his infantile psychotic core a location where only fused "good" representations will be located; safe from conflict with "bad" representations, they allow hope for the development of a healthy path to continue. Surgery gives them the illusion that this has been accomplished, but soon an event reminds them that this is not the case. For example, the transsexual man, after turning into a "good" woman, dreams of possessing a penis—"the badness." Then "she" resumes the search for more surgery and more perfection. If the patient develops other ways of dealing with the infantile psychotic self that are more typical of a psychotic personality organization, the exaggerated focus on surgery may disappear.

Early mother–infant experiences that set up the infantile psychotic self in true transsexuals include depression in the mother as well as her unconscious fantasies that the infant is essential for her psychic and bodily existence. Later, representation of an actual trauma organizes the nature of the transsexual's clinical picture. Usually this actual trauma occurs when the child is at the oedipal age. For example, he might have experienced physical harm to his genitals, have witnessed the death of his father, or have seen the actual castration of an animal by an adult. Issues from higher levels of development get condensed with the influence of the infantile psychotic self.

A BOY AS A PRODUCT OF TWO MEN

A 9-year-old transsexual boy was treated by Dr. James Kavanaugh while I treated the boy's mother for 2 years (Volkan 1980). For 13 years she was engaged in an affair with a man much older than she who urged her to become pregnant. When she did conceive, she was uncertain whether the father was the lover or her husband. She developed a fantasy that her son was a product of both men; she thought it possible that semen from both had fertilized her. When the child was born, she wanted to name him after her lover, but fearing that this would betray their relationship, she gave him a name that differed from her husband's in only one letter. She insisted, "My son was born two people. I know this sounds like a fairy tale, but it is the truth."

I observed that she routinely put her child between her husband and herself. The child was an aggressive penis, and he clashed with her husband. When her husband was not present, however, she saw her son as the representation of her lover; she indicated in her therapy that this older man had represented her mother to her, as well as her own loving and nonaggressive penis. Sometimes she actually thought of her son as a girl. It is clear that the mother's perception of her infant created a core in his developing self-representation that later could not be separated from her (especially in the area of the representation of genitals) and could not integrate opposing self- and object representations or libidinal and aggressive drive derivatives. His future gender identity confusion could be seen in the mother's fantasies about him, which she deposited into the child's evolving self-representation, where it remained partly psychotic.

It is clear in the next case, that of Carla/Carlos (Volkan and Masri 1989), how a mother's depression and unconscious fantasies influence the establishment of a self-representational matrix in the infant that remains psychotic and influences other uninvaded parts for the rest of his life. In this case, the daughter responded to her mother's unconscious fantasies by developing corresponding unconscious fantasies that were absorbed by her psychotic core as being real. As Beres (1962) stated, we detect the presence of unconscious fantasies from their effects. They become evident in clinical work when the adult patient exhibits their derivatives in free associations, dreams, stories involving transference, and projective psychological tests. Whenever possible in our work with transsexuals, we did extensive diagnostic and therapeutic work with the patients' parents and sex partners to identify unconscious aspects of interpersonal relationships and intergenerational transmissions of unconscious psychological germs (e.g., anxiety, unconscious fantasies) as well as psychological genes (e.g., formed mental representations of others or part objects). Let the case of Carla/Carlos speak for itself.

CARLA/CARLOS

Carla, a pretty girl of 17, called herself Carlos, believing she was a man trapped in the body of a woman. She had felt this way as long as she could remember, and since early childhood had stuffed folded toilet tissue or a sock in her panties to simulate a penis. She hated wearing girls' clothing and recalled that between the ages of 6 and 9 she prayed that Santa would bring her a "weenie." At 14 she read about sex operations and became obsessed with the idea that all her problems would be solved if she could have one. She saw a few therapists, and her parents agreed that she should have a sex-change operation. She came to us for a final evaluation and treatment at a time when she was exhibiting some evidence of depression and had broken off her relationship with a special girlfriend in school. The two girls had been in the habit of lying together and hugging and kissing with a pillow between them. Carla thought that both she and her friend acted as though Carla had a penis although both knew that she did not. Whenever her partner made a seductive remark, Carla would imply that this gave her an erection. Both girls spoke of the illusory penis as "the killer." Carla refused to undress before her friend but masturbated when alone and, thinking of her, rubbed her genitalia on the mattress. Neither girl considered herself a lesbian because both believed that Carla was truly a boy trapped in a female body. When the girlfriend's father learned of her association with Carla, he forbade her to see her friend.

Carla dressed in unisex fashion and was mercilessly teased at school. She became very lonely after breaking off with her friend and was more preoccupied than ever with having a sex-change operation. The time she did not spend at school or her job in a restaurant was spent alone in her room. Her belief that she was a man could not be shaken. She once challenged one of her therapists, saying that if a sonogram examination demonstrated the presence of a uterus in her body she would give up her demand for surgery, so certain was she that the interior of her body was that of a male. Because the therapist's experience indicated the inadvisability of confronting a patient with proof of her delusions, he did not set up a sonogram appointment. Just before becoming Dr. Masri's and my patient, Carla was found to be a biologically normal woman according to a physical examination, laboratory tests, and chromosomal studies at a university hospital.

Maria, Carla's Mother

Carla's mother, Maria, a woman in her early fifties, was born and reared in Spain and spoke with an accent. She was the third and last child in her family and had two sisters, six and five years her senior, respectively. She remembered from her early childhood the dangerous and frightening family milieu, in which her father, who drank heavily, beat her mother. She believed that the authorities had forced her father to join the army to relieve the family. Eventually, however, he returned home and continued beating his wife.

When Maria was an adolescent, her mother fell ill with appendicitis and, as a result of poor medical treatment, died within 2 months. Maria remembers seeing a needle stuck into her swollen belly as she lay in the hospital. The news of her death made Maria laugh, and this reversal of affect characterized the way she handled events in later life, denying grief and concealing depression. She was unable to cry or to go through the normal grieving process at a time when she was biologically becoming a woman. She clung to a representation of her mother as a victim unable to meet her child's needs. She went to her mother's funeral and watched the casket being lowered into the ground although she had been unable to view the corpse; to Maria her mother was not really dead, and she exhibited symptoms of the perennial mourner (Volkan 1981a, Volkan and Zintl 1993), haunted by her mother's ghost over and over in her fantasies and nightmares.

Her two sisters married within the year of their mother's death, and Maria was left alone in the family home with their father, who was often drunk and who approached her sexually. His overtures were hard to resist. Her Catholic training made her feel sinful and guilty in this situation, and her self-esteem was reduced.

For the next 9 years, her sisters took turns taking her into their homes to ensure her safety. The two families had, in time, six children altogether, and Maria felt left out; she still needed a mother and maintained in her mind the image of a caring mother alongside a rejecting and unhelpful one. She felt guilty about resenting her sisters' children, to whom she had to play second fiddle, and her self-esteem was reduced even further. Vowing never to have children herself, she viewed a woman's lot as one of suffering. Hiding her depression, she smilingly cared for the children of her sisters until she contracted tuberculosis at the age of 21 and was sent to a sanatorium. This experience contributed further to her identity as someone masochistic and depressed. Released from the tuberculosis hospital, she returned to her sisters and found employment in a store. She also met Tom, an American soldier stationed in Spain, who represented a way out of her traumatic existence. They soon married.

When she arrived in the United States with Tom, Maria knew no English and found the environment alien and hostile. Although she had vowed not to let herself become pregnant, in the fourth year of her marriage she gave birth to a girl who almost died of intestinal obstruction. Womanhood and motherhood seemed horrifying to Maria. When her first child was 15 months old, Tom was sent to the Philippines, and Maria returned to Spain, living alternately in the homes of her sisters. The situation created by the loss of her mother was being repeated because of the "loss" of her husband, and she still searched for someone to mother her. The sisters' children were no longer young and had preoccupations that made Maria feel unwanted. One sister lost her husband to cancer and a son to a traffic accident a few months later.

A little over a year later, Maria joined Tom, who was now stationed in Germany. They had a few years together before he received another 15-month assignment and she returned to Spain. This time she rented an apartment of her own, living with her daughter in a state of open depression and great loneliness.

While awaiting Tom's return, Maria developed a rich fantasy life to ward off depression, fantasizing that various Spanish male movie stars were her lovers. She refrained from taking a lover in reality because she considered it sinful. She was, however, very much aware of her sexual hunger and her fantasies. As soon as Tom returned, Maria wanted to get pregnant, and when she succeeded, she thought of the child she was carrying as a boy. Tom spent much of his time drinking with other men and at home showed little interest in her. Maria was persuaded that her new baby would be a boy who would grow up to be quite different from her husband. For 2 months after Carla's birth, Maria referred to her as "he," because she had a firm mental representation of the baby as a son. She was to say later, "This sounds silly, but is it possible that I could transmit my thoughts about this to my daughter?"

Maria considered Carla difficult and frustrating, but she could not bear to be separated from her child physically and psychically. The baby often cried, and the mother was deeply aware of sexual hunger, which Tom was unwilling or unable to satisfy. She daydreamed much of men and the penis and often masturbated. When Carla was 5, Tom left for another 15-month tour in the Philippines, and the relationship between mother and daughter intensified. Eventually, the family regrouped in the United States, only to move to Germany again before settling in the States permanently. During these moves Carla had language and cultural problems in trying to adjust to her peers.

Maria was aware of having thought of Carla before her birth as a boy but was not conscious of regarding the child as a psychic

reservoir for a representation of a penis. She consciously acknowledged her loneliness and sexual hunger and thought of Carla as
special. The child slept in her parents' room and often in her
mother's bed, as though she were her mother's extension. Maria
clung to the child as though she were something secret, finding it
difficult to take her out in public. In this respect, she was like a
man who is not supposed to exhibit his penis to others. She
rationalized that the child was too active to be seen by others and
treated her as a nonhuman entity. She thought of her as "a
Martian," and her description of Carla's activity brought the
phrase "prick-like" to my mind.

When Carla was a baby, a physician had told Maria that the
child's vagina was not properly opened. Although it is unclear
whether an actual physical anomaly existed, the diagnosis is
important because the mother was instructed to massage Carla's
vagina with a prescribed cream as often as possible. When Carla
was 3 her mother obtained what must have been a speculum,
which she inserted to keep the vagina open. This intrusion into
Carla's body was the actual trauma necessary for the specifics of
true female transsexualism (Volkan and Greer 1995). Although
Maria stopped the focused intrusion when her daughter was 6, she
continued to peek at Carla's vaginal area for years when dressing
her, and so on. Was she searching for a fantasized penis? Was her
finger or the speculum perceived as a penis they shared? Certainly
this sexually focused interaction symbolically created a representation of a penis in the psychic space between the two and allowed
the crystallization of Carla's infantile psychotic self, in which her
representation and her mother's representation remained fused at
the genital body level.

Maria's conscious daydreams indicated that she was
searching for someone to make love to her, and by thrusting her
finger into her own vagina to masturbate and by putting it also in
her daughter's, she was making love to herself and her daughter
with an illusory penis. Although when she grew up Carla could
differentiate her self-representation from that of her mother, her
perception of her genital area remained at best confused and
ambiguous. I also suspect aggression in Maria's intrusion into
Carla's body and recall that Maria's memory of her own dying
(rejecting) mother was that of a belly with a needle thrust into it.
Her symbolic, forced sex with Carla was also Maria's way of
expressing in action what her father had tried to do to her, and

seen in this way, the illusory penis can be viewed as invested with aggression.

Maria's search for something in her child's body was so compelling that when Carla got tonsillitis at the age of 6, she displaced her concern from Carla's vagina to her mouth. The child would refuse to open her mouth to take a pill, and her mother would pinch the child's nose until Carla opened her mouth to breathe, whereupon the mother would insert her finger. Maria boasted that it once took six people to open her daughter's mouth!

Carla's Unconscious Fantasies as a Response to Those of Her Mother

In response to Maria's behavior toward her, Carla unconsciously began to fantasize that she had a penis. The fantasy was given to her by her mother or developed for the mother or was shared in order to mark a special, partly fused relationship—or was paradoxically used as a tool of aggression by both to counter the fear of fusion between them. Carla's symptoms included her refusal to eat meat or eat in the presence of her mother. These seem to echo the vagina-mouth equation already noted. By her refusal Carla was defending herself against her mother's penetration. Like Arja covering the mirrors in her home, Carla found another way to change her physical environment. It was a defense against the influence of her infantile psychotic self. It prevented her from fusing with her mother more completely. Furthermore, the delusional penis was clearly perceived as being tinged with aggression, and Carla built a defense against it when it belonged to her mother.

In her treatment, Carla remembered nothing about penetration by her mother's finger or the speculum. Only recently, at the suggestion of a previous therapist, did Maria tell her daughter about her vaginal difficulty and the remedies attempted, but she left out many details and Carla took the information only as further evidence that she lacked a vagina and had a hidden penis. Carla had, however, a screen memory that may have reflected the long-repressed reality; I believe that she was symbolically remembering a real trauma. In this memory, Carla is a small child sitting on the steps of an apartment building in Spain when she sees a "small seed of something" and sticks it up her nose. Thus, her earliest memory was one of entering a body orifice.

The following delusion and its pictorial representation indicate the intertwining of the actual trauma with unconscious fantasy formation. Carla had a delusion that her skin could be zipped open, and she could step out of it with a penis as Carlos. As her request for a sonogram showed, she was confident that male characteristics lay hidden in her body. The dreams of her childhood reflected, even in manifest content, these unconscious fantasies. For example, her dream of a giraffe ended with her astride the animal's long neck, symbolizing a phallus. This was not altogether a happy circumstance in the dream, for the giraffe was sometimes aggressive, and this made the child astride its neck apprehensive. Her dream world was also full of obviously phallic symbols; like dreams of her mother, they were mostly about such aggressive objects as exploding missiles. It is no wonder that her delusional penis was named "the killer." Her custom of placing objects in her vagina and her desire for a penis of flesh were more direct expressions of her unconscious fantasy.

The Father

The psychodynamic patterns of Carla's father, Tom, indicated that he is what we have come to expect of the father of a female transsexual; like his wife, he lost his mother when he was 12, and his recollection of her centered around her being in such pain from cancer that she chewed on her feeding tubes. Two years after her death, the father remarried, and Tom lived with his father, stepmother, and stepsisters until he joined the military, which literally became his home and family.

Tom was born with a cleft palate, which was surgically repaired, but later in life an opening in the roof of his mouth required further surgery. Cautery and skin graft were performed, but for some time he felt that he had a soft spot in his mouth. The reconstructive surgery he had undergone lent support to his daughter's belief in corrective surgery. In an interview, Tom readily opened his mouth to show the scar on its roof, and although I cannot fully understand what a hole in the mouth meant to this man, it was clear that his preoccupation with his scar was echoed in certain family behavior; it will be remembered that Maria had wanted to see not only into Carla's vagina but into her mouth as well. One of Carla's childhood fantasies was that she had been born with a penis that had been burned off soon after her birth—after all, she had heard about her father's mouth being burned soon after he was born.

Tom spent most of his time with his military comrades, often drinking heavily and playing poker, and his behavior seemed indicative of a conviction, also held by Maria, that women, like his mother, were all born victims. He suffered from premature ejaculation and had only "hit-and-run" sexual intercourse with his wife, whom he left from time to time. This added to Maria's feeling of sexual hunger; at this time in his early fifties, he had for the last 10 years had intercourse with his wife only a few times a year. For 6 months or so, he had been unable to achieve an erection but refused to consult a doctor. Having abandoned fantasies of making love with a movie star, Maria dreamed of small animals entering her body. I do not know if there was a physiological reason for Tom's hyposexuality, but I do know that he associated intimacy with a woman's getting cancer.

Although Maria had thought of Carla in utero as a boy who would grow up to be the opposite of his father, she saw close similarity between Tom and Carlos. After all, her fantasy did not come true; Carla/Carlos would end up yet another sexually ineffective man. "They are like two drops of water in the same bucket," she said. In response to this, Carla perceived her maleness as super strong when she became Carlos.

It was little wonder that Carla spoke of "the killer" and wanted to become a boxer after the proposed surgery. The aggression was clear, and I suggest that through it Carla wanted to protect herself from the representation of the intrusive mother. I saw psychological accuracy in the observation of Carla's conventional older sister, who often accused Carla of "killing their ["bad"] mother." At the lowest level, Carla wished to get rid of her mother's and her own aggression, kill the "bad" representational unit associated with unbearable affects, and create, through surgery, a representational unit that would be strong enough not to crumble from "bad" affects. This is why she wished such drastic changes in the external world, including the external appearance of her body. My experience told me that, unfortunately, she would fail miserably.

9

Attis

Attis was Jesus Christ; there was no doubt about this in his mind. The crucial sign had come on the previous Sunday when his congregation—all but one woman he knew to be the devil's agent—had gazed at him in adoration while he preached of God, his Father. As a young Methodist minister, he knew that as Jesus on Earth, he must save sinners, right wrongs, and eradicate injustice. If he submitted himself to his Father and thanked Him, he need not fear the evil woman in his church.

On Monday morning after receiving the sign, he left his house next to the little country church, which was his first charge as an ordained minister, and walked into the nearby deep woods, climbing to the mountaintop. As he walked, he tore his clothing from his slender, well-muscled body; there should be no barriers between him and his God. He was slashed by branches as he walked naked, and the oozing blood made him look as though he had been savagely whipped. On the mountaintop, he threw out his arms as though he were nailed to a cross and stood motionless to receive his Father, whose power he felt in the rays of the hot summer sun that began to burn his torn body.

When people in the little mountain town realized that their 27-year-old minister was missing, they formed search parties. Three days after he left home, they found him exhausted, dehydrated, and nearly dead. Covered with dried blood and badly sunburned, he looked so much like an animal that the man who found him seized his right hand to make positive identification; it was common knowledge that the young minister had lost a finger on that hand. After being taken to the psychiatric section of the hospital, he was diagnosed as being schizophrenic.

This account came from Attis's hospital record. He became my patient 11 years later in another part of the country. I call him Attis (or Atys), in reference to a story in Greek mythology, which has several versions. It focuses on preservation of body parts and came to mind in connection with this man, whose finger had been severed but saved. A poem by the celebrated Roman poet Gaius Valerius Catullus relates the story of Attis and is recognized as a powerful literary work. I have read modern versions of Attis's story as told by Kerényi (1960) and Erhat (1972).

According to one version, Zeus fell asleep on the Agdos Rock and polluted it with his semen. Because the rock had taken the shape of the Great Mother, it became pregnant and delivered Agdistis, a savage bisexual being who could not be tamed. Dionysus thought to trick it and turned water into wine, which the thirsty Agdistis drank until it fell into a deep sleep. Dionysus then tied the male member of the sleeping Agdistis to a tree and when this bisexual being sprang up from sleep, the male member was castrated. The earth consumed the blood and the severed member, and from these grew a new tree that had potent fruit. Nana, the daughter of Sangarios the river god, put the fruit in her lap and from it conceived a male child. Sangarios exposed the infant in the open to die. A he-goat tended it, however, and it survived. He was named Attis and was so beautiful that Agdistis, now lacking a male member, fell in love with him. Midas, King of Pessinous, hoping to separate

Attis from Agdistis, gave Attis his daughter in marriage. Agdistis appeared at the wedding and drove the guests mad with the notes of a syrinx, whereupon Attis castrated himself and died. Repentant, Agdistis asked Zeus to return the young man to life, but all that Fate would allow was that his body would never putrefy, his hair would continue to grow, and his smallest finger would stay alive and be capable of movement.

A psychoanalytic study of this myth appears in one of the earliest papers of Edith Weigert (1938). It accounts for the name I gave this patient in that he, as a child of 4, had lost a finger when his brother was chopping wood, and the severed finger had been preserved in a bottle.

Attis's case illustrates a different fate of the infantile psychotic self. Dr. Martinez's infantile psychotic self (see Chapter 7) had remained encapsulated until it sprang to life in his forties. In Arja's case, the encapsulation was not successful; however, the influence of the infantile psychotic self was absorbed by her uninvaded part. The two transsexuals I discussed were able to differentiate their self- and object representations except in the area of genital body self. The case of Attis, however, illustrates a combination of psychotic personality organization as well as schizophrenia. He probably had episodes of childhood schizophrenia, but his uninvaded part absorbed the influence of his infantile psychotic self and, instead of full-blown and continued childhood schizophrenia, a psychotic personality organization evolved. At the age of 27, he experienced a prototypical adult type of schizophrenia that was later replaced by a psychotic personality organization. At the age of 38, when I first saw him, he was again acutely schizophrenic after experiencing terror and catatonia in a typical fashion.

HIS LIFE STORY

Attis's case is unique. It enables us to observe the lifelong influence of infantile and adult psychotic selves and the modification of the latter through psychoanalytic psychotherapy and other life experiences. This chapter reports the key events in

Attis's life, and the following chapter focuses on his treatment and follow-up, during which I was able to learn the details of how his mind functioned.

The Groundhog

Groundhog was the name Attis gave to his adult psychotic self. Its connection to his infantile psychotic self was clear because he, the fourth child of a farmer's family, had been born on February 2, Groundhog Day, when, according to tradition, the groundhog emerges from hibernation. If it sees its shadow, the groundhog returns to its hole, indicating another 6 weeks of winter weather can be expected. As far as I know, Attis had been a healthy infant. His mother, however, had often spoken of the bad storm that raged at the time of his birth, and he, later in life, came to feel the storm was a sign of a malignant destiny.

I concluded while working with Attis that his mother did not have mature mothering qualities. She was unable to help her children effectively through separation-individuation phases. I learned, for example, that she kept all her children in diapers longer than usually necessary. As we will soon see, she could not even separate from the severed body parts of her family members. She dominated her offspring, and consequently all of her children were traumatized, although only Attis became schizophrenic. Attis, the Groundhog, was driven back into the Mother Earth (fusion), not because he had seen his shadow but because the weather (early mother–child experiences) was so bad that he could not tolerate individuating fully from his mother's representation, nor did he have the necessary psychological tools to do so.

When Attis was about 20 months old, his mother bore twins, a boy and a girl. At about the same time, two neighbor women also had twins, and the new mothers were highly competitive with their offspring. His mother's preoccupation with the twins, and with a deaf sister born a year after them, further deprived little Attis of the mothering adequate for normal negotiation of developmental tasks. I thought that she may have felt guilty for not having enough time for him, and that she unconsciously responded to this by clinging to him.

Several events occurred when Attis was between 3 and 4 years old that supported the notion that his life depended on his mother as his external ego, and that he must cling to her if he were to survive psychologically as well as physically. Their house caught on fire twice, once when Attis was sick in bed with a high fever. On both occasions, his mother rescued him and never let him forget to whom he owed his life. The fires left psychological scars and contributed to Attis's preoccupation with hell, which, by choosing to become a minister, he later hoped to avoid.

A Finger in a Bottle

When Attis's finger was severed, his mother rushed him to the hospital, thinking that the finger might be reattached, but she found she had "forgotten" it. She later put it into a small brown bottle of rubbing alcohol and kept it until her death, a year before Attis, then 38, became my patient. After his mother's death, Attis kept the bottled finger in his bedroom. When experiencing schizophrenia, he thought of it as alive. It was so mummified and shrunken by then that it was little more than a hard, dark piece of material. It was, nonetheless, magical and functioned as a kind of fetish he shared with his mother, as a triumph over the threat of bodily disintegration, separation, and castration. His mother's regard for the finger conveyed the unconscious idea that it was still alive to her son. The piece of finger served as a link between his and his mother's representations. As with transsexuals, there was a fusion in his mind of aspects of his and his mother's body parts. Therefore, in his later unconscious fantasies, he felt that his fragile core, his infantile psychotic self, was bisexual, and later he experienced his adult psychotic self as bisexual. Family members spoke of him as being tied to his mother's apron strings, and it was clear that in his psychic reality, the finger at times represented the penis of his omnipotent mother. She was proud of the grim object and displayed it to visitors. Even before the time of oedipal struggle with his father, Attis's mother controlled whether he was mutilated or castrated, and Attis maintained the idea that his bodily damage could have been reversed. Attis always felt that the brother who had accidentally chopped off his finger had acted as his mother's agent, and that she could still have taken it to a surgeon and have had it sewn back in place.

The stump on Attis's hand had not yet healed when he had his first experience with surgery—a tonsillectomy. Much later, at 24 or 26, he had more throat surgery. In the year of his first tonsillectomy, he fell from a ladder into a bin of cottonseed and thereafter was afraid of being buried alive. He related this possibility also to the groundhog, which buries itself in the ground; this represented fusion with his mother's representation.

The Oedipal Phase

Attis reached the oedipal age with notably unresolved pre-oedipal object-relations conflicts and anxiety about bodily harm. His father was sadistic and could do little to help him to modify his infantile psychotic self and its influence on his personality. Attis could not be released from his preoccupation with fusing with or separating from his mother or her represen-tation, at least on the genital-body-self level, or with staying close to or moving away from her. I learned about this aspect of his life through his transference expectations of me when he was in treatment. He had once seen his father force a stick up the anus of a recalcitrant mule and suspected him of being capable of homosexual assault. Although he wanted to draw closer to his father in order to move away from his mother and form a firm boundary around his infantile psychotic self, this seemed dangerous. He had to submit totally to the powerful God/father (later, as Jesus, he attempted this) or submit to the father's homosexual assault (inverted oedipal position). He saw his surroundings as menacing and for a while was preoccupied by the story of a worker at a nearby farm who had gone into a cave and severed his genitals with a knife. When he spoke of this as an adult, Attis trembled with anxiety. At the age of 8, he had a back injury that not only left a scar on his hip but also strengthened his belief that life is full of danger and that his bodily self could never be fully differentiated and protected.

Latency and Adolescence

Attis's period of latency did not push his irrepressible and untamed aggressive and sexual impulses into the background. As a latency-age boy, he was fearful of sharp objects, vaginas, and penises. Images of aggressive part-objects existed everywhere and at any time. He related to the world in a paranoid orientation. His stories of this period of his life suggested to me that at times he was openly psychotic.

While Attis was in puberty, in the midst of his second individuation (Blos 1979), his father had an appendectomy and his mother asked to be given the appendix, which she kept in a bottle, as she kept her son's finger. Like Zeus, she was a protector of body parts. But instead of being an omnipotent god, she was simply a sick woman. Whatever her reasons, she seemed to have a fantasy, perhaps a delusion, that body parts could be saved and perhaps brought back to life under her control. This indicated that Attis's initial identification with her mothering functions included a break with reality. This reminds me of the case of Ricky (see Chapter 3), whose mother gave him on his birthdays a series of wedding rings that would not fit his deformed finger. What I want to emphasize here is that the disturbance of reality testing in a future schizophrenic may begin with the earliest identifications. Attis's eventual preoccupations with bisexuality, death and rebirth, "living" part-objects, incest, mutilation, castration, the domination of rejecting and "murderous" parents, and the search for an omnipotent being who would save (at least in part) his body and life, along with other themes closely mirrored in the classical myth, can be traced to his early experiences.

Attis recalled gazing as an adolescent at the bottles with their strange contents and deciding that the appendix was larger than the bit of finger. His oedipal desire to identify with a strong father as a way of moving away from his mother's orbit (reaching up as a defense [Boyer 1961, Volkan 1976]) was not fully repressed. Wishing that the larger bit of tissue—the appendix—belonged to him, he introjected (psychologically ate) the appendix/father's phallus; when he became openly schizophrenic, he had the delusion that he felt it in his stomach.

Effective repression is available when the healthier part of one's personality protects itself from the influence of the infantile psychotic self and/or encapsulates it and includes differentiated and integrated self- and object representations. Because Attis had never fully developed an effective defense mechanism of repression, he was unable to repress completely his incestuous wishes toward his mother; he would describe her vagina in detail, claiming he had seen it when he was 8 or 9 months old. This must have involved a screen memory because it is unlikely that a visual image from that early an age would persist. When he was schizophrenic and excited at the thought of his mother's vagina, he felt tingling in (1) his real penis, (2) his cut finger, and (3) the introjected phallus of his father in his stomach. Furthermore, because his infantile psychotic self-representation was fused with his mother's representation (genital body part fusions), he spoke of two vaginas in his armpits.

Adulthood

Attis reached adulthood with a psychotic personality organization. He had poor reality testing and fluctuating, unstable primitive defenses such as splitting, and on and off he was hypochondriacal. He was not openly schizophrenic as long as he was at home and submitting to his mother's whims.

Complaining of severe stomach pains when he was 20, Attis had an appendectomy. This time, his mother did not add the excised appendix to her collection. The operation reactivated his notion of having his father's penis in his stomach. The father's introjected penis might be removed by surgery; did he or didn't he wish this? Instead of having a definite answer in mind, he had a conflict. He wanted to retain his father's penis/appendix within himself in order to identify with the strong oedipal father who could save him from the pull toward fusion with his "bad" mother's representation; on the other hand, a separation from the mother's representation would mean that he would have no hope of restoring the integrity of his body. His operation also reactivated the memory of earlier attacks on his body, which on one level seemed to be punishment for incestuous desires, and on another (lower) level, an exacerbation of object relations conflicts. He felt that he and his mother could be psychologically separated only if he or she were mutilated or "killed."

When Attis was 22, his father died, and unrepressed oedipal issues and preoccupation with his father's sadistic images intensified. He was convinced that his father had been buried alive and would return to castrate him. As long as he could reach up to oedipal issues and be obsessed with them, he could escape pre-oedipal object-relations conflicts and maintain a sense of self that absorbed and concealed, to a degree, his infantile psychotic self. He could function in a limited way in his day-to-day life and continue attending school.

Psychotic Adjustment to Life

In college Attis was inhibited by internal fears and the awareness of his mother and her representation. He tried, for example, to restore his body image through athletic activity. But his mother compared his unfavorable efforts to the athletic successes of his brother, who was responsible for the loss of his finger and who also attended divinity school and was subsequently ordained. Attis's interpersonal relationships were colored by his paranoid thoughts, and he could not develop real friendships. His commitment to religion arose less from sublimated spiritual ideals than from fascination with the magical aspects of religious belief, which, along with dogma, helped him to conceal his infantile psychotic core. Although on one level he realized that the church was not his mother, on another level it was, and he related to it in a complicated way.

After much difficulty in a well-known college, he left for a second-class divinity school, from which he graduated at 25. He was then ordained a Methodist minister, and the reality of his situation made him think of himself as an adult separated from his mother and her representation. His first schizophrenic episode occurred soon after. Reading the hospital records of that time, I could not identify any other external event that triggered his schizophrenia. His going to the mountaintop suggested to me that he was attempting to identify with his father/God to receive assistance for psychic separation from his mother's representation.

Life as a Minister

The church authorities did not unfrock him after his trip to the mountaintop. He had been mentally ill since childhood but managed to continue being part of the Methodist church, which treated him well, although they labeled him an "oddball" and thought of him as "a little crazy" or, occasionally, "very crazy." Aware of his chronic mental condition after his acute catatonic schizophrenia, the church reassigned him to small rural churches where, I surmise, religious belief and customs are unsophisticated, good and evil seen as issues of black and white, and signs from beyond taken seriously. In such a milieu, he could conceal his delusions most of the time, making a psychotic adjustment to his real world. He reestablished a psychotic personality organization, but his history suggests that on and off he was openly psychotic.

Between open episodes of disorganization he could control the processes of his infantile and adult psychotic selves mainly by obsessive-compulsive and phobic mechanisms. He used extensive ritualization, intellectualization, avoidance, and isolation. He had a recurring nightmare in which he saw a door drop like a guillotine on a snake and cut it in two; this reflected the severing of his finger. News of a fire or mutilation served as an external stimulus for recalling conflict from any level of psychosexual development and application of his obsessive-compulsive or phobic defenses. Although he did not appear markedly phobic or severely obsessive-compulsive, the untrained observer would still see him as a neurotic. One could, nonetheless, glimpse his psychotic core through the cracks of his seemingly high-level defense mechanisms. For example, he ritualized closing his closet doors to exclude his father's ghost, but when stressed, he hallucinated his father's grinning face and adopted more defenses, shouting three times to it to leave him alone and becoming temporarily catatonic if it remained. And he could not leave the house without being afraid he had left something burning and needed to return to check the stove and the security of all the locks. This behavior reenacted his childhood fear of being unable to survive without his mother. He was the mother who checked on and saved the child in a burning house. Furthermore, the house stood as a representation of his mother: to leave her was to "kill" her. He wanted her death but feared that she would take the representation of his finger/penis with her, precluding the chance of his ever having an intact body.

He also used much displacement and projection, identifying in his congregation a woman he thought "a bitch" to represent his "bad" mother. He struggled with her in a paranoid way, being conscientious about serving others in the church, who represented the "good" mother.

Marriage

Attis's mother decided that he should marry and found a woman for him. Two weeks before the wedding day, Attis learned that his fiancée had had an affair with an older man of ill repute. Attis wanted to cancel the wedding, but seeing her as an extension of his mother, he did not. He discussed the affair with his fiancée and managed to make her feel guilty. I con-

cluded that she had masochistic traits and married Attis to
escape from a bad liaison. Staying with him as if undertaking
penance, she endured this "psychotic" marriage by maintaining a life of her own as an apparently successful social work
administrator. Attis thought her repulsive. With unrepressed
incestuous feelings he fantasized—even hallucinated at times—
that his father was grinning sadistically at his sexual performance.

His Mother's Death

Attis's mother died when he was 37, which greatly disturbed
his fragile adjustment to his internal and external worlds. He
could not grieve normally, for her omnipotent representation
lived in his mind, influencing him. He was more preoccupied
with thoughts of her now than when she had been alive. At the
time of her death, he lived in a rural parsonage next to the
church cemetery, where he claimed to see lights at night.
Although his family was not buried there, he feared visits from
their ghosts.

The year after losing his mother, Attis could hardly tell his
wife's representation from his mother's. Making love to his wife
seemed incestuous on one level, but on another, he feared
losing himself in intercourse through fusion. His body perception changed in the act of sex; before orgasm he felt himself to
be a frog between his wife's legs, facing the mouth of a walrus,
which most likely represented vagina dentata. (Cortes [1978]
has noted a connection between frogs and genitalia in numerous paintings and sculptures from medieval and Renais-
sance Europe.) When not intimate with his wife, Attis longed for
freedom from his wife/mother. Although he wanted a divorce,
he could not propose it because primary-process thinking told
him that only death would separate them psychologically.

A Murder Attempt

Attis impulsively tried to kill his wife one night when she lay
sleeping at his side. He left the house to get an ax, taking care

not to be seen by his dead father, who might emerge from the nearby cemetery. Turning back toward the house, ax in hand, he felt terrified and then went into a catatonic state much as he had done 11 years before on the mountaintop, submitting himself to God/father. This state seems to have been a massive defense against actually committing murder, and it persisted until he was taken to the hospital, where he became my patient.

Ten

Thirty-Seven Years with Attis

I was still in psychiatric training when I began to work with Attis and had little experience treating schizophrenics. I learned much from our work together. During the late 1950s, psychoanalysis and psychodynamics dominated many psychiatric training centers, including mine. Medication was considered so inappropriate for the mentally ill that I was sharply criticized for giving an aspirin to a mental patient who complained of a headache. We were expected, under supervision, to use ourselves as therapeutic tools. Neurosis, character disorders, psychosomatic conditions, and psychosis were attributed to psychogenic causes; therefore, psychological remedies were applied.

I was influenced early by Paul Federn's (1952) understanding of schizophrenia and Frieda Fromm-Reichmann's (Bullard 1959) techniques of treating it. I considered schizophrenic symptoms an expression of and a defense against anxiety and believed that "the goal of dynamic psychotherapy with schizophrenia is the same as that of intensive psychotherapy with other mental patients" (Fromm-Reichmann in Bullard 1959, p. 208). I had great admiration for Harold Searles (1951, 1960, 1961), who described his psychotherapeutic work with schizophrenics, and for his understanding of their inner worlds. I began treating Attis in accordance with Searles's methods.

I was still adjusting to life in the United States, to which I had only recently come from Cyprus, and my "regression" may account for the empathy I felt for Attis's chronic regressive state. Kemal Atatürk, the founder of modern Turkey, was my ego ideal, and I was imbued with what I considered to be his belief that religion as practiced in the Ottoman Empire had kept the Turks from entering the modern world. My parents had been fervently devoted to his mental representation (Volkan and Itzkowitz 1980), so my Moslem background dealt more with traditions than with any deeply felt religious convictions. Thus, I was an outsider to Attis's religious preoccupations and considered anything he said about religion suitable material for analysis. I never made my religious background a subject of comment, but I felt that my being an outsider was a great comfort to him—and to myself as well.

At the time I emigrated, Cyprus was turbulent with ethnic tension, extreme nationalism, and terrorism. A schoolmate to whom I was devoted had been a victim of the latter, and I had not yet completed mourning his loss and the loss of my homeland (Volkan 1979). These circumstances made it possible for me to listen almost dispassionately to Attis's murderous rage. In retrospect, I believe that this orientation more than compensated for my lack of therapeutic experience.

AN OVERVIEW

During his first 3 months in the hospital, I saw Attis privately in his hospital room five or six times a week for 50 minutes. After he left the hospital, he was my outpatient for 5 years. During the first 2 years, he was admitted to the hospital three times, each stay lasting from a few weeks to a few months. As an outpatient he had to drive between 150 and 300 miles to see me, depending on his assignment for church duty, which limited his visits to no more than twice a week. Winter weather cut his visits further; he could usually manage to come once a week but occasionally had to skip a week. I moved after the first 5 years of therapy, and this more than doubled the distance he had to travel to see me. I knew that patients with the symptom complexes Attis presented should have more intensive treatment than I was able to provide, but my training obligations and reality factors allowed me to adopt only the schedule outlined here. At no time, incidentally, did he receive any medication for his mental condition from me or any other physician. His 5 years of continuous treatment taught me greatly how to advance the evolution of my understanding of such patients. I have chosen to report his case chiefly because he is now 75 years old. Thus, I have a 32-year follow-up on the value of his treatment with me.

His adult psychotic self had been modified by our first 5 years of work, but I knew that much more treatment was required and suggested that he become a patient of an able colleague of mine practicing near his home. After seeing him a few times, Attis decided that he did not want to become involved with a new therapist. He had become my *satellite* (Volkan and Corney 1986), and his transference attachment to me was too strong to make him comfortable with a change. His visits became more infrequent, once a month or so at first, and he then settled on two to six visits a year, a pattern that he followed for 32 years. He called me on the telephone for brief consultations once in a while. I took a sabbatical in the twelfth year of our connection. I told him about this and supplied my overseas address, but he did not write. He resumed his infrequent visits on my return to the United States.

Attis retired after serving a number of different churches. He lost several close associates to death, made new friends, and had some physical ailments, including heart trouble, with which he was rather seriously ill. Six years ago he had a heart attack that necessitated an emergency triple bypass. After his recovery we resumed our visits.

I grew fond of him over the years. During these years I changed jobs, but despite our long connection I still conducted our therapeutic sessions in the usual way and addressed him as Mr. Attis. If there was something in his 50-minute session that I could clarify or interpret, I did so, emphasizing the interaction of his inner world with external reality. I gave no advice nor did I attempt to manage his life. Although I revealed nothing about myself, I believe he sensed my affection for him. I believe that our infrequent sessions enabled him to maintain what he gained from our first 5 years of continuous work, encapsulate and shrink his infantile psychotic self, put his healthy part on the right developmental track, and keep it there, for he continued to improve psychologically, however slowly, and mastered new ego functions. He never became schizophrenic again, proving that, at least in his case, psychotherapy, even when not intensive, was of benefit in schizophrenia.

Attis's Support System

It was necessary during the first 2 years of his treatment to admit him to a hospital in the absence of an external support system—when, for example, his wife, who usually supported him, became frightened. But I was careful not to hospitalize him often, lest he become dependent on an institution instead of struggling with his deficits and conflicts. I was willing to take a risk and anticipate his nearly adequate functioning as an outpatient. His wife, Gloria, during the first 3 years of her husband's treatment, consulted a therapist in order to better understand her husband's illness and its management. Armed with much self-esteem from her own professional status, she chose to stay with him, although she was aware of his murderous impulses. Her therapist consulted with me when necessary, but I do not recall sharing with her any of the very private issues in Attis's treatment; she depended primarily on what she learned from Gloria.

During our last 32 years of association, Attis traveled a considerable distance to see me, and often Gloria came along.

The couple stayed overnight in a motel, and Gloria would wait outside my office while Attis and I had a session. She was always pleasant to me when I greeted her; I felt that our ritual of courtesy was important to her and that knowledge of my availability made her feel secure in supporting her husband at difficult times, when he did not feel close to her. More recently, when events brought concern about Attis's physical state, Gloria would chat about it in my office with Attis and me, with his permission. When appropriate, I would offer explanations of the effect of his mental state on his physical health. Gloria was by now devoted to him, and I had grown fond of her.

Although at times Attis took sick leave from his church duties, I never discussed his illness with the church authorities, although I wrote once to inform them (for matters of insurance), without giving details, that he had anxiety attacks. Their response to his special needs was always admirable.

A Thirty-Seven-Year Span

I have divided my 37 years of experience with Attis into seven stages:

1. my initial work with him in the hospital, when he was schizophrenic
2. the first years of outpatient treatment
3. the turning point at which his adult psychotic self began modification
4. the period at which his self organized at the borderline level and he adjusted to his inner world and outer world in a satellite state
5. the slow evolution of his psychic integration to higher, neurotic levels
6. his reactions to life-threatening illness, surgery, and the start of old age
7. his old age

My recollections of my sessions with Attis as an inpatient 35 years ago might have been sketchy without the notes that I took at the time. Although to a degree incomplete, they contain enough information to highlight certain observations. Subsequent notes, taken when Attis was an outpatient, are ampler.

AT THE HOSPITAL

When I first saw him, Attis was in a semicatatonic, almost motionless, state. He communicated nothing, but Gloria established his history for me with the help of a social worker. He had shared much of his early story with her. She said that Attis had salvaged the bottled finger after his mother's death and had kept it in the bedroom he shared with Gloria. She was aware that it held magical properties for her husband and knew that he feared the ghosts of his parents. She knew how fearfully he watched the nearby cemetery at night for their return.

Attis's main preoccupation was his wife—his need of closeness to her and his dread of the same (see the need-fear dilemma, Chapter 3). He had begun to call her by his mother's name, and his parishioners were noticing drastic changes in his personality. He seemed gripped by fear and was barely able to discharge his responsibilities. Gloria sometimes found him peeking into closets while mumbling to himself, and she had the impression that he was hallucinating. His anxiety was particularly acute following intercourse, during which he spoke of turning into a frog.

As was usual in that time and place, his nurses in the hospital were not intrusive, being psychodynamically oriented; they took care of his needs simply as a matter of course. I saw him every day except on weekends. He would lie on a daybed in his room while I sat on a chair facing him for 50-minute intervals.

When we first met, after introducing myself I told him that I was willing to understand whatever bothered him whenever he was ready to talk about it. After a week of silence, I found him in the fetal position under a blanket. Nurses reported that he had begun leaving his room for meals but that he would suddenly scurry back into his room and take shelter again beneath his blanket. I told him I would not harm him if he would emerge from beneath the covers. My English was not good then, and I was timid about pushing him.

When I was a resident in psychiatry, I saw a film on the treatment of a schizophrenic patient by a therapist whose name escapes me. He sat silently in his patient's room at regular intervals for 6 months before the patient nonverbally acknowledged his presence. Attis did not take that long to speak. He was about 17 years my senior and in fine physical condition, so he— on a realistic level—probably did not see me as dangerous. I always wondered if his uninvaded part sensed that both of us were handicapped, in my case because of my struggle as an immigrant to adjust to a new culture.

One day I found him sitting up with his blanket wrapped around his body, his head uncovered so he could see me. He began letting his toes and fingers peep out from under the blanket and then drew them back. He talked about a guillotine cutting a snake into pieces, and I saw this as representing the amputation of his finger (or toes, or penis) by an ax. I sensed that he was testing the external world and showing distrust by retracting his fingers and toes. When he hallucinated snakes in his room, he did not fear them but feared their being hurt. He always concealed the stump of his finger beneath his other hand, and it was years before he could show it to me without anxiety.

Attis introduced himself: he was a monster with two vaginas, he said, pointing to his armpits. He claimed to have four penises, which I later learned were his real penis, the amputated finger, the finger in a bottle, and his father's penis, which he had internalized into his stomach. He seemed effeminate from time to time, but at other times he behaved as though powerfully masculine. He was able, with a little encouragement, to give an unrepressed history, including his life as a child, his desires and fears, and his later ascent to the mountaintop. His reporting was, however, subject to bizarre interruptions, such as his seeing snakes and guillotines in the room or breaking into a cold sweat with staring eyes. He began to be better organized and ritualistic. He clung to me. Because I was inexperienced I felt the need to interpret and pointed to a possible connection between those hallucinations and the loss of his finger. He obliged me in acknowledging a possible connection but was obviously not convinced or interested in such explanations. He sometimes spoke openly of sexual matters, telling in minute detail how a glimpse of his mother's vagina had excited him and how afraid he had been of his father. In the midst of a calm session, he would call me a vulture, and then he would become a vulture and spread his arms out, looking like a bird taking flight, ready to pounce on me. Then he would quickly return to being a frightened groundhog. After 3 months he left the hospital, obviously not well but sufficiently organized to attempt a return to his daily life. He clung to Gloria. We made arrangements for him to be my outpatient and for her to continue seeing her therapist.

ATTIS AS AN OUTPATIENT

As an outpatient Attis had a paranoid orientation. He talked endlessly of funerals, hallucinating his father's face, being repelled by his wife's vagina, and being terrified by "bad" objects, such as the woman parishioner he so disliked, and alternated between aggressive attacks on me and compliance. Gloria was frightened by his aggressive outbursts at home and sent him to the hospital a few times in a period of 2 years; I saw him daily then.

Like many schizophrenics, he brought nonpsychotic aspects of himself into treatment and displayed what seemed to be a caricature of transference neurosis, regarding me as representing aspects of his parents and siblings and sometimes standing for his desires and his defenses against them. I eventually explained, without using technical terms, how he had more and more displaced his dead mother's representation onto his wife. He was conflicted by this and was sexually dysfunctional with her because of incestuous implications, fear of retaliation from his father's representation, and dread of fusing with her. His hold on such interpretations was very tenuous at best. I soon learned, however, that any effort to work through his difficulties via interpretation of transference neurosis was unavailing. Slowly I was learning what a transference psychosis (Searles 1965) was all about. He began dressing like me, talking like me at times, and transiently becoming me, as if to gain temporary control over his symptoms.

I learned from him that one should approach a schizophrenic differently from the way one would approach a neurotic, and I began dealing with events in the external world that triggered his endless variety of symptoms. If he had a cold sweat after telling me about a policeman he saw on his way to the session, I linked his distress to the sight of authority but refrained from making genetic (psychological) interpretations that the officer might represent his brutal father. I simply illustrated that Attis's mental products were connected with actual events. Such exercises seemed to lead to better reality testing. He appeared more obsessional and brought to his sessions lists of grievances and lists of people whom he saw as agents of annihilation and castration. I realized that as long as he anticipated external dangers, he could believe that he was not yet psychologically killed or castrated. He needed detached body parts to be complete, the part most at issue being the bottled finger, which was sometimes represented by an object that was not truly symbolic but protosymbolic (Werner and Kaplan 1963) and experienced as though a detachable member of his own body.

One day he arrived looking healthy and happy and no longer paranoid. Much to my surprise, he was in this state for three sessions. I could not account for the sudden change until I heard that he had bought a car he said was flesh colored. This represented the bottled finger and his/his mother's detached penis. The car seemed to repair his psychotic sense of self; he felt complete at the cost of a break with reality and perceived the car as truly an extension of the representations of his mind and body. When he had the car serviced and the attendant raised the hood, Attis experienced tactile sensations in his "penises," and when the exhaust pipe needed repair he developed hemorrhoids. The details of how a psychological phenomenon evokes bodily responses are not known, but this actually happened with Attis. He again became paranoid after deciding that the new car ran poorly, and he accused the dealer of having tricked him.

In his fourth year with me I noticed an exaggeration of his fusing with my representation, but something was different. He was attempting to identify with my functions so that, paradoxically, his need for fusion would lessen. He spoke less about the magic of religion and his sermons became explanatory, as if he were interpreting for the benefit of his flock. He became more openly curious about me and my background but anxiously tried to conceal his interest. In his sermons he would use statements I had made during our sessions. Meanwhile, he began to offer me a more organized account of his life than before and to see that his childhood had much to do with his current problems. He did not lose his symptoms but kept them under control.

THE TURNING POINT

Toward the end of the fourth year of treatment, Attis lived more than 150 miles from my office, and travel became difficult because of heavy winter weather. Therefore, he canceled a series of appointments with me, adding that he had to officiate at an unusual number of funerals. At this point, he was trying to separate further, intrapsychically, from the therapist/early mother, and these efforts accompanied his increased references to people who had died or reference to himself, who might die. I sensed that concepts of death and intrapsychic separation were intertwined in his mind.

On one level, the cancellations of the sessions represented his wish to separate from the early mother/therapist. The winter weather helped him to materialize, as well as to defend, this wish. He felt that if he came to therapy hours, I might engulf him. Were his and my representations to fuse we could never be separated. I believe that our rather extended physical separation helped him to keep me as a "bad" entity from which he could be safe by maintaining distance between us. He had more opportunities for distorting reality when not in touch with me.

When he called for an appointment, a new secretary asked the reason for his earlier cancellations, and he greatly resented her "aggressive curiosity." He thought of her as my extension, a representation of his intrusive mother. He opened his next session with a rather calm complaint about her pointed questions and spoke of a quarrel in his home town: the owner of a funeral home had discontinued ambulance service because it was unprofitable, and the townspeople objected. Attis said angrily that he thought of their criticism as unjust persecution; he felt involved because a community leader had suggested to him that the finances of the mortuary should be investigated. Attis wanted to preach a sermon in defense of the funeral director, although this would endanger his own image in the town. He did not seem to see the parallel between my secretary's question and the suspicions concerning the funeral director, although in each a persecuting "bad" object tried to intrude on a "good" and victimized one.

Around this time Attis became upset and resumed looking into closets for his dead father. Although in the past he had hallucinated his father's presence, he now looked for one particular aspect of his father—his punitive and haunting grin—in reference to a temper tantrum his father once had, which Attis connected with his own murderous rage. Although he did hallucinate his father's image, he knew at this point that what he saw was not real.

He said that he had thought of turning around and going home while on the way to my office. I knew he was afraid of losing control over his anger; he wanted to protect me from it and considered not coming, but he kept his appointment nonetheless. He was angered further when, while parking his car outside my office, he was "tricked out of" an empty slot by a big man, although Attis had located it first. This anger triggered emotions associated with other episodes he spoke of during the hour.

As Eissler (1954) and Peto (1968) long ago observed in patients who, like Attis, have defective ego structures, an emotion accumulates new energy by activating other memories that feed it. At this same session Attis recalled the brother who had cut off his finger, and felt anger because he had been the favorite of their mother, who had given Attis second place. At a basketball game a week earlier, he had been reminded of his brother's prowess in athletics as a teenager and how he himself had given up athletics because his mother disapproved of his participation. There were two brothers in the game he saw; Attis thought that the younger was the better player but "for psychological reasons" had refrained from shooting the ball into the basket. Although these incidents contained aspects of the oedipal struggle of a sibling in a triangle, Attis emphasized the dyad of himself and his mother within the triangle. He became more and more angry as he poured out these memories.

At this point, he was not conscious that these memories served to support his anger, and he could not separate one event, with its accompanying affect, from another. Suddenly rising, he started to attack me but became catatonic. I slowly overcame my natural fear and realized what was happening: he had recalled, in feelings and action, what had brought him to the hospital where I first saw him. The murderous rage about his mother/wife, father, brother, and all persecuting objects was reenacted between us, and I felt that I must help him understand and master it. I called his name as if to give him a healthier identity. My response helped him to get out of his catatonia.

He could now recall in detail the night he left his house to get the ax to kill his wife and the catatonic state that resulted. He said that the paralysis of his overwhelming affect was like playing possum, and he thought the catatonia he had experienced then was similar to what had overtaken him now. By this time, he had to some extent identified with my observing ego functions, and they now belonged to him. He could describe his adult psychotic sense of self when it was saturated with rage and thought of himself as a swollen, balloon-like monster of indeterminate sex. He vaguely imagined bursting and destroying everything around him. When I called him by name, he saw his adult psychotic self as a groundhog, something much tamer than a monster. I told him in lay terms that the groundhog also symbolized the core of earliest affective relationships between himself and his mother (his infantile psychotic self). Behind his rage lay a more dreadful emotion—anaclitic depression and the inability to feel his mother's love for him and to survive without her representation. He had to defend himself from hunger for love and protect himself from annihilating helplessness and other unnamable "bad" affects by whatever means he could summon. His catatonia (paralysis) was a primitive and massive defense against his infantile and adult psychotic selves saturated with helplessness and rage. If he moved, he could destroy his sense of continuity and destroy me. Catatonia allowed him to have an illusion about future object relations.

He was able to feel and understand his rage against a love object from which he wanted to separate and individuate, but his dependence on external objects and their representations was such that without them he was at the mercy of an infantile psychotic self filled with unnamable and unbearable affects deriving from an early lack of mothering. When he could handle saturation with affects, and know and name them in secondary process thinking, he came face-to-face with the unknown enemy. One can defend oneself in more adaptive ways when the enemy is known and its whereabouts understood.

Attis then indicated further identification with a new object: my representation. Months after tolerating saturation with affect and avoiding catatonia, he came to me looking pale. He spoke of eating a turkey dinner on the previous day and being anxious ever since. Although accustomed to eating turkey, eating it as he attempted to identify with his Turkish therapist made turkey a concrete symbol, or protosymbol (Werner and Kaplan 1963). In his fantasy he had eaten me; introjection and eating concretely became the same process. He spoke of having had fantasies of my destruction while en route to my office. I first interpreted the positive aspect of his fantasy: his wish to be like me by "eating me up." Then I spoke of his subsequent fear that he had destroyed me because he had eaten a turkey dinner. Realizing that the suit he wore was like mine, he confirmed the attempted identification; he had purchased this suit, along with a shirt very much like mine, on the previous day. My interpretation of his bizarre wish to eat me humanized his fantasy and brought his primary process thinking under control of secondary process thought, and he relaxed.

He then asked what I thought about the Supreme Court's decision about prayer in the schools and speculated about my religion. The tenor of my response was, "Look, if you want to be like me, you need not make the resemblance an all-or-nothing business. You can get useful things from me, and you may reject other aspects of me. You can choose." He wore the same lookalike clothing to our next session, saying he had been impelled to do so. Before starting his therapy hour, he went to the bathroom, where he produced a hard stool. I felt that he had to rid himself of "bad" aspects of the therapist introject, and I made a remark to this effect, in a sense giving him further permission to rid himself of unwanted aspects of the introject. Formerly, when perceiving his father's representation as "bad," he would eject his father's penis from his belly through his rectum, indicating primary process thought about having eaten the bottled appendix/penis. He would eventually feel this introject inside himself again.

An introject is a special type of object representation that falls just short of assimilation into the self-representation (Volkan 1981a). It is active, functional, and influential on the self-representation. Attis fantasized his own death as the hour went on, and I interpreted his destructive fantasies about the therapist introject, his desire to identify with it, and fear of his own death. Toward the end of the hour, after working through his fear of new identification with my introject, he reported a sensation of getting out of his shell and developing a new personality, with which he wanted to take a long vacation. Thus he spoke openly about starting to hold on to a new self-representation to replace—or at least modify—the earlier, adult psychotic one.

Attis had never traveled out of the state in which he had been born, his emotional illness having kept him out of the military. Remaining close to home reflected his difficulty with separation-individuation. Like the groundhog who stayed in his hole, he could not leave his state/mother representation. The new personality that emerged could be expected to change this immobility by dissolving his adult psychotic self and corresponding positive changes in his uninvaded parts.

Attis expressed a desire to travel out of state and have adventures. He could do so by identifying with that function of me that could leave a mother-representation (the state) behind. He spoke of my immigrating to the United States from Turkey as a highly adventurous undertaking. In one of the next sessions he set Philadelphia as his travel objective. This did, in fact, involve a considerable journey for him. His associations centered around the Liberty Bell in the City of Brotherly Love, which indicated a need for symbolic celebration of the birth of his new personality and the modification of his adult psychotic self. As we discussed the proposed trip, I said I had once visited Philadelphia (implying that the trip was not a dangerous enterprise). In retrospect, I suspect he was very anxious about finding his liberty and turning from aggression for the castrator brother/mother/father toward love, and that my remark was a response to this intuition. I needed to protect him, and probably myself within him (his identification with my representation), by giving such reassurance. Thus, my response was determined by my countertransference, but I think it was a proper one.

Before long he took a 6-week vacation in Philadelphia. On his return from the successful trip, he visited the brother who had amputated his finger. "I wanted to show him my new personality," he said and reported being amused at hearing his brother, only 4 years his senior, call him "son." When he returned for his next appointment with me, Attis overheard office personnel speaking about my wife's recent delivery of a baby girl. I had never spoken of being married, and what he overheard gave him a ready-made opportunity to repeat his early life history. Here he was being born again, but as in his childhood, he had to compete with newborn siblings (the twins and the deaf sister) and face a mother (therapist) who might be preoccupied with the siblings (my baby).

He kept referring to my baby during the hour that followed, speaking of "him" although he knew I had a new daughter. I think this also reflected a wish that it was he who was my child. I said that it might have been unfortunate for him to overhear something about my life, that hearing about my baby might be burdensome to him, and that the meaning of what he had heard needed analysis. Although he seemed to relax, he went for a thorough medical check-up after this session. I felt he was seeking an examination for psychological reasons, that he wanted reassurance that his new personality was healthy and that his murderous rage about the mother/therapist and envy about sibling(s)/my daughter had not damaged him.

Feeling that he had been born again, he became anxious about whether the newborn "son" would be treated like the original one (himself), who had been under the shadow of the early mother. In transference, I became that early mother. This time, however, the transference was mostly neurotic because he did not fuse my representation with his archaic mother's. He knew that my metamorphosis into his mother was only symbolic, but the symbol made him anxious. Was he playing second fiddle to my new baby? Would I be able to give him my attention now that I had a new baby at home to distract me? On other occasions, my new baby was Attis. I reminded him that when the twins and the deaf sister were born, he had to play second fiddle in competition for their mother's attention. He soon became anxious, fearing that the newborn "son" might be castrated as the original one, symbolically castrated at age 4, had been. He ceased having sexual relations with his wife. His old flesh-colored car once more became "alive," a penis. He wanted to sell it in a gesture of self-castration.

My new object and his new personality images were in conflict with his mother's dominating images and his corresponding submissive images. His sessions were full of descriptions of competing self- and object images (Abse and Ewing 1960) and jealousy of one internal object representation of another (Searles 1986). He wanted his more mature self- and object images to prevail, to be victorious, but he was unsure of the outcome. He decided that his mother had been like Nikita

Khrushchev, who at that time was regarded in the United States as an aggressively invested "bad object" representation, and that the brother who had "castrated" him resembled Fidel Castro (castrator). His therapist was from Turkey, which was allied with the United States. He reported that although his mother had warned him against trusting strangers (foreigners), he felt that he could trust me. Turkey was an ally, a new but foreign object. He reached for assurance, but instead of giving it, I helped him to see his inner processes and the reason for his anxiety.

In a later session, he expressed gratitude to me for saving him from "fire"—the influence of his psychotic selves. He recalled that when his mother had saved him from the burning house, and when she had preserved his finger in a bottle, his obligation to her had necessitated his being in her shadow, unindividuated. He wondered now if I would demand total submission of his new self to me. His mother had stolen his penis, although at the same time preserving it, and he was afraid to be free of her lest she destroy it. He saw me as a homosexual in a new transference situation and began referring to me as one. I knew that his thinking of me as a homosexual involved projection and displacement from both the oedipal and the pre-oedipal levels, but in dealing with him I focused on what was "hot" and what would help him continue on his developmental path. I interpreted the pre-oedipal mother transference that was making him feel uncomfortable and told him that if I were homosexual I would emulate his mother in keeping his penis and keeping him from individuation. This would maintain the status quo, with which he was unhappy. If, on the other hand, I were not homosexual and not in search of a penis, I would be different from the mother of his childhood. This would mean that he could separate himself from her influence. Because this was a new situation for him, it might make him so anxious that he would choose to maintain the status quo, even at the cost of being unable to progress. He responded positively, and I postponed dealing with his wish to see me as homosexual in defense against his castrating father.

He slowly but steadily continued to modify his adult psychotic self and began to crystallize and maintain a new sense of self on the level of a borderline personality. I assumed that by dissolving his adult psychotic self he also modified his infantile psychotic self. Nevertheless, I knew that his infantile psychotic self was not dissolved, but more effectively encapsulated. Our work was by no means completed. At this time, however, I moved to a new post some distance away.

SATELLITE ADJUSTMENT

At the time of my move, I was becoming more and more influenced professionally by Margaret Mahler's (1968) work on child development and childhood psychosis and her description of autism, symbiosis, and separation-individuation. Harold Searles (1965) was using her ideas to treat regressed patients. Although at times in our professional careers we come under the influence of colleagues and become their professional allies, it is well to keep in mind the historical continuity of our specialty. At that time, I read more Mahler and Searles than Federn and used a concept based on the writings of Mahler and her associates (Mahler and Furer 1966, Mahler and La Perriere 1965) in dealing with Attis's adjustment to me and to life in general after we ended our routine therapeutic work because of my move. In 1968, Corney and I published a paper describing Attis's adjustment with reference to the *satellite state*. Margaret Mahler wrote to me expressing her approval of the concept of the satellite state and its usefulness in assessing certain clinical phenomena. The formulation corresponds to what we know now as borderline personality organization, but it did not attract much attention at the time that object-relations theory, which reflected the intrapsychic aspect of Mahler's findings in a systematic way, was being developed and adopted by the psychoanalytic profession. Much later, another analyst, Salman Akhtar (1992a,b), who also has been greatly influenced by Mahler, extended our understanding of clinical manifestations of disturbed optimal distance.

I believe that the satellite state formulation is most suitable to describe Attis's adjustment in a graphic way and to give it meaning. Explanation of the borderline organization with this conceptualization does not compete with or replace the concept that Kernberg (1975, 1984) championed and I elaborated on (Volkan 1976, 1987) and still support. The same picture is simply seen from a different angle.

I had about 6 months to prepare Attis for my move, which would double the distance between us and which I anticipated would bring an end to our association. He was anxiously trying to relate to me as a strong father figure who could help him to separate intrapsychically further from his mother's representation. Although he made a cool response to my plans for departure and withdrew, he never returned to psychotic disorganization. After consulting a few times with the psychiatrist to whom I had referred him, he asked to resume work with me, indicating his willingness to make the long journey. I noted that he was adapting to life on a borderline level and had become my satellite.

In the Greek myth, Daedalus, imprisoned on Crete, found escape from the island difficult because Minos kept watch by sea and had offered a large reward for his capture. So Daedalus made wings for himself and for his son, Icarus. As they began to fly away, he warned his son not to fly too high lest the sun melt the wax with which his wings were attached, nor too low lest the feathers become wet in the sea. Disobeying, Icarus began soaring toward the sun, and when the sun melted the wax, he fell into the sea and drowned.

The danger involved in flying higher than the father has received some attention in psychoanalytic literature in reference to oedipal problems. For example, Bond's (1952) study of military pilots during World War II indicated that Icarian fantasies were common among fliers who developed phobias about flying. Bond believed that aircraft held a symbolic meaning and involved a narcissistic love for one's own body. He also noted that there was evidence for this in many phobic fliers who saw the renunciation of flying as equal to self-castration.

In working with Attis, I was aware of the second proviso in Daedalus's admonition—that his son should not swoop too low lest his feathers become wet and he be drawn into the sea. It is my clinical observation that Icarian fantasies involving the second proviso refer mainly to unresolved problems of separation-individuation. As I saw in Attis, however, Icarian fantasies and dreams are condensed with problems of the oedipal level, but it is also recognized that a deeper and more prominent problem exists at the pregenital level.

Separation-individuation is a gradual intrapsychic developmental process—separation of the self and the start of the establishment of individual identity. Mahler and Furer (1966) specify that they do not mean physical separation from the mother but, rather, intrapsychic separation that normally occurs when the mother is physically present. I adhere to this view but feel that in certain adults for whom separation-individuation problems remain, the experience of physical separation can tip the balance, throwing into bold relief the vulnerable individual's earlier unresolved separation-individuation problem and causing clinical difficulty. For these persons, the experience of physical separation becomes primitively symbolized and represents psychic separation. This was the case with Attis, who experienced the physical separation between us as an intrapsychic separation.

The main function of the ego associated with his uninvaded parts had been to contain his psychotic selves. The ego development he achieved now served the important function of maintaining a satellite relationship with me. I represented his childhood mother—a source of instant gratification but at the same time a dreaded force that pulled him toward fusion. He would not leave me too far behind because of his continuing dependency on me; he was obliged to orbit around me. During the first years after my move, after his visits and telephone calls became more infrequent, he reported having dreams in which he or a representation of himself circled around a central object. A characteristic of these dreams was the orbiting state of the dependent satellite, which never seemed to leave orbit.

I came to realize that these satellite dreams fulfilled two wishes: first, they permitted expression of an extreme degree of dependency without consequent loss of identity through fusion;

second, they kept aggression under control by allowing the desire for freedom to be expressed without interrupting the satellite state. Aggression against the mother's representation, as in Attis's efforts to separate from her influence, was seen as the same as destroying her and, as such, was also equated with the death of the satellite. A prototype of his satellite dreams would be: "I dreamed of a huge steel ball like the Earth, and an eagle. Every hundred years the eagle would fly by and would brush the ball with the tip of its wing." His association to this dream involved his object-relations issues. He was the eagle, and he was doomed to spend an eternity aloft, he said, until the steel ball was worn out; only then could he be free from the representation of the mother/therapist. On one level, he experienced his visits, which were 2 to 6 months apart, as though we were separated for a century after each one.

Kohut (1971) reported similar satellite dreams as part of narcissistic transference; he saw the narcissistic patient's avoidance of spinning out of orbit as protection against psychosis, and the effective pull to the center as narcissistic transference. His perceptions supplement what Corney and I described earlier; I think they are not incompatible with our interpretation of such dreams from the point of view of separation-individuation as well as of object relations.

In time I made it clear to Attis that his satellite position occupied in the developmental sequence a place between the symbiotic relationship with his mother and the freedom of intrapsychic life apart from her without loss of identity. I also spoke of his ability to maintain an image of me even when far from me for months at a time. Deferring to his remarks about me, I told him how he was seeing me in terms of black and white, reminding him that we had worked together for years. I suggested that as he came to trust himself, I would not intrude into his personality or coldly abandon him even though I was physically distant from him, and that he would be increasingly less obliged to circle around me but would have a more integrated perception of me.

When he spoke to me of his visit to the Liberty Bell, I suggested that he had made at least one important symbolic gesture toward internal freedom and that having done this once, it was possible that he would achieve further freedom, although he would have to consider surrendering the comfort of a compromised position. Corney and I had noted that

> [an] individual so compromised must remain dynamically like the child passing through the sub-phase of "practicing," in need of repeated "refueling" from mother (or other source of instantaneous gratification). Such an individual is in essence a captive body, forever doomed to orbit within the gravitational field of an intense unsolved dependency. [Volkan and Corney 1968, p. 287]

In my infrequent sessions with Attis I reminded him of our work history and the original determinants of his problems and pointed to the possibility of further development; by then he understood about being a captive body. I saw no evidence of progress with him for some years, however; nor had I really expected much. As long as he circled around me as he circled around the church, never totally committing himself to it and always longing to abandon his role as pastor, he functioned without developing a clinical psychosis or returning to schizophrenia.

There is an element of safety in the satellite state; it permits a certain freedom of functioning as long as stress is not too great and the illusion of the availability of the source at the center is maintained. One must be careful to stay in orbit; if one comes close to the center, one can be engulfed. If one goes too far away from the center, however, one can be without regulatory power. What ego does develop does so in the service of perpetuating the condition of compromise. When the center is perceived as "good," the one in orbit feels close—but not too close to it lest it turn out to be "bad." When the center is perceived as "bad," one keeps one's distance from it, but not too far lest it again turn out to be "good." The need-fear dilemma (Abse and Ewing 1960, Burnham et al. 1969), which is prominent in schizophrenia, is handled at the borderline level by the formation of a satellite position; reality testing is maintained because there is no fusion of self- and object representation, and the dependency needs are responded to without fear of losing altogether the external object or oneself.

FURTHER DEVELOPMENTAL MOVEMENTS

For twelve years after his proper therapy ended, Attis would "brush me with his wing" a few times a year. I represented his mother, but elements of a father transference were present also, in time overshadowing the mother transference. The father transference evolved after he did more exercises to separate himself from women and to achieve a more integrated image of them.

He was routinely transferred from one church to another every 3 years or so, and each move brought a heightening of his obsessional symptoms, which now controlled his satellite position. He knew he was reacting to change and separation. In each congregation he identified an older, "bad" woman, a "bitch" he knew represented his early mother in a symbolic way. His acknowledgment of what she represented did not keep him from being anxious in relating to her, but he did not fuse a representation of a "bitch" with that of his mother or of himself, nor did he engage in excessive introjective-projective cycles with her representation.

Afraid of these "bitches," he fought bravely against them. Whenever he became very anxious, he would tolerate his anxiety, call, or come to see me. I continued to refrain from giving advice but clarified and interpreted the intrapsychic processes in which he was involved. His "fights" with these older women were his basic psychic exercises in further attempting to achieve separation-individuation. Twelve years after I moved and our regular sessions ended, these women no longer gave him much anxiety, and he reported taking pleasure in "saying no" to them; saying no to the representation of a "bad" object is evidence of further individuation (Volkan 1982b). Saying no has different meanings at different times of development; its use at this time by this patient showed strengthening of the border between self-representation and the representation of an object.

During his infrequent sessions with me, Attis gleefully described in some detail how he had overcome fear of the "bitches" and could now put them in their place. Rather than encouraging him, I continued to explain that this activity was in the service of his intrapsychic freedom and progress. His vacillation between being dependent on and being hostile to his wife was no longer so marked, and he no longer thought of her vagina as a walrus's mouth. The bottle containing his finger had been put away in the attic, and although it still had a spell over him, he behaved as though it was no longer magical.

When involved in conflicts with his "bad" women, he began regarding me as the strong father with whose functions he wanted further identification so he could leave the women behind and enter a man's world. Progress from a satellite state was made by further identifications with experiences with me. He perceived me as a tough, venturesome immigrant able to stand up to "the bitches," against whom he wanted me to speak. He joked and laughed about them.

He occasionally spent his time with me reporting items about Turkey that he had read in the paper or in news magazines. Although he had graduated from college, he was no intellectual, and his interest in Turkey was motivated simply by a desire to integrate me. His relation to men in the environment improved drastically the more he came to see me as a benign oedipal father. Formerly on guard with other men, he began to enjoy their company, especially on the golf course. I recalled that when he was dominated by his adult psychotic self, he had tried golf, but he would suddenly perceive the balls and clubs as sexual organs and fear picking a ball out of a hole lest a walrus bite him. On a lower level, he was afraid that if he put his hand in a hole, the earth would suck him in and that he would disappear, as a groundhog would. When his anxiety increased, as it did sometimes when playing, he had psychosomatic disturbances such as stomach pains, fainting, or diarrhea and would wait for months before playing again. Now sports competition no longer brought homosexual or engulfment fantasies and the anxiety they entailed.

His preoccupation with the "bitch" women helped him to separate from his "bad" mother's representation, and he began to find good qualities in some of them. When they became "good" or better integrated, however, he anxiously speculated about how I would regard him as a sexual man. Would I castrate him? He began to anticipate castration less from woman/walrus and more from male competitors. He still had sensations in the severed finger that represented his penis but no longer felt that it *was* his penis. He had long repressed the notion of his father's penis being lodged in his belly and did not make references to it. As stated earlier, the finger in the bottle was tucked away.

About 12 years after I moved, Attis began to tell me of several lively flirtations he had with women and his consideration of having affairs with them. He still perceived his wife as his mother, but not on a psychotic level, and the representations of the two women were no longer interchangeable. His interest in women showed an attempt to crystallize his separation from the representation of his mother/wife and to compete with me as his oedipal father in the hope of ultimately identifying with me. After kissing and hugging a willing woman, he would be turned away from further pursuit by anxiety and would return to his wife with hostile submission. I neither encouraged nor discouraged his advances toward women, but when it seemed appropriate, I compared him to a teenager just learning to date. His behavior expressed a further developmental push.

Sometimes he expected me to be a punitive father but came to see that I was simply curious about his intrapsychic operations. I felt comfortable with him, and he felt comfortable with me. He began something he would not have been capable of earlier: trying, shyly and with some anxiety, to be amusing, telling me jokes that I found entertaining. His only jokes had been formerly at the expense of "the bitches," and he told them with anxiety. But now he seemed to joke to see if we, two men, shared good feelings and some attitudes. I saw psychosexual implications in some of his pleasantries but made no comment. Because I felt that the chief reason he was letting me in on these jokes was to establish a man-to-man relationship with me, I smiled at them.

He had no children, and as his identity as an adult male became better established, he spoke of wanting to adopt. He and Gloria discussed the possibility but abandoned it because of his history and their age. Our meetings then were very poignant; he grieved over his childless state and tried to be philosophical about his life and the years lost to his psychotic personality organization as well as his schizophrenic episodes. I stood by while he mourned. Mourning allows further refinement of reality (Volkan 1981a); a mourner comes to realize that some things are gone and makes an effort to integrate the experience of loss with reality so life can go on (Pollock 1989). Attis's ability to mourn in an adult fashion gave further evidence that his adult psychotic self was dissolved; a schizophrenic or a person with a psychotic personality organization cannot engage in what we know as the adult mourning process, and even persons with a borderline personality organization find it difficult to experience grief and sorrow (Searles 1986). Attis's mourning indicated psychic growth.

In his late fifties and after a long courtship, Attis became the lover of a married woman. The couple was very discreet. The woman was a few years younger than Attis, had no children, and was unhappy in her marriage. At first Attis treated her like an idealized woman; his wife remained in his mind as potentially "bad." He still used splitting in a stable way as a defense, although he could also use repression and other sophisticated higher-level defenses. In time, he developed a deep friendship with his lover and a more integrated perception of her. At the same time, he developed a more realistic perception of his wife and friendship with and understanding of her also. He could then acknowledge his conflicts about his ministry, his marriage, and his mistress. Becoming "philosophical," he decided to maintain his affair because he felt that he had, until now, missed having a loving and sexual relationship with a woman he could integrate. His wife did not complain when, for all practical purposes, they no longer had sex together but became better companions.

Attis and Gloria moved after he retired, bought a house, and settled in a nice neighborhood, while his lover stayed in the town where he had first met her. Attis visited her from time to time, keeping her a secret from his wife. In his sixties, he reported happiness he had never before experienced and sexual freedom he had never before known. Gone were his old fears of women and their genitalia, his father's ghost, his disintegrating anxieties, and his metamorphosis into a frog. And he reported that his wife began enjoying him more as a companion because he was more relaxed.

What is the therapist's role in dealing with a patient's infidelity? I made no distinction between Attis's reports of extramarital or other activities. I was as curious about the meaning of his affair as I was about the meaning of his other activities. When it was appropriate, I told Attis that he had made a new adjustment to life in accordance with the new growth in his psychic system; his wife, in the past, symbolized his mother, but he had separated from her and found his own woman—but one who was married to another man. Thus, he still had to work through issues about the reality that he was married and about the triangular relationship. I suggested that there were possibilities for new adjustments, new commitments, and new responsibilities in working out his oedipal conflict, although I did not use that technical term. Attis had become a neurotic personality in his sixties. He was well aware of some of the things I brought to his attention and of his age, his past, and the relatively pleasurable life-style he had attained. He had no more paranoid fears and no torturing fights with his wife or the "bitches."

He had a genuinely good time with his lover. He had golfing companions in his retirement, had become respected in his community, and had reasonably good relationships with most of his living siblings, although there had been some problems over inheritance when their parents' farm was sold. The brother responsible for the amputation of Attis's finger had kept the place to himself and claimed more than his share of the proceeds of its sale. Attis led the rest of the family in taking the case to court, where they prevailed.

When he had a psychotic personality organization or schizophrenic episodes, Attis had been preoccupied with hell and ghosts and interpreted his religion in accordance with primary process thinking, using it to hide his infantile psychotic core. At the borderline level, he had used the church as his mother—both "good" and "bad"—in a split way, orbiting around it. His ministerial functions centered around the borderline position in respect to object relations, and he looked for "bitches" or allies among his parishioners, addressing his sermons to them as he perceived them. When he reached the neurotic level, however, he used his role as a minister according to his identification with me as a therapist and became more interested in the personal and social problems of his parishioners. He was very good at listening to their difficulties and their grief, and people readily came to him for consultation. Dedicated to his work, he made himself available except when stress brought a temporary regression. He was particularly good with teenagers, understanding them and advising their parents how to deal with them. He saw in them the sons and daughters he had never had, and there were indications that they represented also his neurotic self, their lives reflecting the teenage years he had not been able to enjoy as an integrated person. He joined in life with these youngsters, finding excitement in exploring it, despite transient feelings of depression that never developed into a full-blown depressive state. What was most heartwarming for me was that he did all this realistically and without much anxiety. After his parents' estate was settled he was able to extend a friendly hand to the brother who had cut off his finger and who had pressed his claim, and in time they resumed a relatively friendly relationship.

Attis was not ready to move up further, perhaps, because he could not do so without proper treatment. His treatment had shrunk and effectively encapsulated his infantile psychotic self, and dissolved his adult psychotic self and put him on the right developmental track. He was telling me that while he traveled on this path he had passed many stations, but this was the station he wanted to settle in and where he could be content.

PHYSICAL ILLNESS

As Attis passed through his sixties, he faced a number of traumas against which his neurotic personality organization stood firm. When he began having dizzy spells nearly 16 years ago, his psychiatric experience led him to seek a possible psychological cause. Attis's reasoning made me recall from many years before a mental image of myself on my analyst's couch, analyzing away a symptom I was having—regurgitation during sleep. My analyst had suggested that this might be caused by a hiatal hernia, which proved to be the case. Remembering this, I did not accept Attis's explanation of a psychological cause of his dizziness but suggested that he have a physical examination. I heard from his cardiologist a month later that he needed a permanent transvenous pacemaker. He had a sick sinus syndrome, which causes a spectrum of Brady arrhythmias and, occasionally, Brady arrhythmias following tachycardia. The cardiologist noted that Attis did not want metal in contact with his skin and raised the question of a psychological reason for this aversion. When Attis consulted me, it was obvious to both of us that metal in contact with his skin represented the ax that had removed his finger. He agreed to obtain a pacemaker if necessary, but when the cardiologist told him that his heart problem would progress slowly and its advance was unpredictable, he decided not to get one and continued a normal physical existence, playing golf and taking vacations as before and reporting for yearly check-ups. Nine years after first seeing the cardiologist, he had an attack that necessitated triple bypass surgery.

He had played golf three days in a row during his wife's absence from home and had experienced some chest pains. He went to a hospital, where he had a heart attack and fainted. Surgery was performed to save his life, but he knew nothing of what had happened until it was all over. In his postsurgery mental state, he felt confused and uncertain about whether he was dreaming or hallucinating. He had seen his mother, who opened her arms to him, calling "Come to me!" This frightened him. His physical trauma apparently evoked memories of acts that made him feel guilty, and the recollection made the assault on his body seem a punishment. He recalled playing at sex with a cousin as a child, and he felt guilty about his marital infidelity. For a day or so after his operation his mind was filled with images from his childhood; he dreamed of mules and of how his father had thrust a stick into the anus of one. "Everything disturbing came back to me," he said on the phone after being discharged from the hospital. His comments, and the fact that he had not called me until 3 weeks after his operation, impressed me with how much self-analysis he had accomplished in order to get rid of his disturbing feelings and symptoms before getting in touch with me.

He said he had hallucinated seeing fire in the recovery room. "I knew it was psychologically motivated," he explained. "I wouldn't tell anyone." During the first few days after his operation, he had a feeling that his mother knew all about his sins, and he wanted to ask her forgiveness. "I sensed my old fusion feelings, but I did not really merge with her although I sensed her presence."

He was unable to urinate after his operation, and when a nurse laughed at him and called him "the bladder boy," he felt that he was being harassed as he had been as a child, in an intrusive, frustrating environment. When he complained of a full bladder, the nurse, a large woman, screamed at him, "If you say another word, I'll tie you to your bed." Feeling humiliated and childlike, he planned to report the incident to his doctor, telling him that such a woman should not be allowed to practice. He decided, however, not to disturb the physician's feelings by criticizing one of his workers. The physician and the other nurses were very nice to him. He saw the big nurse as "a bitch," a bad woman—as in truth she was—and he classified his nurses into "good" and "bad" categories.

After the initial shock of surgical trauma and the effects of medication lessened, Attis reorganized himself at a neurotic level of personality, and his observing ego began to function fully. One night he was able to cry, and he felt better on the following day. He survived his ordeal well in the long run but was still restless and slightly depressed. He received a postcard from his lover, who thought it indiscreet to visit him, and he spoke to her on the telephone after being discharged from the hospital.

He called me every few days during the next 3 weeks as though making progress notes. He steadily improved. "The wound on my chest healed beautifully," he reported, adding, "I guess I also had a psychological wound, and it is healing too." He had many visitors and was delighted to realize how many friends he had. Bad dreams, for example, the one of his mother inviting him to join her, disappeared. He did dream that someone was asking him to do construction work for which he was not yet ready. He associated with its manifest content by saying that his recovery was like doing construction work and that he was not physically and psychologically ready to complete it.

He did more and more physical exercise some months after his operation and got out of the house more often, resuming his golf. He called to make an appointment with me. "I have something funny to tell you," he said. Prior to coming to see me, he had purchased a light brown car. When he drove it for the first time, he had a sensation in his missing finger and began to laugh when he realized that he had symbolically repeated the purchase of the flesh-colored car. On one level, he had experienced his surgery as castration, which he was undoing with the purchase of a new car. Recalling what I had said about his original flesh-colored car representing his finger/penis, he told himself, "A car is a car!" He reported greatly enjoying his new automobile and spoke of having driven to see his lover and talking with her.

When he came to see me for the first time after his surgery, he looked much thinner than before. He was now 70 years old, but he said that he felt fine and repeated his observations of himself after the operation. It was obvious to both of us that this

man—once "Jesus Christ," a would-be murderer, and a bisexual monster—had a great capacity for self-observation and
for reorganizing after the regression that had been forced on
him by his surgery, medications, and helplessness in a hospital
bed.

He wanted to share with me the idea that perhaps it was
time for him to take the next step—to say good-bye to his lover.
Her husband's health was failing, and she was responsible for
and busy with his care. Also, throughout his surgery and
recovery he had felt very close to his wife and highly appreciative of her genuine concern for him. He felt comfortable with
her. Although she had once been willing to be his wife in name
only, they resumed sexual relations, now finding sexual union
comforting. He had discussed with his lover the termination of
their affair. I listened to him but offered no opinion.

Attis continued to see his lover but with less and less
frequency over the next years. His perception of her and his
experiences with her were always pleasant and rewarding; he
understood the meaning of intimacy and could share with her
his innermost thoughts and feelings. He also became fonder of
Gloria and observed rituals of companionship, reading and
walking with her, although with her he never felt the sexual
excitement that he experienced with his lover. At this time he
had skin cancer and cysts, one on his neck and another on the
hand that was missing a finger. These were treated surgically,
as he reported rather laconically.

Four years ago the brother who had amputated Attis's
finger had surgery for a malignant prostate tumor. Driving from
a visit to his brother in a hospital, Attis visited his lover and they
made love. It occurred to him that his brother's operation fell on
the anniversary of President Kennedy's assassination, and he
had the insight to see that he had unconscious death wishes
concerning his brother and father. He recalled that his brother
had given him a beautiful coat; he had never given him anything before, and the recollection of it led Attis to review his
childhood while driving to the hospital. He found the rest of his
family there and they were all pleasant and spoke together of
their childhood. Attis realized that his siblings had largely

repressed their childhood memories and traumas and seemed a rather stereotyped, conventional family. He felt that he had a special, more realistic view of their early family life, and this reinforced his sense of self.

He dreamed that night of seeing a man plow a field and cut a sewer line. Awakening, he understood that he was the man who was damaging the sewer lines (his brother's prostate). This uncovered his repressed desire for revenge on the dying brother who had taken his finger. He was enjoying sex soon after the mutilation/assassination of his brother/father/President Kennedy, and although this evoked feelings of revenge and guilt, he had no symptoms. Four months later I learned that Attis also faced prostate surgery, and he considered that his feelings of revenge toward his brother might have backfired. He came to see me 4 days before his operation to ask about talking with his brother about their childhood; he wanted to share his own perceptions of it but was not sure his brother would understand. He seemed to want to tie up loose ends before his brother died; by then he knew that he had been the luckier of the two because his own tumor was not malignant. He joked about having paid doctors' bills all his life.

His experience with the prostate surgery reminded him of some of the incidents that had followed his triple bypass heart surgery. When he woke up in bed, he found that a nurse had tied a blue ribbon on his penis, and he felt humiliated. His report of this gave us a chance to review once more his early feelings that his mother lacked empathy for him. His prostate surgery was successful, and he later reported fantasies of taking a trip to the Grand Canyon with Gloria, which he felt an urge to visit, instead of taking their usual vacation at the beach. Interest in the Grand Canyon coincided with his prostate surgery, and he was curious about its psychological implications, concluding that "the surgery made me anxious, reminded me of my old fears." "The Grand Canyon is a big vagina," he decided, "my mother's—which would mutilate or castrate me. My wish to go to the Grand Canyon is my wish to conquer my fear. At my age, I'm not going walking around the Grand Canyon! It's good to know where this unusual wish comes from."

He recalled having seen his mother's vagina (the walrus) when he was 4. He had wanted to touch it but his mother hit his hand (perhaps the one later castrated by her agent). Then he wanted to touch her breast, but she would not allow it, saying that her aunt had big breasts that he should fondle. He recalled awaiting a visit from this aunt, who forbade his fondling her breasts. He now realized that those of his lover might represent the aunt's in his transference. He was creating an aunt/mother who would not reject him but would take him to her bosom and give him pleasure and affirmation instead of a fragile self-representation.

OLD AGE

In his early seventies, Attis experienced more heart problems. One morning he woke up with severe chest pains and was taken to a hospital where he underwent further heart surgery, which was minor in comparison to his previous triple bypass operation. While he was still recovering in the hospital, his lover's husband, who had been ailing for some time, died. Attis had to wait a while before he could visit with her. He found her grieving and, therefore, less responsive to him. He understood her reason and encouraged her to grieve further. He was able to be compassionate during his later, now infrequent, visits with her. She was once more very loving to him as a friend and as a lover.

While Attis's response to his lover's husband's death was appropriate, he gave a more anguished response to the death of his brother. His old idea that his brother was the agent of his mother returned, but this time in his dreams. He also dreamed about his mother and wished to push her away, but he would wake up without doing so. He came to tell me that he was having a difficult time grieving over his brother and that his brother's death had reactivated his old separation-individuation difficulties. On the way home from this session, he asked Gloria to stop at the town where his brother used to live. Gloria did not want to do this because after the problem with his parents' estate, her sister-in-law had not been welcoming. Attis told Gloria that they did not need to visit with his brother's wife, and that he simply wanted to visit his brother's grave. Gloria understood, and they stopped at the cemetery. Attis walked to his brother's grave site alone and prayed for his brother's soul. The next day he called to tell me that his mother's representation had appeared in a dream the previous night, but this time there was no struggle about her leaving him behind. She opened the door of the room, where both of them were standing, and just walked away.

Today Attis is old. His mind is still keen, but he must take heart medication. I find his personality better integrated than ever before. During one of his more recent visits, I told him I had never seen him so well mentally, and I noticed that his eyes watered. I had tears, too, and I felt worried about his physical well-being. He looked pale and tired; he and Gloria had driven hundreds of miles to see me and had checked into the same motel where they had stayed before Attis's appointments with me. He seemed in need of more sleep and spoke of how difficult it was going to be in the future for him to make a trip to see me. He was having occasional chest pains; his doctor was uncertain whether they were caused by his hiatal hernia or the start of another heart problem. When the couple left I found myself wondering if I would ever see Attis again. In any case, the representation of him will always be with me.

DISCUSSION

Attis's treatment was not the type of intensive treatment I usually undertake with patients suffering from the same mental problems, the techniques of which I describe in Part III. I believe, however, that his case, his treatment, the evolution of his psychic changes, and his responses to real-life situations provide, when examined longitudinally, a most unusual and fascinating illustration of the causes and meanings of symptoms owing to the influence of an infantile psychotic self on schizophrenia.

I now know more clearly that at the start of our association, I used Attis as a target of my own projective identification. With his impaired psyche, paranoid fears, and separation as well as mutilation anxieties, he was a suitable target for the projection of a new immigrant whose own fearful feelings about separation from familiar surroundings had been activated in a strange environment. Until an internal and external adjustment to a new country takes place, an immigrant feels crippled in many ways (Volkan 1993a), and the projection of my "impairment" onto Attis helped me to control and tame my own adjustment anxieties. It may have even helped me to develop as a psychiatrist, psychoanalyst, and teacher.

Throughout the past 37 years I have often wondered why Attis and I stayed so long in a working relationship. The psychology of our initial period together may be a factor because although he was asked to seek treatment nearer his home many times, he refused, choosing to stay with me. Each of us has since gone his own way now, but while I helped him, he also helped me and taught me a great deal. In the following section, I focus on theoretical and practical aspects of treatment concerning the modification of infantile and adult psychotic selves. Some of this information came to my attention through our long period of work together.

Part III

TREATMENT

11

Treatment of the Psychotic Personality Organization

Treatment strategies leading to beneficial structural changes in either an infantile or an adult psychotic self and modification of defenses in the uninvaded parts are not the same in the case of nonschizophrenic and schizophrenic patients. In this chapter I focus on the treatment of the psychotic personality organization. Before proceeding, I should explain that what I mean by *treatment* is restricted in that therapeutic neutrality and the use of interpretations are the same in classic psychoanalysis when applied to high-level personality organizations; however, strategies in the treatment of the psychotic personality organization differ from those used with neuroses and other high-level personality organizations. For example, when an analyst treats a person with a psychotic personality organization, he or she needs to focus first on object-relations conflicts instead of analyzing oedipal issues. The analyst meets the patient at a level where his or her needs and wishes, and defenses against them, are "hot." I also refer to *treatment* as one that evolves to become eventually identical with the technique and strategies used in classic analysis—except for considerations such as the return of pre-oedipal issues at the termination phase for a last review and final resolution.

AN OVERVIEW

Treatment of Borderline Personality Organization

Borderline patients have a more advanced personality organization than those who possess infantile psychotic selves. Once in treatment, however, after the initial year or years of therapeutic work, an individual with a psychotic personality organization begins to travel through the same therapeutic grounds with which borderline patients are familiar. Therefore, the reader may benefit by reading my (Volkan 1987) findings on the treatment of borderline patients as a preparation for studying the technique I apply in the treatment of psychotic personality organization. I have described six steps or constellations that appear sequentially in the treatment of borderline patients— with expected regressions and progressions—throughout the years during which the patient is seen intensively on the couch four or five times a week. A borderline individual, already regressed, initially relates to the analyst as he or she relates to all intimate others. The patient relies on splitting and related defense mechanisms and develops a chaotic *split transference* (Volkan 1981b). Eventually, the borderline individual undergoes a *therapeutic regression*, during which he or she exhibits a focalized transference psychosis. When the patient comes out of it, he or she can follow a developmental path and evolve through experiences and identifications with the analyst and integrate self- and object representations. In other words, the patient goes through a *crucial juncture* (Kernberg 1970, Klein 1946, Volkan 1993b, Volkan and Ast 1992, 1994), the point at which a borderline or narcissistic patient pulls together opposing representational units and corresponding opposing drive derivatives. It "is reached when the patient becomes able to tame his exaggeration of aggression, which is invested in his 'bad' self- and object representations, as well as his exaggeration of the idealization of 'good' representations'' (Volkan 1993b, p. 279). The patient is then ready to develop a transference neurosis. At this time, vicissitudes of the Oedipus complex are evident, genuine in the sense that they are experienced with integrated self- and object representations for the first time. Also, for all practical purposes, the mechanism of repression replaces splitting as a defense. In the termination phase, the previously borderline individual usually reviews, overhauls, and resolves conflicts of his or her object relations as they are reactivated by knowledge of the impending separation and are unrepressed.

The key concept of my findings on the treatment of borderline patients is the therapeutic regression of an already regressed patient. I believe that therapeutic regression is necessary in the psychoanalytic treatment of any type of patient, including patients with psychotic personality organization. Loewald (1982) stated "it is not regression per se which is therapeutic, but the resumption of progressive development made possible by regression to an earlier stage or to a 'fixation' point" (p. 114). He goes on to say that we notice and analyze defenses that interfere with this resumption. He also emphasizes that the analyst validates the patient's regressive experience as a genuine one, having its own weight, claim, and title "despite its incompatibility with the accepted normal organization of external reality, object relations, etc." (p. 118). To accomplish this validation the analyst must have a corresponding therapeutic regression of his or her own (Olinick 1969, 1980) so that the patient is "not left alone" (Loewald 1982, p. 118). In other words, as Boyer (1983, 1990) and Searles (1979) emphasize, the analyst needs to be cognizant of his or her countertransference.

Differences in Initial Treatment Periods: Borderline versus Psychotic Personality Organization

It is easy to differentiate between individuals with typical and stable borderline personality organization and those with psychotic personality organization. But a differentiation between psychosis-prone borderline personality organization (Boyer 1986, Gunderson et al. 1975, Volkan 1987) and psychotic personality organization can be very difficult. I described the former in the following way:

> Such patients know where they end and others begin; they all have psychic boundaries that, while not intact, remain distinct when close to those of others, although with drugs or some other regressing influence, representations of others sometimes flow into the self-system through boundary flaws. The regressive influence may be psychological since these patients are quick to develop transference reactions to others. A female friend, for example, may very quickly become almost altogether a mother representation, and when this occurs, the patient may lose his psychic boundary to a considerable extent when relating to her, although he maintains it in less critical relationships. [1987, pp. 29–30]

A closer examination of psychosis-prone borderline individuals and those who have a psychotic personality organization points to differences. A psychosis-prone borderline individual may regress under internal and external circumstances and act like a person with a psychotic personality organization or may even exhibit temporary psychotic episodes. If the individual is borderline, he or she eventually returns to a level of functioning that uses stable splitting and related mechanisms (e.g., denial, idealization, devaluation, and projective identification) as primary defenses. The main aim of the defenses is to keep apart self- and object representations with their associated drive derivatives to protect the individual from the tensions of object-relations conflict.

The person with a psychotic personality organization does not use such splitting as a main defense. To be sure, the individual does use splitting, but it can never be kept stable long enough. In fact, the self- and object representations are often fragmented into many part-objects. The individual's main defense mechanism is centered around introjective-projective relatedness, which aims to find a fit between internal and external worlds so that a sense of reality is maintained.

When a borderline patient begins treatment he includes his therapist in the chaotic split transference he has been using in relation to everyone and everything he perceives as intimate. The split transference of the psychosis-prone borderline patient is even more chaotic, and he exhibits, along with the splitting, a more active introjective-projective relatedness, and even fusion and defusion, although always returning to splitting as his main operation. When a patient with a psychotic personality organization comes to treatment, he initially includes the therapist's representation in the reenactments that appear as various actions and symptoms to find an echo in the environment for the demands of his infantile psychotic self and to keep the illusion that he can replace his core saturated with "bad" affects with one saturated with "good" affects. As long as these reenactments provide such an echo and illusion, the patient protects himself against experiencing psychotic episodes and the unbearable or unnamable "bad" affects that are associated with his infantile psychotic self. His reality depends on these reenactments, which are accompanied by the patient's extensive use of projections and introjections.

Strategies in the Treatment of Psychotic Personality Organization

The initial strategy for the therapist in treating an individual with psychotic personality organization is to allow enough time—perhaps a year or so—for the patient's tendency to include the therapist's representation in his reenactments. The patient experientially learns that his expectation of the therapist's response in these reenactments does not usually come true. He then begins to experience the therapist genuinely as a new object, in the sense described earlier. At appropriate times the meanings of reenactments are interpreted.

When a typical borderline patient reaches therapeutic regression, he develops a transference-related, focalized psychosis, which eventually gives way to a progressive movement. When a patient with a psychotic personality organization reaches a therapeutic regression, his transference-related psychosis may become more generalized. If therapy is going well, the transference-related psychosis is contained within the sessions; it is up to the therapist to pay attention to and protect his and his patient's observing ego and their therapeutic alliance. Therapeutic regression of the person with a psychotic personality organization starts the surrender of reenactments and related defenses that are attempts to control the influence of his infantile psychotic self. When such reenactments and related defenses are given up, the therapist becomes involved in a more direct fusion-defusion and/or introjective-projective cycle with the infantile psychotic core. At the same time, the patient alternately experiences the therapist as a repetition of the original mothering person or as a new object. When he differentiates the therapist and his representations from the archaic object representations, the patient is on his way to lessening the fusion-defusion cycle and using introjective-projective cycles less for defense than for development. The introjective-projective cycles lead to the patient's identification with various ego functions of the therapist in order for the patient to deal with both original defects and primitive object relations conflicts. The therapist's interpretations at this phase are aimed to help the patient give up resisting the differentiation process and adaptive identifications. The treatment is experienced as a new version of early child–parent relationships.

Most patients with infantile psychotic selves are aware of the existence of their fragile cores and often make statements such as, "I am like a doughnut, my middle part is missing." Often there is reference to the affect in this core, for example, "There is a bad seed planted in my soul." Sometimes, like Attis, they refer to their psychotic core as if it is nonhuman, for instance, an animal. The treatment now allows the patient to capture experientially the infantile psychotic self and reframe it with a more advanced symbol. For example, the appearance in dreams of a deformed baby or a terrible looking animal reflects the patient's ability to put a boundary around and name his or her fragile core. Sometimes the therapy effectively encapsulates the infantile self. At times, even further progress is possible. The patient symbolically bids farewell to the infantile psychotic self, dissolves it, and mourns its loss. This, of course, reflects a better therapeutic result than effective encapsulation.

As the infantile psychotic self is effectively tucked away or dissolved, further ego development and maturation of self- and object representations takes place. During this process, the patient behaves as if he has a borderline personality organization; he then starts to discover his developmental splitting and a way to the crucial juncture. A transference neurosis will later appear for the first time with differentiated and integrated self- and object representations. Although I describe the therapeutic process as sequential, the expected two steps forward and one step back—regressions and progressions—do occur throughout the years.

INTRODUCTION TO DOGMAN

In the next chapter I illustrate the treatment process of a psychotic personality organization by giving a total case example. William Greer, Ph.D., treated a patient with psychotic personality organization for 5 years, throughout which he consulted with me. This case illustrates most of the treatment formulations previously mentioned. I do not know if the sequential appearance of different treatment constellations as well as the outcome would have been different if I had been the primary therapist. Certainly being in the room with the patient and being able to respond with my personality and experience might have given me observations that perhaps escaped my attention during consultations. It is perhaps more useful, however, to report Dr. Greer's case because while consulting with him, I was able to see issues of his countertransference more clearly. Furthermore, in writing this case I can point out technical issues as the treatment unfolds, as I did while working with Greer.

Greer and I called the patient in this case study "Dogman."

His attempt to change his body image did not go as far as a transsexual's; he did not seek surgery to become a dog. He often wore a dog costume, however, and at times behaved like one. Like many other individuals with a psychotic personality organization, he used many actions and symptoms to create a fit between his infantile psychotic self and the external world and to avoid his unbearable and unnamable affects, which included psychosomatic manifestations, assaults on his wife, pedophilia, rape, fantasies of violence against women while masturbating, clowning, lying, and inhibitions (e.g., never learning to drive a car), as well as a higher level of compromise formations. While in treatment he had brief psychotic episodes when he could not maintain control over his infantile psychotic self and let us see what was behind his multiple defenses, most of which centered around projective and introjective moves.

We considered Dogman as having a psychotic personality organization. Deutsch (1942) might call him an *as-if* personality, and Winnicott (1960) might refer to him as having a *false self*. Shengold (1988) has written about people like Dogman and described the syndrome that results from certain pathological experiences as *soul murder*. Our patient's soul was "murdered" in his infancy and early childhood, and he had an infantile psychotic self. In the fifth year of treatment and after many stormy experiences with Greer, he reframed and symbolized his infantile self in a memorable dream, which will be reported.

I wrote the next chapter with Greer, who took extensive treatment notes. In turn, as is my habit, I also took extensive notes during supervision. Greer also presented this case to David Rosenfeld, and Greer and I gratefully acknowledge his insights into and contributions to the case.

12

Dogman

The aim of this chapter is to report the psychoanalytic psychotherapy of a patient who had a psychotic personality organization. After his life history is described, his 5-year therapy with
William Greer is presented. As the patient's therapeutic process
unfolds, remarks are included to illustrate the meanings of
various clinical phenomena and technical issues.

JOSEPH: A PEDOPHILIC WIFE-BEATER

The patient, whom we call Joseph, was in his late thirties when
he sought treatment because of a facial tic and concern over a
bad marriage. What Joseph referred to as facial tics were
recurring facial grimaces that made him look like a snarling
dog. He also sniffed the air involuntarily, like a dog trying to
catch a scent wafting by. He had been unhappily married for
about 20 years and at times felt that it was impossible to live
with his wife because of her constant jealous accusations of

infidelity. On occasion he lost his temper and assaulted her when she interpreted some insignificant detail of behavior or conversation as evidence of her allegations. It was one of these altercations, during which he had struck his wife in the face with his fist and then tried to throttle her, that instigated his search for help. He was afraid that he might lose her or perhaps even maim or kill her. These fears exacerbated his tics, over which he had become extremely self-conscious. He recalled having similar tics that had lasted a year or so when he was in his latency.

Joseph was college educated and a successful plant manager with a local food-processing company. The company's logo depicted a funny-looking dog, which Joseph had volunteered to represent in the company's frequent public relations events. By wearing a dog costume, he became the company's official clown. This role suited Joseph perfectly because of his penchant for clownish antics around his staff and friends. He reveled in the thought that he was another Bob Hope. He did, indeed, have a wry, pungent wit, which he often used both to express and to conceal his anger. Before official appearances he would frolic about the plant in his dog costume, snarling and hiking up his leg, pretending to urinate on the amused employees. From the beginning of his treatment there were indications in his tics and sniffing behavior that Joseph might have unconsciously identified with a dog, and that he voluntarily accepted "becoming" a dog in serving his company.

Besides becoming a dog, he frequently lied about himself and his background. For instance, he once told his young son a story about his exploits as a professional boxer because he thought it might make him proud of his father. In casual conversations he would insinuate information about himself to impress others. He often daydreamed of himself as an invincible, omnipotent, superman-like hero. On the other hand, he "forced" others to take care of him. A good example of this was that he never learned to drive a car. His wife drove him to work and picked him up at the end of the day. While on official business, dressed in the dog costume, he would be driven by a chauffeur in the company's limousine.

When Joseph's son (who was in his late teens when Joseph began his treatment) was 3 years old, Joseph sucked the little boy's penis. He had never told this to anyone before for fear of the legal consequences. (A more detailed account of this and other incidents of pedophilia will be presented later.) He enjoyed films about graphic violence directed toward women, films that he purchased through the mail. He routinely masturbated as he viewed them, fantasizing raping and beating women. Except for his wife, he had never raped a woman, nor did he ever have intercourse with a child.

Greer considered rightly that Dogman was not suitable for psychoanalysis proper. He knew that the classic technique needed to be modified. Joseph was offered and accepted psychoanalytic psychotherapy.

After being seen face-to-face for a couple of months, Dogman was treated on the couch. With patients like Dogman, who grossly distort the therapist's representation even at the beginning of the treatment, I suggest initially meeting face-to-face for the establishment of a *reality base* (Volkan 1987, p. 85). Such an initial and direct face-to-face experience with the therapist is useful when the patient later develops a full-blown transference psychosis and looks for memories and realistic perceptions of the therapist to fall back on in order to tolerate it. No medication was prescribed for Dogman's mental condition. He was instructed to free-associate. His treatment lasted for 5 years, during which his infantile psychotic self was modified. For reasons we will describe, however, he did not reach a mutually agreed-upon therapeutic termination.

The Early Environment

Joseph was born into a poor Catholic family in a small industrial town. His father, a factory worker, was an alcoholic. He deserted the family when Joseph was 2 or 3 years old, and Joseph's mother had to look after him and his sister, who was 5 years older, by herself. Apparently she had required intermittent psychiatric hospitalization since Joseph's birth and was thought to be a schizophrenic. When she was away, a widowed maternal grandmother took care of the children. If the grandmother was unavailable they were placed temporarily in an orphanage.

Aside from an ineffable feeling that there was no warmth in the house, Joseph had few conscious memories of his early childhood. To this day we do not know if there had been a real dog in Joseph's early environment. He did have one when he started his treatment, and at times he seemed to identify with it. For example, when his wife was harsh with the dog, Joseph felt its pain.

When Joseph was 3 years old, his mother had one more hospitalization. As he was later told, she was diagnosed as suffering from an inoperable brain tumor but not from schizophrenia, although she may have had both. Joseph retained three memories of her after she returned home: one of her lying ill on a sofa, throwing up in a bucket; another of his rousing her from sleep to tell her the house was on fire (he and his sister had "accidentally" set the house on fire by playing with matches); and still another of her falling down the steps as he rushed into her arms to hug her.

She died when he was 6 years old. With the exception of one incident that occurred in the funeral procession, he recalled little of this time. The memory he did recall clearly was riding in a car with his sister and an aunt on the way to the cemetery to inter his mother. His aunt inadvertently sat on his mother's picture, which his sister had brought along, and shattered the glass. It is possible that this is a screen memory reflecting the little boy's perception of death and psychic damage. After the mother's death, the children returned to the Catholic orphanage, with which they were already familiar.

While in the orphanage, Joseph contracted streptococcal meningitis, from which he nearly died. He remained in a hospital for months and slowly recuperated from the illness. The neurologist who cared for him evidently became very fond of him, intimating that he might adopt him, and Joseph recalled being utterly crestfallen when he did not. It is difficult to tell how much of this was a wish and how much reality, but in any event he was sent back to the orphanage, where he remained until his maternal grandmother took him and his sister to live with her on a permanent basis.

The grandmother was an impecunious, alcoholic woman who had been widowed for years. Unable to adequately care for the children, she perpetuated their neglect. With almost no guidance or discipline, the children were forced to look after themselves. When not in school, Joseph spent most of his time on the streets with children similarly dispossessed. He started to smoke when he was 7 because he thought it manly. He was inclined to play with younger children because he thought he could acquit himself more advantageously in their games and squabbles. He recalls being perpetually scared as a child, of his own aggression and that of the other boys. He consciously worried that if he got into a fight with one of them he might seriously injure or perhaps kill him. He developed inhibitions against activities that either challenged his competence or were imbued with aggressive symbolism (as reflected in his inability to drive a car).

Joseph's sister and grandmother used to dress him up in girl's clothes and parade him around the neighborhood. Although acutely humiliated by this, he rarely complained. They stopped this practice, however, as he got older. One good friend occasionally rescued him from these women. This friend regularly invited him over for dinner and to other family activities. Joseph recalls being on his best behavior around these people for fear they would not ask him back again. Around this time he was molested by men who offered him rides. There was no actual intercourse, but they fondled his genitals and kissed him. Aroused by their seductions, Joseph participated.

Although he had inadequate support for his overall psychological development, Joseph received guidance for his intellectual growth. His early psychic deficits and object relations conflicts remained part of him, but he grew up in respect to intellectual relationships, as exemplified by his being an excellent student in parochial school. He remembered the Catholic nuns who taught him as harsh, stern women, singularly insensitive to children. They sometimes threatened the children with corporal punishment for the most minor infraction of the rules. Joseph often recalled one incident that particularly injured his pride: a nun chastised him in front of class for wearing the same pair of frayed and dirty trousers to school each day. She then threw a donated pair at him as a replacement and directed him to put them on. He could see that they were too large and baggy, but despite his feeble protests she insisted that he wear them. He was flooded with a sense of humiliation and shame at this treatment. The school, however, was probably the most stable institution in his life.

Adolescence

The neglect that characterized his childhood continued into his adolescence. There was virtually no warmth, support, or discipline given by the grandmother. She often was too drunk to talk to him, so he would retire to his room or go out on the streets to hang out with his friends. She once asked him to scrub her back as she bathed. He was so repulsed by the sight of her shriveled breasts and state of decrepitude that he excused himself and fled the house. His relationship with his sister was not much of an improvement. She would invite him on her dates, during which he was privy to her lovemaking with boys. He was convinced that she must be the "town pump," given the steady stream of boys that courted her. To escape all of this, he frequented his maternal aunt's home. Unfortunately, she, too, was an alcoholic, and she allowed him to fondle her breasts when she was intoxicated. He would get so aroused by this that he would rush into a bedroom and masturbate.

Joseph recalled almost nothing about his father until after his mother's death. Although his father lived nearby, he rarely visited his children. Joseph poignantly recalled the many times his father arranged to see him, only to fail to appear at the appointed time. He would sit on the front steps in anticipation of his arrival, expecting every car that turned the corner to be his. His anticipation would turn into acute disappointment when it became apparent that he was not going to come. When Joseph eventually saw his father, there were never any explanations or apologies, only more empty promises, and he grew to despise the man for his unconscionable treatment.

On the rare occasions when he did keep his promise to visit, his father would take his son to a tavern he frequented. When intoxicated, the father would provoke fights with other patrons. When in a more sanguine mood, he would ask Joseph, who was a talented vocalist, to sing ethnic ballads, to the pleasure of the father's friends. Other than this rather narcissistic exploitation of his son, he gave him little warmth or kindness.

When Joseph was in his early adolescence, his father married a divorcée with a daughter about Joseph's age. He invited Joseph to move in with them, an invitation Joseph accepted with misgivings. In his perception, there was little warmth or affection from either of his parents. On weekends his father would routinely drink heavily, becoming aggressive toward anyone who crossed him. Joseph silently rankled at all of this until he could no longer contain his rage. His stepmother instructed him to mow the lawn one afternoon when he was engaged in something else, and he hurled obscenities at her. When his father was advised of this that evening, he went berserk and chased his son around the house. Terrified, Joseph took refuge in the tool shed and locked the door, but his father tore the door from its hinges and assaulted him. Joseph told his recently married sister about the incident, and she promptly moved him in with her. It was there that the patient committed his first pedophilic act.

Joseph's sister regularly baby-sat for a couple in her apartment building who had a toddler of about 3, and sometimes she left her brother in the care of this child while she ran errands. On one such occasion, Joseph noticed that the child seemed to get excited when he bounced her on his knee. This, in turn, excited him, and he began to fondle the child's genitals. He repeated this on several other occasions.

Adulthood

After graduating from high school Joseph joined the military. While stationed overseas he met a native who was to become his future wife. The courtship was brief and he soon proposed marriage. His fiancée could hardly speak a word of English, was poorly educated, and had no job skills. Nevertheless, they married within a year and lived with her parents until he was transferred back to the United States. By this time his wife was pregnant with his first and only child. After his son's birth he became envious of the attention his wife lavished on the child. His incestuous pedophilic activity occurred on an occasion reminiscent of the first such incident. Asked by his wife to care for the toddler, he became flooded with sexual fantasies. When he changed the child's diapers he became so excited at the sight of the toddler's penis that he impulsively sucked it. He described the experience as something close to a state of beatitude. Afterward he loathed himself for this act and vowed never to do it again. He kept his vow with his son but constantly worried that the child might have been damaged by this deed. A year later, however, he molested a little girl who had been left with his wife to baby-sit. The fact that his wife was a foreigner whose skin color was different from his symbolized to Joseph, as we learned in his psychotherapy, that she would be a different woman than his mother and grandmother. He later became disappointed with her and thought of his marriage as horrible.

Joseph was able to attend college with the money he received from the military and became employed after graduation. His father died 12 years before he started treatment. He had no close relationship with his sister or, for that matter, anyone other than his wife, whom he beat occasionally.

TREATMENT

The First Year

Joseph presented himself as if he were two entirely different men. One was a competent and respected plant manager, perceived by his associates and those who reported to him as a normal man, especially when he did not act like a clown. The other was a frightened, bewildered, paranoid, helpless, enraged, infant/child suspended in a time warp. The first Joseph had to manage the second and change the external environment to respond to the latter's internal needs, mainly through various actions (e.g., wife abuse, pedophilia, and clowning).

Joseph's abject dependence on his wife was immediately evident. She drove him to the therapist's office and then went shopping, returning in 50 minutes to fetch him. As Joseph was driven to and from his sessions, it was not unusual for him to fantasize that something dreadful, or even fatal, would happen to his wife. Hearing an ambulance siren would make him extremely anxious that his wife might die at any moment from some inexplicable cause. He would then think that he was responsible for her misfortune and should turn himself in to the police. It occurred to the therapist that perhaps his childhood fantasy of being culpable for his mother's illness and death was being relived.

At his workplace thousands of food cans were found to be contaminated and had to be destroyed. Joseph oversaw this operation, but the company's failure to produce perfect food led to his notion that thousands of penises and much fecal material, symbolized by the contaminated cans, were being thrown at him. His thinking almost felt real, and the therapist thought he might be delusional. The people he supervised did not know this part of his inner world, and he continued to perform as a good supervisor.

Joseph became aware of a need to prepare and rehearse material for his sessions en route to the therapist's office in order to appear profound and witty. He recalled that when young, he had behaved in the same way to please his one good friend and his friend's family, without whom he would have had no one to pay attention to him. If Greer was silent behind the couch, Joseph would fantasize that he had slipped out of the room. "If I don't keep my act going . . . the whole edifice will collapse," he said. Boyer (1967) and Volkan (1987) speak of the *noisy phase* in the treatment of already regressed patients. In treatment individuals like Dogman will not tolerate the therapist's silence at first. Silence increases the intensity of such patients' fantasies and may bring them to a delusional level. Thus, until a firmer therapeutic alliance is established, the therapist makes noncommittal sounds. It is important that the therapist does not interfere with whatever relationship the patient works out with him. Joseph said, "If I do not walk the straight and narrow, I will be abandoned." He was also sensitive to any sign of illness in the therapist. The meaning of this was readily available to Joseph, who spoke of his mother's vomiting spells.

He referred to world destruction fantasies, but they were not on a delusional level. Destruction of the world meant the destruction of both Joseph and his therapist. He was concerned that his world destruction fantasies might be threatening to the therapist, and that Greer "might get scared and run out the door." Then he stated, "I scared my mother to death." Joseph recalled his childhood wish to push his mother down the stairs when he rushed into her arms to hug her. The therapist told Joseph that he was aware of his patient's caution about being openly hostile with others. Danger lurked everywhere. Joseph's clownish antics and buffoonery were related to his desperate need to engage others, but in his paranoid orientation to life, the specter of loss hung over him like the proverbial sword of Damocles.

In the second half of the first year of Joseph's treatment, the therapist was included in the patient's introjective-projective cycle, which was contaminated with feelings of helplessness and murderous rage. If Greer made a false move, Joseph threatened to attack him with the pen knife he carried with him for protection. On the other hand, he wanted to protect Greer from harm. For example, if Joseph heard a noise as he waited for the session to begin, it provoked fantasies of Greer being attacked and brutally assaulted by an enraged patient, a displaced representation of Joseph. Then he fantasized that he would rush into the office, save Greer, and earn his eternal gratitude. A dream narrated at this time conveyed the magnitude of aggression and helplessness with which Joseph was struggling. "I had a gun," he said, "with which I was randomly shooting people on the street. I also had a hand grenade, but it made no 'bang' when I threw it. I woke up terrified." Some persons who actually commit a murder or a series of murders have psychological backgrounds similar to Joseph's. To his credit, Greer was able to tolerate the derivatives of aggression Joseph was bringing to sessions. He also knew that the therapeutic relationship he was involved in with Joseph might be the patient's only hope to modify his psychic organization.

As he grew more anxious about being abandoned by his therapist, Joseph reported fantasies of being greeted by him with thunderous applause. Joseph readily saw his grand entrance as a famous personage as a defense against his irrepressible fear of going absolutely unnoticed. In turn, the therapist readily joined Joseph in exploring the connections between what he was bringing to his treatment and his childhood experiences. In other words, transference interpretations and their association to the patient's childhood history were offered. After a while the therapist noted, however, that such interpretations were not effective and understood that they served to escape the intensity of affects that Joseph induced in himself and in the therapist. The therapist and his supervisor noted that a patient like Dogman does not use transference and/or genetic (psychological) interpretations at this phase of the treatment to initiate psychic change.

The following illustrates a more effective response made by the therapist. When Joseph began coming to his sessions in a rather disheveled and unhygienic condition, the therapist noted that he was involved in another reenactment but said nothing about it. Joseph had become the reincarnation of a neglected child needing physical care from a mother figure. This time, instead of interpreting the transference and its genetic connections, Greer allowed the reenactment to continue. Joseph came to his sessions without a bath or a shave for weeks. Greer tolerated this behavior, but ultimately explained to the patient that he believed his actions demonstrated how Joseph needed to be cared for. He added, "You have given me a first-hand experience of your need and of how important it is for you that someone, in this case me, know this." Soon after this, Joseph stopped coming to his sessions so unkempt, but for a long time he continued trying to find out if the therapist loved him. If the check he wrote to Greer was not cashed promptly, Joseph fantasized that Greer did not need his money, that his love could not be bought, and that Greer would abandon him. That Greer did not abandon Joseph made him a new object (Giovacchini 1972, Loewald 1960, Volkan 1976). The newness of the therapist's representation is based on the therapeutic reactivation of early developmental paths. In order to follow this path, the patient needs to make therapeutically regressive moves.

The Second Year

As the close of the first year of treatment approached and passed, Joseph's intensely sadomasochistic relationship with his wife underwent some changes. His sexual attraction toward her waned along with their ritualized daily intercourse, which had nothing to do with an adult love relationship. It was another reenactment so that Joseph would have the illusion that he could daily find a mothering person to change the "bad" affects in the early mother–child unit into pleasurable ones. Because he occasionally raped his wife, the daily intercourse was also in the service of discharging his rage. A libidinal child–mother (husband–wife) fused representation could not be maintained.

The waning of interest in his wife was accompanied by increased interest in a pubescent girl across the street, whom the couple had befriended after their son went away to school. Joseph, overcome by erotic fantasies about this girl, became overtly seductive with her, and she readily reciprocated. When his wife was out of the room the girl would sit on Joseph's lap and tickle him, much to their mutual delight. She would brush against him with her exposed thighs, and pause over his hand. Joseph began reporting memories of being intensely aroused by his sister's sexual activities with her boyfriends when he had accompanied them on dates. He told Greer of his boyhood fantasy of his sister performing fellatio on him. He also remembered the incredibly intense excitement he felt when he had fondled his drunken aunt's breasts and how he rushed into the next room to masturbate to relieve his tension. As he put it, "Lust has no scruples." Meanwhile, he became "afraid of everybody and everything." He thought he would feel safer if he went incognito, so he purchased a pair of dark glasses that he wore everywhere. In his fantasies they were like mirrors, reflecting and deflecting images of dangerous others. Like Arja (see Chapter 7), who covered mirrors and reflecting surfaces, Joseph was attempting to slow down the introjective-projective cycle.

Although a therapist may find it easy not to interfere prematurely with a patient's reenactments (e.g., Joseph turning himself into an unkempt child), it is obviously more difficult not to respond when a reenactment is hurtful to an innocent party, such as a child. The therapist and his supervisor decided that if the therapist remained in the therapeutic position, he might, in the long run, be more helpful in the modification of Joseph's pedophilic and related activities. The therapist decided that he should at least try an interpretation to see if it would stop the patient's behavior with the young girl. In essence, what Greer told Joseph was that he was defending against memories of being deprived of early maternal care. He was seeking a child with whom to have a mother–child oneness, through which he would feed, get fed, and be blissfully gratified. In his unconscious fantasies, he was both mother and child in this relationship.

Rather than working with this interpretation, Joseph chided the therapist for what he perceived to be efforts to transform his heinous deeds into psychoanalytic excuses. He became involved about this time in a new action and arrived for a session mildly intoxicated. Greer voiced his hunch that Joseph was behaving in a provocative manner to get his therapist to punish him for his pedophilic and similar activities, and that his representation in his patient's mind was that of someone who either prematurely forgave or punished, with neither being a useful reaction in the long run. He added that he preferred to continue as Joseph's therapist and asked Joseph to join him in exploring the deeper motives of his actions.

In the next hour Joseph disclosed that he was having fantasies of sucking Greer's penis and connected this with his sucking his son's penis. Pedophilic activities were thus in a sense brought into their sessions. Greer felt that Joseph's fantasies about him were connected with both a wish for closeness and an expression of aggression and thought that he should deal first with his patient's need for closeness and leave the exploration of aggression for a later time. With Greer's help, Joseph further understood that as a child he had hungered for a good relationship. Now both therapist and patient could speak more comfortably about how Joseph, in his pedophilic experience with his son, was attempting to create his own mother–child interaction, control it, and make it pleasurable. In reversing roles, Joseph made the infant a nurturing mother, a nurturing penis/nipple, fused with it, and sought a pleasurable experience.

Not long after speaking of his childhood "hunger" and lack of a nurturing environment, Joseph reported excruciating abdominal pain and bloody stools. Concerned that he might be developing a peptic ulcer, he arranged a consultation with an internist, who confirmed his suspicions. Conservative treatment was initiated, and his symptoms remitted. They were to wax and wane over the next several years in conjunction with the therapeutic work. (A study focusing on the psychosomatic aspects of this patient has been published elsewhere [Volkan 1992b].)

After Joseph received physical help for his peptic ulcer, his mood changed. The aggressive aspects of his early mother–child experiences surfaced once more. Joseph noticed that he was more irritable and given to rages toward his wife; jealousy was all the provocation he needed. At work, heretofore the clown prince, he found himself more sardonic with his co-workers. His banter and repartee were used more to hurt than to entertain. This change of mood was ushered in with the remark, "I am like a lump of ice that has started to melt."

Toward the latter part of the second year of treatment, a new symptom emerged. Joseph observed with jocularity that when angry with others, he would cast a dirty look at them. He played with fantasies, which were like delusions at times, in which this look would annihilate its recipient. These fantasies were particularly active on his way to the therapist's office. He would stare at drivers that offended him, visualizing their cars swerving off the road into the woods. These images were almost invariably accompanied by memories of being in his mother's funeral procession with his sister and the aunt who sat on his mother's picture. Once when he heard an ambulance siren, he suddenly felt the urge to assault his wife, who, it will be recalled, chauffeured him. The therapist commented that perhaps the siren reminded him of the dying mother whose death had deprived him of his childhood.

He confided that he had felt flawed and damaged as far back as he could remember. Half seriously, he said, "All I want is a Mommy and a Daddy to grow up with and leave me an estate in the Bahamas. What I need," he continued, "is a primal scream therapist." Greer, moved, simply replied that he could hear Joseph's pain. Greer felt as if he were a nurturing mother, who, despite her child's having a painful temper tantrum, still could maintain the child's welfare in mind.

The transference began to include symbolic anal elements; for example, Joseph worried that the grease from his hair tonic might soil the therapist's couch. If so, he was to be told so that he could bring in Handy Wipes to clean up the mess. Joseph also became aware that he averted his gaze from the therapist as he entered his office in order to protect the therapist from his dirty looks. A little later, Greer saw him scanning his desk as he went toward the couch. Inquiries into this behavior revealed only that he was worried that something was different about this piece of furniture (there was not). The therapist thought of the desk as an extension of himself and as symbolic of the dying mother, so he mused aloud that perhaps Joseph was anxious that his destructive fury (anal sadism) might have given the therapist a brain tumor. The patient then sheepishly admitted that he made faces at the therapist as he lay on the couch, gloating at the thought that he could humiliate him with impunity. He understood this behavior as an expression of the enraged feelings he had when he was "too weak and too small to voice them." In another session Joseph became aware of clenching his teeth when he spoke, eliciting fantasies of himself as a vicious dog. Within weeks the sniffing "tic," so prominent when he first came into treatment, reappeared. All this time Joseph struggled with his pedophilic fantasies and impulses toward the girl across the street, who was now in mid-adolescence, more curvaceous and sensual, arousing him whenever they were together. His fantasies ranged from passionate trysts on romantic isles to raping her. The sight of her with boys her own age evoked jealous rage. He acted the part of the spurned lover bent on revenge. His conversations with her were marked by tart barbs that hurt her feelings. His wife, at last, sensed his affection for the girl and ordered her out.

At times the therapist found Joseph's activities with the girl across the street repugnant, but he kept his feelings to himself and told him only what was in the service of protecting the therapeutic relationship and alliance. He warned, however, that in the real world, his activities with underage girls might get him into legal difficulties and make it impossible for him to continue his treatment. "Would you let me suggest to you that you put these impulses into words and thus allow me to protect the continuity of our relationship?" the therapist asked.

In the next session Joseph reported a fantasy in which he had sucked the girl's breast, sucking so voraciously that he sucked out all her fluids, killing her. The therapist told him that he was continuing to remember his childhood in his fantasies about this girl, and that fantasies could be better analyzed than actions because actions would actually change the external world. Joseph was clearly driven to recreate a mother–child experience, but because in reality his experience with his mother had been replete with frustrations, his experience with the girl eventually allowed his aggression (the wish to "kill" her) to surface. The therapist interpreted that his first flagrantly pedophilic activities and then his fantasies about the girl were his major resistance to owning his angry, hungry, helpless, and humiliated core (his infantile psychotic self). He further explained to him that as a child, he had been subjected to many humiliating events and was recalling them by sexualizing them

and by reenactments. Although trying to change his helplessness and humiliation through experiencing sexual pleasure
might provide temporary release from tension, it took real
courage to allow himself to verbalize these impulses and feelings. Joseph responded well and spoke of how he had been
sexually abused as a teenager, being kissed and fondled without
actual intercourse. This theme was further expanded in a
dream in which he saw his son as a statue with a knife stuck in
it. His associations brought feelings about his own sexual abuse
and his jealous rage at the sight of his infant son at his wife's
breast. In turn, he had sucked his son's penis in order to kill
him. By now, both meanings of his pedophilic activities, the
wish to have a nurturing mother and the wish to kill the "bad"
mother, were understood.

Joseph ceased his pedophilic activity and his involvement
with the young girl. This was accompanied by an increased rage
toward his therapist; he spontaneously revealed that as a child,
even after his mother's death, he used to have fantasies of
killing her. He seemed to be owning and expressing the "bad"
affects of his infantile psychotic self instead of using pedophilic
and related actions as a defense against them.

The Third Year

Not long after the beginning of the third year of treatment,
Joseph told the therapist it was his birthday and that his wife
had forgotten it and his son had sent him a smoked salmon. He
was incensed with both of them for their perceived thoughtless-
ness. How dare his son send him such a gift, which he derisively
referred to as a penis in a box. He added, "I suppose he sent it
to remind me that I had oral sex with him." He suddenly
fantasized being in a catatonic state, intuitively understanding
this as a defense against his rage.

Joseph became obsessed with motorists once more as he
was being driven to his appointments by his wife. More overtly
aggressive now, he made obscene gestures to them, bellowed
oaths, and shook his fist. All of this made him quite anxious,

however, because he feared that some enraged driver might shoot him. The therapist explained that being enraged and frightened in a car was what he remembered being in the funeral procession as a boy. He then connected this with the patient's inhibition against driving, which represented a defense against his conscious fantasy that he had killed his mother.

In the early part of his third year of treatment, amorous fantasies about women with whom he worked preoccupied him constantly. Every morning when he arrived at the plant he sought them out and, under the guise of humor, made inappropriate professions of love to them. His suggestive remarks and overtures were good-naturedly received by some, but they offended others. If the women failed to respond as he wished them to, he felt acutely rejected and humiliated. Then violent criminals of current notoriety would come to mind—criminals with whom he identified.

An incident occurred at a picnic for the company employees and their families, where Joseph wore his dog costume. About to be overcome by heat, he retired to the back of the air-conditioned limousine where he could remove the full-head mask without being seen by the children. Some of his acquaintances opened the door as he rested. Several children saw him. He thought that the children who knew of him in costume as a real dog would know now that he was an impostor. This thought was accompanied by an image of himself in the back of the car at the funeral procession. What was inferred from this incident was that his efforts to be both mother and child happily engaged with each other were unmasked and that the "killer" (of his mother) was exposed.

As a dog/clown, Joseph wished to change the horrible affects that saturated the fused child–mother representation in his infantile psychotic self. Beneath the pleasure-giving dog/clown, there was a dog, a sense of self as being less than a human infant. When saturated with "bad" affects, the dog would be vicious. We recall how a nun made him wear large baggy trousers and how his grandmother insisted on parading him about dressed as a girl. These incidents may have played a role in his unconscious choice of a dog symbol to represent his fragile core's psychic tissue. As a dog, he invited love and nurturing but also expressed snarling aggression. Through his humorous antics and acerbic wit he could express his enormous aggression yet maintain object ties. Furthermore, by being a dog/clown, he could reach up (Boyer 1961, Volkan 1976) and try to establish a relationship with the representation of his father. It should be recalled that his father used Joseph to entertain his friends in a bar. As an entertainer he received his drunken father's approval while still hating him. This understanding of different meanings of the dog symbol was interpreted at appropriate times.

After the dog was unmasked, Joseph came to his sessions anxiously searching for the therapist's car. Even if he saw it, he expected to come to his office and find him gone (as were his other caregivers and his father). He felt agitated on the couch, saying he needed a pill to calm himself. He then paused reflectively for a moment and with insight said, "A pill is a nipple, isn't it? And a nipple is better than a penis." With mock hostility he enjoined the therapist to speak to him and threatened to kill him. "You know, my anger has no stages. Either I am in control or I am not." His aggressive thoughts and fantasies became more explicit and graphic with each session. His dreams were full of scenes of murder, rape, and paranoid fears of attack. Reanimated infantile rage led to verbalized fantasies of mutual fellatio between him and the therapist.

An already regressed patient, Joseph was experiencing a therapeutic regression. His infantile psychotic self, flooded with unneutralized aggression and other unnamable affects, as well as his wish and dread to fuse with the mother/analyst representation, was being presented to the therapist without the benefit of defensive buffers. As this process continued, the therapist noted that Joseph was able to keep the therapist's new object representation more effectively within himself. When his fellatio and other homosexual fantasies about Greer peaked, Joseph dreamed of a police officer arresting an aggressive man and forcing him to submit to anal intercourse. Through this dream, which recalled his sexual abuse by men, Joseph also provided associations indicating that he was anally taking in the therapist's representation (his words) and keeping it. Through such an identification he was learning to control his rage. In the dream, the aggressive man represented Joseph's enraged infantile self, but the policeman was also Joseph, containing such an infant self.

The Fourth Year

Most of the issues Joseph dealt with in the latter part of the third year of his treatment were also present in the first part of the fourth year. As an infant and a child, he had little experience with what can be termed *trust*, so his therapeutic experiences with Greer's representation could not readily be made trustworthy and so maintained. Any frustration with Greer would push him, once more, to reenact old ways that ranged from more pedophilic thoughts to desire for the teenage girl across the street to physical abuse of his wife. At times he felt paralyzed in his attempt to get out from under the influence of his infantile psychotic core and expressed his frustration with Greer by saying, "If you get a package with the salutation 'Dear Shit' on it, you will know where it came from."

In the second part of the fourth year, Greer returned from his vacation to find Joseph flooded with pedophilic dreams. Rather than engaging in actual pedophilic involvement or related activities or being flooded with fantasies about them, he now seemed better able to control his actions and fantasies as they were transposed into his dreams. The other actions continued, however. During his therapist's vacation, Joseph often had grabbed at his wife's breast in his sleep so aggressively that she would be forced to awaken him to keep from being injured.

As his therapeutic regression became more noticeable and "hot," everything seemed to be centered around his relationship with Greer. When Greer was a minute late for their appointment, Joseph felt ignored, forgotten, and mistreated. If Greer parked his car in a space other than the one in which he ordinarily parked, Joseph felt that it was done intentionally to make him anxious. He feared that Greer would find an excuse to terminate his treatment if he became too aggressive with him. Joseph dreamed of being with a woman who put a leash around his neck and treated him like a dog. She represented the mother/analyst to whom he was connected with an umbilical cord (the leash). His main fear was that his new object relationship with Greer might be modeled after the first one. Greer interpreted this fear.

As Joseph's transference relationship became more and more intense, there were indications of improvement in his life in the external world. His relationship with others, especially with men, became more mature at his workplace. He reported a rebirth fantasy in which he would go to a nearby bridge, remove his clothes, and make it appear as though he had jumped over the side and drowned, a suicide victim, but he would dress in other clothes and vanish, never to be heard from again. Thus he would be separated from his wife. He wished to be reborn again, to be away from his nonnurturing mother and to have a hope of being better parented in his new life. This was a portentous fantasy, as later developments clearly showed.

In their sessions Greer began perceiving Joseph as more like a neurotic individual than one bewildered by object-relations conflict. He certainly had not worked through such conflicts completely, but he could more genuinely and more readily connect their appearance in the transference and extra-transference relationships to their genetic (psychological) causes. He could now work with his dreams as a neurotic might. In one dream he was hungry and went to the refrigerator to get something to eat, but the refrigerator suddenly turned into a coffin. He did not open it and kept repeating, "I just want lunch." Intuitively he understood this sequence of images to mean that he was going to have to face the fact that as a child, he could not get the necessary narcissistic supplies from his dead mother. Notwithstanding this, he persisted in his unconscious search for a nurturing mother in his relationships and in his dreams. For example, he dreamed of performing fellatio on a small boy whose penis grew larger and larger as he sucked until it was nearly the size of an adult's. The therapist addressed the progressive aspect of this dream, telling Joseph that he was seeking a nurturing mother whose breasts he could suckle in order to become more independent and free to grow up as a man.

As he often did, Joseph recalled and reexamined his pedo-philic experience with his son and his wish and his dream of performing fellatio on his therapist. He then thought of fero-cious dogs and the pleasure he derived from needling the women at work. Greer pointed out the terrible dilemma that the patient had to face as a result of his untamed aggression toward the very objects he needed badly. The ferocious dogs repre-sented Joseph's oral sadism, which he could now own not by reenactment but by dealing with it in the psychological realm. There followed a dream in which Joseph kissed a little girl whose mouth had a strange taste that reminded him at once of sour milk. The therapist explained that it was his rage, along with his mother's unavailability, that soured the milk and motivated his interminable search for a good mother.

As the fourth year of treatment came to a close, the pa-tient's relationship with the young girl had receded into the background. She came to his house one day and announced that she was a lesbian. Joseph became extremely agitated and had to go to bed with his wife and perform fellatio on her. But in his next session he asked rhetorically whether he was so deprived of love that he could accept anything as the genuine article. Not long after this, instead of being involved in an action, he dreamed of the girl. She came into his yard, removed her blouse, and was forced to perform fellatio on him against her will. Joseph knew that the dream represented his losing his mother and other caregivers and that in order to deny his deprivation, he took what was being withheld.

After Greer canceled one appointment, Joseph dreamed of a woman at work who had a child every other year (a super-mother) and whose last name implied that she prepared meals for others. In the dream she wore a T-shirt through which he could see her protuberant nipples. He tenderly embraced her "instead of sucking her breasts," he sobbed. The dream was initiated by the cancellation of an appointment; an improvement in his condition could now be expected inasmuch as he could now cry and accept the loss of the nurturing experience in his infancy and childhood.

The Fifth Year

As the fifth year of Joseph's treatment commenced, he was in considerable emotional turmoil, attempting to mourn over his childhood developmental losses and to modify and/or dissolve his infantile psychotic self. He was also changing some of the defenses his previous uninvaded part had employed to keep his infantile psychotic self in check. In the past Joseph had avoided learning how to drive a car. A car was an aggressive tool, and thus he avoided the possibility of killing someone (his mother). Furthermore, an important memory of his childhood was riding in his mother's funeral procession and his aunt's crushing of his mother's photograph. The car was like a childhood *linking object* (Volkan 1981a) for him and represented a link to his mother as well as the fragmentation of her image. Without telling Greer, Joseph began to take driving lessons, and soon after this he began to drive. He feared at first that he might hit and kill a child, but when he understood that he really wanted to kill the helpless, aggressive infant within, he drove more freely.

Once Joseph became more independent and no longer needed to be driven to work or to sessions, his wife got a job. This drastically disturbed the balance at home. Joseph perceived that his wife possessed many of the same character traits as his mother, but she tolerated Joseph's physical and verbal abuse without leaving him. He would hit her on the head in a conscious and unconscious attempt to create another brain-damaged woman. She was part of an external environment he created to meet his internal demands.

Joseph wished now to be free of all of his symptoms. As he improved, his wife became more paranoid. Joseph was no longer after little girls, but his wife continued to accuse him. One day his wife wondered what he and his therapist were doing during their sessions. She asked, "Do you suck each other's dicks?" The question made Joseph uncomfortable because he actually had such fantasies. That night he had a dream in which a piece of cylindrical fecal material came out of his mouth and then turned into a cobra. Joseph once more was able to examine his earliest infant–mother relationship and the associated "bad" feelings as well as unconscious fantasies. His associations to the dream indicated that in sucking his son's penis and later fantasizing taking in the therapist's, he was in search of his mother's "good nipple." The reality was, however, that she had frustrated him. In consequence, he had projected his infantile rage on the nipple/penis and turned it into a fecal cobra/penis. It was internalized as such and was assimilated into his infantile psychotic self. He now wanted to spit it out.

After working on this dream Joseph improved even more. He knew that, at least in part, his wife stood for the nonnurturing, brain-damaged, ineffective mother representation. In turn, he knew that his wife had played such a role and that their marriage had been a stormy, pathological one. He had no realistic hope that she would change and meet him at his improved level. He attempted to discuss these issues with his wife and asked for a divorce. Both of them agreed that this might be the best solution. The idea of actually separating from his wife/mother representation made Joseph anxious, however. By separating physically and intrapsychically from a "bad" mother, he might be utterly alone. He was having fantasies about making a woman at work his future wife. She was, in fact, a healthier and a more appropriate choice than his present wife. At the peak of Joseph's considerations, Greer took a 2-week vacation, which he had planned earlier. The patient reacted to this with a psychosis-like episode in which he lived out a version of his rebirth fantasy.

Joseph disappeared from his home in confusion and lived on the streets, as he had done as a child and an adolescent. When the therapist returned from vacation, he received a call from Joseph's wife, who informed him that her husband had failed to return from work the previous afternoon and that she was extremely frightened for his safety. She had already notified the police, who advised her that it was too soon to declare him a missing person. During the fourth day of Joseph's disappearance, Greer received a call from Joseph, who disclosed his whereabouts. Joseph had been told by the director of the shelter where he was staying that he should admit himself to a hospital, and he came to Greer's office later that day to discuss the issue. The therapist, unaware of the countertransference being induced in him at this time (to be discussed later) and not noticing the progressive aspect of what Joseph had done, concurred with the advice. On a conscious level the therapist was feeling uncomfortable, because while everything was going so well, his patient appeared to be disorganized. This embarrassed the therapist, and he became concerned about what the shelter director or other professionals would think of his reputation.

Joseph quickly admitted himself to a local psychiatric hospital, where he remained for 30 days. This, to a great extent, crystallized in his mind that whatever experiences he had with Greer would not change his fate, and that in the long run any caregiver, such as the neurologist he grew fond of after his meningitis, would reject him. The neurologist had saved his life but did not adopt him. Greer saved Joseph from his psychological prison, but now he was rejecting him and sending him to be cared for by others. At this time, neither the therapist nor his patient realized that Joseph's seemingly psychosis-like behavior was a reenactment of his rebirth wish and that, indeed, it had a progressive aspect. With the help of the supervisor, who later learned what was going on, the therapist came to understand his reactions. The therapist was the anxious, enraged, and bewildered child whose mother had disappeared, and Joseph was that mother. In turn, Greer "rejected" his patient.

Upon discharge from the hospital, the patient returned to his sessions. The first hours were devoted to an account of his activities while in his psychosis-like state. He had lost his identity temporarily and found himself at a nearby resort, where he sat on a bench next to a prostitute, whom he initially perceived as an idealized woman. She told him that she had resorted to prostitution to raise money to care for her infant daughter. After they made love in a motel, Joseph found himself acting very maternal toward the woman. He soothed and comforted her, offering to send her money to help her care for her infant. Her story about being a destitute mother too proud to accept charity moved him to tears. Greer understood this as an enactment of the patient's search for an idealized mother–child fusion during his therapist's absence. Obviously the patient was still having difficulty verbalizing this search.

But the therapist sensed that Joseph's latest psychotic-like episode was different from his previous ones because this time he was able to keep or to restore quickly his observing and working egos and be curious about his experience, connecting it with his childhood losses and his rebirth fantasies. He was aware, perhaps for the first time at a truly affective level, of his emotional hunger. He sensed what he called an empty feeling in his stomach as he devoured a birthday cake at a fellow employee's birthday party. Several days later he experienced another episode of a bleeding duodenal ulcer, which was treated by his internist. Soon, however, we felt that the developmental path from somatization to verbalization of affects had been opened in Joseph. He seemed to be flooded with unnamable "bad" feelings, reporting that they were the cause of the "hole" in his stomach. As Herbert Rosenfeld (1985) states, in patients like Joseph "psychotic aspects . . . may leak out in psychosomatic symptoms" (p. 381). Through his psychotic-like behavior and psychosomatic reactions, Joseph's infantile psychotic self was dislodged, and he could reframe and resymbolize it and get a better hold on it.

A memorable dream followed this episode: Joseph saw himself holding a baby that looked like an underdeveloped fetus with a swollen stomach. They were in a kitchen with a black woman who was wearing make-up. The black woman asked Joseph not to talk to the baby. Joseph, angry at the woman for this directive, told her that she was no longer needed in the kitchen and she could leave, which she did. Joseph looked at the baby and knew that this underdeveloped infant was himself. A thought came to his mind that at last he had seen how he looked as a baby (his infantile psychotic self). The baby looked almost dead. Joseph knew that when the baby died he could bury him. In reality, Joseph had heard that the funeral director had put a great deal of make-up on his dead mother. "The black woman is my mother, the corpse," he declared with confidence. He realized that now he might be ready to genuinely separate from her representation intrapsychically and ultimately free himself from his fusion with her representation. He could now "talk" to the baby, own and separate it from the rest of his personality, and repress (bury) it.

FLIGHT FROM TREATMENT

Belatedly, after the patient's hospitalization, the therapist understood that Joseph's recent regression into a psychosis-like episode and his development of a psychosomatic symptom were in the service of progression. It was like a disorganization that occurs during adolescence, followed by a new reorganization of the personality (Blos 1979). In actual treatment, therapeutic movement phases (mentioned in the previous chapter) do not always take place in the neat and orderly fashion that is described by theoretical formulations. Many therapeutic regressions occur and are followed by progressions. By going two steps up and one step down, and by repeating this process, the patient slowly improves. Joseph exhibited a drastic therapeutic regression that ushered in the recapture of his infantile psychotic self. We were impressed with Joseph's intrapsychic improvement, but he faced what proved to be, for him, two untenable dilemmas. The first one pertained to his wish to crystallize in the external world the intrapsychic separation from his mother's representation by divorcing his wife. The second one involved new complications in the transference-countertransference axis.

The first dilemma was that Joseph wanted a divorce, but anxieties about being on his own without the support of a "mother" were paramount in his thoughts. These anxieties about being able to function competently by himself evinced themselves in a dream in which he was walking on water (a narcissistic defense), supported by an unseen canoe. The therapist empathized with Joseph's anxieties as he strove to move in a progressive direction. He cautioned him that despite his wishes to resolve his infantile anxieties, this was a process that could not be hurried because he continued to depend on a mother representation (the canoe that probably also represented Greer) from which he drew strength. He emphasized that they needed to do more therapeutic work.

Joseph was convinced that the real proof of his being well would be tried in the complications of divorce proceedings. He understood why he had married his wife in the first place and what kept them in this relationship. As he separated his "brain-damaged" mother representation from his wife, he developed empathy for his wife and her unhappy task. He urged her to consult a therapist, which she did for a short while. There was, however, no change in her paranoia and, moreover, no motivation to change as far as he could ascertain. In the end, however, Joseph could not bring himself to divorce her, and he felt that further therapy would only keep his worries about this torturous and conflicted issue indefinitely and painfully open.

The second dilemma was that the therapist, unconsciously responding to the patient's projection of the "hungry" infant representation onto him, had concurred with the advice of the shelter's director that Joseph should admit himself to a psychiatric hospital. This led to the therapist becoming identified in Joseph's fantasies with the neurologist who had saved his life when he was a boy but who later abandoned him. After an unexpected and unplanned encounter with Greer's wife and adopted daughter at his office, therapeutic matters became even more complicated. Because the child belonged to a different race, Joseph knew immediately that the therapist's daughter was adopted. Joseph then spoke of his wish to be adopted by the therapist's family and felt frustrated. This request and Greer's assent to his hospitalization kept Joseph from leaving the hospital altogether after his month's stay; he continued to be very much involved with the hospital's treatment program for recently discharged patients after he resumed work with Greer. This program, for all practical purposes, was undermining the intrapsychic work Greer and Joseph were attempting to do in order to work through the recent complications in the transference-countertransference. It was as if, disappointed with the mother/neurologist/therapist, Joseph had gone to an orphanage. Thus, in his mind, his therapist had become similar to object representations toward which Joseph felt murderous rage. At the same time, Joseph wanted the therapist to remain as a nurturing mother. To protect the "good" therapist from his rage, Joseph escaped from treatment and remained married to his wife.

It has been a little over a year since Joseph left treatment, and Greer and I assume that he functions with high-level borderline personality organization. We suspect that he still keeps his wife as a "bad" object representation while Greer's representation, which Joseph keeps at a physical distance so that he cannot be contaminated with his "badness," remains a "good" one. Evidence of this formulation is our knowledge that Greer still preoccupies Joseph's mind. Less than a year after Joseph prematurely ended the treatment, he called Greer "to say hello and explain why I walked out on you." He then proceeded to say that he knew that he had used something the therapist had said as a pretext to terminate his sessions abruptly. His complaint was that the therapist's interventions had become repetitious, which they had not. The implication is that Joseph needed a reason to distance himself from Greer to keep him as a "good" cushion to fall back on in the future. Joseph sent Greer a poem that captured with poignant clarity the torturous inner world about which he seemed to have great insight now and into which both men had traveled in order to make drastic modifications in Joseph's infantile psychotic self. Joseph is being encouraged to return to treatment and finish the therapeutic task.

13

Psychoanalytic Psychotherapy of Schizophrenics

Many psychoanalysts consider the schizophrenic patient's uninvaded part highly important because it permits therapeutic engagement. The implication is that the therapeutic work is done with the patient's nonpsychotic part, which is so strengthened and modified that the patient gains better control over the adult as well as the infantile psychotic self. The uninvaded aspect of the patient is certainly important in establishing a therapeutic alliance and a working relationship, but the type of treatment I describe here focuses on the typical patient's adult as well as infantile self. The analyst must get directly in touch with these psychotic parts in transference–countertransference relationships in order to modify them. In this process we must consider the concept of therapeutic regression in the already extremely regressed patient. In the case of a schizophrenic individual, this will evoke two major phenomena that constitute turning points in treatment.

The first is a return to the patient's experience of terror and loss of maintenance mechanisms. The schizophrenic established his adult psychotic self following the terror and, in treatment, through therapeutic regression, he returns to it, finding himself now able to tolerate it through identification with the therapist's functions that can handle extreme anxiety. Before revisiting it, the patient will have established some *work ego* (Olinick et al. 1973) and benefited from the structuralizing effects of interpretations. He has thus been helped to loosen his hold on his adult psychotic self.

The patient's main resistance to the surrender of the adult psychotic self is fear of experiencing terror again; thus he stubbornly tries to cling to it. Frosch (1983) wrote of this resistance in reference to the *fixity of delusions* (p. 117). Having done enough therapeutic work, he allows himself to regress therapeutically and to experience a new terror, which may result in his giving up the adult psychotic self, and replacing it with a healthier one.

The second phenomenon is the patient's return, in further therapeutic regression, to his earliest experiences with his mother, which constitute a channel through which all physiological and psychological elements of development pass. This permits him to undergo these experiences with the new object, putting new ingredients through the reactivated developmental channel. Once the infantile psychotic self dissolves, the patient never need be schizophrenic again. According to Boyer (1971),

> such patients may in the therapeutic situation achieve a controlled and adaptive regression . . . to a period which has attributes of a more optimal mother-infant relationship than existed when the patient was an infant; when such a relationship has developed, innate maturational tendencies can continue to unfold accompanied by alterations of the far-reaching effects of early learning, provided ill-timed actions of the psychoanalyst do not interfere. [p. 74]

These two phenomena often appear dramatically in the clinical setting. The appearance of Attis's terror-catatonia in one of his sessions is an example of the first (see Chapter 12), and Jane's *cosmic laughter* (see Chapter 14) is an example of the second. These phenomena may appear in subtle ways, however, and one should not expect only one occurrence of each in the course of treatment. There may be many experiences of terror leading to the adult psychotic self, just as there may be many attempts to re-experience and tolerate them; these lead to the development of healthier and expanded uninvaded parts. It is usual for one or more such occurrences to appear dramatically. Likewise, the patient's original developmental channel may be re-created more than once through the interaction of the analyst's representation and the patient's corresponding representation of himself in early childhood. These revisitings may allow the patient to form a healthier core self-representation.

The therapist should not interfere with the appearance of these reversed sequences that lead to progress but make his mature functions available to the patient for new identifications (Volkan 1994a). My observations on treating patients with psychotic personality organization (see Chapter 11) apply also to the treatment of schizophrenics: the therapeutic work includes the evolution of the patient's differentiated and integrated self- and object representations and his passage through the oedipal phase for the first time with such mature representations.

I should clarify what I mean by *treatment* of schizophrenics, because there are many types of treatment that are used. For example, in Finland, Alanen and his co-workers (Alanen 1993, Alanen et al. 1991) designed a method called *need-adapted treatment*, which includes family therapy. Their record of success is impressive. As biological treatment methods came to dominate the psychiatric scene, many psychoanalytically oriented therapists began to combine psychotherapy and medication. Such approaches have ranged from sophisticated (e.g., Marcus 1992) to very unsophisticated, and medication is sometimes used to satisfy the requirements of insurance coverage. When I refer to treatment, however, it is limited to psychotherapy based on psychoanalytic theory and techniques. Strategies are used in the initial years so that the treatment eventually evolves to become identical to classic psychoanalysis. I have no experience combining this psychoanalytic approach with medication in the treatment of very regressed patients, including schizophrenics.

SEARLES ON THE PHASES OF TREATMENT

As far as I know, Searles (1961) was the first analyst to state that "successive phases . . . best characterize the psychotherapy of chronic adult schizophrenics" (p. 523). He was influenced at the time by Mahler's (1952) work with autistic and symbiotic infantile psychosis and by Balint's (1955) writings on phenomena of early ego formation, which he encountered during psychoanalysis of neurotic patients. Searles named the first of the successive phases the *out-of-contact phase,* explaining that he preferred this term over the *autistic phase* because, for him, the word *autistic* had certain connotations he considered invalid. Also, *autistic* conjured up Freud's (1911) psychodynamic formulation of schizophrenia as involving withdrawal of libido from the external world and subsequent investment in the self-regression to narcissism (see Chapter 2, London [1973a, b] on Freud's specific theory). Searles's own view at the time was that in schizophrenia a regressive differentiation toward an early level of ego development occurs, "which has its prototype in the experience of the young infant for whom inner and outer worlds have not yet become clearly distinguishable as such" (p. 525). The out-of-contact phase dominates during the early months, sometimes even over years of treatment. The patient's feelings are not available to him, nor can he convey them to others in interpersonal relationships. The therapist in turn experiences little feeling in response to the patient's behavior but instead senses something strange and alien. This does not mean that the patient and the therapist do nothing in this phase.

> The patient is . . . no inert vehicle which needs to be energized by the therapist; rather, an abundance of energy is locked up in him, pressing ceaselessly to be freed, and a

hovering "helpful" orientation on the part of the therapist would only get in the way. [Searles 1961, p. 526]

The therapist remains an investigator instead of feeling compelled to help and to love the patient despite prolonged silences and obscure conversations.

Searles called the second and third phases the *phase of ambivalent symbiosis* and *the phase of preambivalent symbiosis,* respectively. It is interesting that his first three phases reverse the phases by which the schizophrenic illness was originally formed and run parallel to the idea of regression in already regressed patients.

Searles (1961) observed that the second phase begins with "a progressive weakening of ego-boundaries between patient and therapist" (p. 531). He added that "projection and introjection on the part of each participant is facilitated to an extent which is seldom if ever seen in an analyst's work with a neurotic patient" (p. 531). As the third phase begins, the therapist more and more accepts the feelings of a "good" mother, very important to the infantile self of the patient, and at the same time owns his own infantile-dependent feelings toward the patient, as a "good" mother would do.

The strivings for individuality of the two participants eventually lead to the fourth phase. It is clear that, like Boyer (1971) and Schulz (1975), Searles is appreciative of the patient's innate strivings for maturation, which I call *psychobiological development push.* Once obstructions are removed, and the patient is put into the "natural" developmental channel, his psychic organization begins to evolve more maturely.

Searles's fourth phase is the *phase of resolution of symbiosis,* followed by his last, or *late,* phase—a long phase during which the patient experiences what neurotic patients ordinarily do in psychoanalysis. Boyer (1971) also shows that when "pregenital problems have been more or less satisfactorily resolved [the patients] were able to analyze phallic and genital conflicts with at least moderate success" (p. 74). I have been influenced by Searles's way of conceptualizing the phases in psychoanalytic treatment of schizophrenia and by Boyer's parallel remarks. I later examine these phases under new names, after taking into account metapsychological and clinical data now available.

WHICH SCHIZOPHRENICS ARE TREATABLE IN PSYCHOANALYTIC PSYCHOTHERAPY?

It is a complicated matter to select those schizophrenic patients who would be suitable for psychoanalytic psychotherapy on the basis of a psychoanalytic understanding of their illness. Suitability can be determined by the balance of biological and psychological factors initiating and/or maintaining the schizophrenia. In theory we can assume that when psychological factors are dominant, the patient is a candidate for psychotherapy, although it is very difficult to distinguish the effect of the environment from the influence of the disposition. They are, in fact, intertwined. In the clinical setting, we have seen that meaningful psychological relationships can modify the influence of biological factors, although such circumstances are not yet fully understood.

I select patients for treatment according to my formulations about the meaning of the symptoms they present and the communications they offer in the diagnostic interview. I feel more confident if I can mentally map out during these interviews the patient's fragmented self- and object representations involved in fusion-defusion or introjective-projective cycles and when the patient's childhood history accounts for them. I always try to get an adequate history from a schizophrenic patient, even if it is available only as a mélange of actual recollection and delusion. My ability to make an initial map of the patient's mind reflects my capacity for empathy with that particular individual; this is a clue that guides me (more emotionally than intellectually) in accepting a patient.

A patient of mine named Sanford, a 19-year-old schizophrenic not unlike a patient described by Kafka (1969), often gently cut himself and examined his blood, using it as a transitional object. Mary, Kafka's patient, had been swaddled and bandaged during the first year of her life because of a life-threatening early allergic dermatitis. She became self-mutilating as an adult, and when Kafka studied her dreams and fantasies he learned that "in a sense, as long as one has blood, one carried within oneself this potential security blanket capable of giving warmth and comforting envelopment" (p. 210). According to Kafka, "internal blood was probably linked to the internalized mother, and the patient felt superior to others or omnipotent because she could use her knowledge to make external this comforting mother-blanket" (p. 219).

Sanford had been adopted at about one year old and soon thereafter contracted severe dermatitis. I know nothing of his biological parents, but his adopted parents related to him with extreme ambivalence; the mother was afraid to hold and comfort him lest she damage his skin. After Sanford was seen by a number of dermatologists, his dermatitis eventually disappeared when he was 3. In his teens he started self-mutilation, and in his treatment I learned that he, like Mary, used blood as a mother-blanket.

I accepted him for treatment because I was able to feel empathy for him in our diagnostic sessions, having grasped the meaning of his blood symbolism. Because he thought that the color of his blood differed from time to time, he thought of himself as being a different person each time the color changed, and sought the "true blood." Unlike Mary, he was schizophrenic, and had been since learning, in his teens, that he had been adopted. He tried unsuccessfully to locate his biological parents but soon had delusions of being related to various people. In high school he became interested in blood chemistry and earned praise and good grades from his teachers before his preoccupation with the subject became bizarre. During his diagnostic interview I thought that his interest in blood and his search for "true blood" stemmed from his being adopted and sometimes being treated as though he came from a good bloodline or the opposite. Knowing that he was searching in a concrete way for his bloodline, I understood some things about him at the outset. He could not conceptualize any symbolic meaning in his inspection of his blood. He had an appealing quality in relating to me and asked about the possibility of my having noble ancestry. I was included at once in his psychotic world and felt comfortable with this.

HOW NOT TO BE A MANAGER

Severely regressed and/or undeveloped patients may be unable to come regularly to the therapist's office because of their break with reality, their inability to control their impulses, or for some other reason owing to their general condition. Such patients may need managers, regardless of whether they are hospital inpatients. One of the first considerations for the therapist in this situation is to avoid being seduced into managing the patient's life, because if he or she falls into this trap it is unlikely that a therapeutic relationship leading to the formation of a new structure will be possible. Searles (1961) wrote,

> To the extent that the therapist is free from a compulsion to rescue the suffering patient, he can remain sufficiently extricated from that suffering to be able to note significant sequences in the appearance of such symptoms as hallucinations, verbalized delusions, and so forth, and thus be in a position to be genuinely helpful. [p. 528]

An example of how a therapist may be seduced into becoming a manager is provided by a male therapist who undertook the treatment of a schizophrenic college student unable to continue his studies but electing to stay in the university town for treatment. The student received a monthly allowance from his father, who lived elsewhere; it was adequate to meet his living expenses and treatment fees for a month, but he frittered it away in a few weeks. His therapist felt it would be therapeutically helpful to get the father's permission to open a joint account. One was established, from which the patient could not withdraw money or cash checks without the therapist's signature. The therapist then tried to coach his patient on how to manage money and, perhaps, on how to conduct his life. The therapeutic space between therapist and patient, necessary even when the patient is schizophrenic, was ruined and results were disastrous.

Boyer (1967, 1983) refused to begin treatment with certain schizophrenic patients in the absence of an available manager other than himself. Schulz and Kilgalen (1969) offer a list of twenty-four requirements for a hospital staff to use with schizophrenic inpatients. With some modifications this list can be used by managers dealing with outpatients; it is useful in that it creates an atmosphere attuned to the needs of such patients.

We can expand the therapist's guidelines for not managing a patient's life to include suggestions for the protection and maintenance of the therapeutic setting and the therapeutic space. A woman therapist was treating a young schizophrenic patient who came to her office three times a week on his own. After a year of treatment she found him in her office ahead of time, examining the contents of her purse. To avoid hurting his feelings, she pretended not to notice what he was doing. A few days later he began calling her at home; because she had an unlisted telephone number, she realized that he had found it (and her home address) when looking through her purse. She spoke to him briefly when he called, again trying to avoid hurting his feelings, but later, during one of their sessions, she asked him how he had obtained her home number. He did not answer. She did not push the issue, and a week later, as she was about to sit down to dinner with her family, he appeared at her door. Again, she was careful not to seem rejecting and invited him in, introducing him to her family. The next day she found him naked in her office, with an erect penis, demanding intercourse. Panic-stricken, she called for help, and a week later she presented this case to me for my advice. She was clearly a therapist with a compulsion to cure her patients. Those of us who embark on intensive therapeutic work must always remember that the protection of the therapeutic space and the therapeutic setting is essential, and that no psychoanalytic work is possible without respecting this basic rule.

PSYCHOANALYTIC PSYCHOTHERAPY OF THE SCHIZOPHRENIC

Much of my work has centered around patients who did *not* have chronic schizophrenia and who were able to come to me, except for short intervals, as outpatients. Although my description of the overall treatment process bypasses Searles's initial out-of-contact phase to a great extent, I have had enough experience with chronic schizophrenics to conclude that his description of the first phase is still valid.

A prototypical schizophrenic individual clings to the adult psychotic self and the supporting efforts of his uninvaded parts, which may appear as symptoms, in order to prevent another terror and to avoid losing the balance between the adult psychotic self and the uninvaded self. This creates a most stubborn resistance. The patient must be helped to feel secure enough to come to a point in treatment at which he will revisit the terror; it is assumed that by then the patient has enough observing and work ego (Olinick et al. 1973) when he is through revisiting so that he is able to form a new and healthier self-representation to replace the adult psychotic self.

When the adult psychotic self changes, the infantile psychotic core to which it is linked also changes, but it nevertheless continues to exist. It may even become dormant, so the therapist's task is not finished when the adult psychotic self is no longer crystallized. The healthier self-representation is very fragile and must be solidified with more therapeutic work. This can be accomplished only by the further modification and ultimate removal of the infantile psychotic self and the building of a new psychic foundation. Again, the patient must regress therapeutically in order for his infantile psychotic self to interact directly with the therapist and change entirely. Using new terms, I now turn to consider other selected strategies and maneuvers in the six phases of treatment.

PHASE ONE: THE PATIENT PREPARES TO FACE A NEW TERROR

An Overview

The typical schizophrenic's adult psychotic self dominates his personality, and it is fortunate, in a sense, that it is involved in fusion-defusion and/or introjective-projective relatedness. Cameron (1961) noted that it is possible for the schizophrenic patient "to introject massively with archaic completeness in adulthood and then be able to assimilate the new introject as an infant might so that it disappears as such but some of its properties do not" (p. 93). Both Loewald (1960, 1982) and I (Volkan 1968, 1976, 1994b) expressed a similar view. If the therapist protects the therapeutic setting and does not interfere with the natural evolution of the dyadic relationship, his representation will be involved in the patient's fusion-defusion and introjective-projective cycles. If the patient has chronic schizophrenia and is in an out-of-contact phase, he will eventually relate to the therapist in the same way.

The patient takes in nothing new as long as his fragmented images and representations of the therapist are contaminated with the archaic self- and object images and representations. Images and representations of the therapist are not initially taken in as what Loewald (1960) termed a *new object* and Giovacchini (1972) called an *analytic introject*; therefore, they do not provide the patient with an analytical attitude. It is up to the analyst to differentiate himself from the archaic self- and object representations and images at the outset, and in piecemeal fashion to help the patient alter the nature of his archaic introjects (Abse 1955, Boyer 1971, 1983, Searles 1961, 1979, Volkan 1976, 1990, 1994b). The differentiated images and representations of the therapist compete with archaic ones, but the patient will eventually be able to use them for adaptive identifications that allow him to face another terror (or terrors), overt or not, in order to modify the adult psychotic self.

In dealing with such patients the therapist must initially be able to remain in *therapeutic psychotic transference* (Searles 1965) with the patient for a long time, keeping his or her own observing ego and protecting the patient's, however fragile it may be. After experiencing such therapeutic psychotic transference (fusion-defusion and/or primitive introjective-projective relatedness), the patient can start moving toward a more differentiated existence.

Because the patient's primitive relatedness to objects and

their images and representations naturally leads him to introject the therapist, any deliberate maneuver of the therapist to
offer himself or herself as a model is usually a seductive
intrusion that will cause anxiety and impede the development
of more mature self- and object representations and associated
ego-building. Internalization occurring in the transference may,
in contrast to its use in ego-building, indicate an effort to retain
primitive defenses and a primitive mode of relationship, because any move to individuate evokes fear of losing the existing
sense of self, however psychotic. The patient may sometimes
perceive any attempt by the therapist to promote the internalization process as his or her insistence on continuing this
primitive mode of relating, and sometimes as insistence on the
surrender of the patient's defenses. Searles (1951) indicated
that *incorporative processes* within the transference–countertransference relationship may, when used to defend against
anxiety, account for many long-standing stalemates in psychoanalytic therapy. The therapist would be forcing the internalization of a caricature of himself as a model were he to give
personal information about his own life. The therapist differentiates his representation from the patient's archaic images and
representations by staying in a therapeutic position and using
interpretation along with clarification and nonseductive suggestions that the patient may not hear at first but will subsequently
take in. This gives the patient an environment in which the
therapist provides explanation and nonintrusive therapeutic
protection. There should be no lengthy speeches, but there
should be time for the patient to assimilate, if possible, what has
been said. The therapist may spend much time listening to the
patient's silences.

Reality Base

There is a way for the therapist to give the patient limited
personal information in a specific therapeutic interaction at the
very beginning of treatment. Such information is given in the
service of responding to intrapsychic processes in the sense of
promoting elaboration and development in the treatment set-

ting. I have used a technique I call the *establishment of a reality base* (Volkan 1976, 1987). With neurotics we try to avoid interfering with the developing transference neurosis, but it may be helpful with the psychotic person to establish a reality base before the transference psychosis is fully developed. This will give the patient something to fall back on as he tries to work through the differentiation of the therapist's images and representations from his or her own archaic self- and object images and representations. With the neurotic, a built-in reality base can be assumed because the patient knows that he pays the analyst, whose role is clearly not parental. The transference neurosis is built on the base of reality (A. Freud 1954). In contrast, the schizophrenic patient, who may not differentiate the therapist from the representation of his parents, must be helped to develop and to take into account a reality base in relating to him (Volkan 1976). Such help may also establish the patient's observing ego and become its focal point.

Let us recall the patient Ricky, who in the third hour of our work together tried to take me in as German wine, as an image invested with the Hitlerian image. My response to him was a simple declaration that I am Turkish. Answering his question as to what type of wines Turkey produces, I commented that Turkey produces both sweet and sour wines, as does Germany. I thus gave him "good" as well as "bad" targets for his projections. Had he been neurotic, I would not have interrupted his fantasies about me and my homeland. With Ricky I interfered in order to establish a reality base. The clarification of my national origin arose naturally within this situation. Differentiating my image from those of his archaic objects, as well as my response to his anxiety about sour wine, did not gratify his interest in the details of my life.

Avoidance of Internalization Conflict

Unless he is in the out-of-contact phase, from the outset the schizophrenic patient will involve the therapist and his representation in fusion–defusion and/or introjective-projective relatedness. The consequent contact must gradually be made meaningful and therapeutic. The therapist must absorb the patient's externalizations of self- and object images and projections of unacceptable ideas long enough to make the necessary connections with the intrapsychic aspects and for the patient to be somewhat tolerant in reinternalizing the therapist's image. A quality so acquired may be retained. As Giovacchini (1967) suggested in reference to character disorders, interpretations at the start of treatment may not have much specific content, but the schizophrenic patient makes externalizations and projections, some quite obvious and others subtle, from the initial interview. By constantly and quickly interpreting them, the therapist causes an internalization conflict. The therapist's purpose is to focus on the intrapsychic; the patient gains considerable security when he also succeeds in doing this, and learns through identification with the therapist that he can keep what is projected onto him long enough without becoming disorganized.

Eventually the therapist gently interprets the patient's distortions and contradictions as they become evident in therapy and bring him or her fear, pain, or elation. The therapist does not agree or disagree with the patient's delusions or psychotic behavior; the therapist's aim is eventually to clarify and/or interpret the defensive functions of the psychotic products. We should remember, however, that for a long time the patient may not hear these clarifications and/or interpretations; what is important is that the therapist respond empathically and attempt to communicate without being intrusive, disagreeable, advice-giving, or seductive. Besides involuntary nonverbal and preverbal communications, the therapist uses logical sentences when addressing a schizophrenic patient. The dominant part of the patient's mind may be unable to comprehend fully such speech, but the therapist must start somewhere, and brief empathic statements become, through repetition, the precursors of the patient's new logical thought.

Humanizing Deep Material

What lies on the surface of the patient's relatedness to the therapist and his representations, such as cannibalistic fantasies primitively symbolizing internalization, manifests what we would call *deep material* in the case of a neurotic patient. The therapist should not shy away from identifying and/or interpreting this (Volkan 1968) because it helps the patient to identify his uncanny delusions, fantasies, and experiences—especially the defensive ones—as steps in the developmental process rather than regarding them as grotesque and beyond human experience. For example, the therapist may respond to a patient's cannibalistic desire for him by simply saying that it represents a wish to relate to him, because if the therapist is "eaten," the patient and therapist are together. If the patient tries to spit out the therapist's representation, the therapist can say the patient is experiencing him as something to be feared. Such remarks can allow the therapist to clarify the need-fear dilemma (Burnham et al. 1969) that presents itself in the sessions. The therapist's understanding and verbalization of this phenomenon may initiate an empathic contact between therapist and patient.

A Focus on the Introjective-Projective Process

Boyer (1967, 1983) suggests, and my experience confirms, that the therapist will do better by not concentrating at first on material arising from libidinal drives per se, unless an eroticized psychotic transference threatens to become unwieldy, and by restricting his or her clarifications and interpretation to the aggressive aspects of what is being presented. In time both aggressive and libidinal materials will be examined.

I deal with the patient's disturbing reactions to fusing with and/or internalizing "bad" objects rather than their externalization. When the patient externalizes "bad" object images or representations, he or she feels relatively comfortable until they begin to return. While seeking his biological parents, Sanford met a couple whom he thought of as his biological parents in his delusional state, but when he approached them they treated him badly. In his session a few days later, he seemed panic-stricken and depressed and mimicked their gestures and facial expressions. He spoke of their nonverbal communication, and I sensed that what was depressing him was his internalization of and temporary identification with the couple's "bad" representations, toward which he was directing his aggression, thus treating himself badly. I told Sanford that his self had become a host for the couple because his disappointment with them was strong enough to connect him with them. I directed him to speak further of his actual interaction with them. As he told and retold the story, Sanford began to disidentify with their representations; his frustration became realistic as he perceived the couple as being outside himself.

Sanford's fear of introjecting the "bad" self- and object images or representations, and his defenses for dealing with this process, needed to be respected. A woman patient expressed her struggle when my "bad" representation was involved in her relational world. She put a Lifesaver candy in her mouth during our sessions in order to keep the "bad" therapist out. I did not ask that she take it out of her mouth because I felt that this defense was in the service of saving her psychic existence. After much work with me she became able to speak to me without having a Lifesaver in her mouth.

Boyer (1967, 1983) chooses to focus on depressive material rather than on paranoid ideation because it relates to the introjected "bad" self- and object representations, which in the past we sometimes called *superego forerunners* and/or *superego introjects*. They must be dealt with initially so that the sadistic/masochistic nature of the patient's inner world can be reduced and/or anchored to people or events that exist in reality. This leads to consideration of linking interpretations.

Linking Interpretations

Giovacchini (1969) described linking interpretation as a therapeutic maneuver in which the therapist tries to link events in the outside world to intrapsychic phenomena to promote contact with reality. Linking interpretations are used in the initial phase of a schizophrenic patient's treatment; they not only make the patient more alert in testing reality but also promote psychological-mindedness by nurturing an observing ego.

Giovacchini recalled Freud's (1900) concept of the day residue of dreams. Day residue, an extrapsychic stimulus, is a seemingly irrelevant event that stimulates and fuses with id content. Giovacchini (1969) said, "An interpretation may make a casual connection by referring to day residue which may be the stimulus for the flow of the patient's associations or for some otherwise unexplainable behavior" (p. 180). For example, a schizophrenic had a stomachache when he saw a policeman on the way to my office. I interpreted the link between the sight of the policeman and the pain in his stomach, saying that he had perceived the officer as too "bad" to be stomached. Note that at this point the emphasis was on introjection of the "bad" object (depressive direction). I did not focus on the externalization of his own aggressive aspects onto the policeman (paranoid direction).

PHASE TWO: WHEN THE PATIENT MODIFIES OR RELINQUISHES THE ADULT PSYCHOTIC SELF

Progressive Use of Transitional Relatedness

During my initial work with a schizophrenic I do not forbid him to bring to our sessions objects or phenomena he uses as reactivated transitional objects (Winnicott 1953); they may be simply a piece of cloth, a tape recorder, a turtle, or a snatch of song, a saying, or a way of twisting hair in magical ways. I see such an object or phenomenon as being like a lantern with an opaque side and a transparent side (Volkan 1976). When the patient feels comfortable with me, he turns the transparent side toward me, and the light falls on me so he gets to know me. When uncomfortable in my presence, he turns the opaque side of the lantern in my direction and blots me out. When I eventually explain this to a patient, I make it clear that the magical object or activity in question has both progressive and

regressive aspects (Modell 1968, 1970). I demonstrate that I can
be either reached or obliterated through its use, and that I can
tolerate the latter fate. I make clear my understanding that the
magical item or activity is under the patient's control, suggesting that as he gets to know me better, he will use the
progressive side more often and will eventually give up the need
for magic in loving or hating me.

With the passage of years, and as the schizophrenic differentiates my images and representations more and more from
those of himself and others, he will tend to use the progressive
aspect of the transitional item or activity more often and will
eventually try relating to me without it. This move usually
requires courage and needs the therapist's attention. Because
the patient may regard the surrender of the magic item as
frightening, he should not be pressed to give it up; it is better to
acknowledge the patient's struggle and to encourage him to
wonder about the consequences of no longer having the magical
buffer between himself and the therapist. The surrender of the
transitional object or behavioral quirk indicates greater crystallization of the differentiation of self- and object representations.

Emotional Flooding and Revisiting the Terror

Progress paradoxically leads to therapeutic regression. If there
is no interference from the environment, and the therapist
commits no major technical errors, the patient will visit his
terror and emerge from it with progressive development. This
revisiting is a turning point in treatment and initiates dissolution of the adult psychotic self. This experience, which I have
called *emotional flooding* (1976), corresponds in many ways to
Pao's (1979) organismic panic.

Although the original terror, followed by shock, induces
personality change and the appearance of the adult psychotic
self, emotional flooding in the treatment setting and with
connections to transference helps to modify and resolve the
adult psychotic self and initiates establishment of a healthier
one through the expansion and modification of the uninvaded

part. The revisiting of the terror occurs when a patient presents an accumulation of memories and fantasies (flooding in the ideational field [Volkan 1976]) that support the same emotion. The patient may scream and seem to lose his human identity. The gesture or verbalization of "no" appears as a massive defense against the anxiety of giving up whatever self-continuity existed:

> Patients capable of reporting their experience of emotional flooding after the event usually indicate that strange perceptual changes took place. They underwent a "metamorphosis" during the experience, becoming monstrous and diabolical when signal affects were replaced by primal affects closely related to the aggressive drive. If the primal affect was close to the libidinal drive, however, there was another kind of change, the kind reflected in poetry or prose when a lover tells his beloved, "I love you so much that I am a new person." . . . In this state, the representation of the affect becomes the patient's perceived self. [Volkan 1976, p. 185]

Patients may not be aware that tolerance of their emotional flooding marks the start of a healthier self, one that modifies and/or replaces the adult psychotic self. During the flooding the self is experienced as the representation of the affect, as if it were a sponge soaked with emotion or a balloon swollen with it. They may call themselves "swollen monsters" when over-whelmed with aggressive affect.

The ability to tolerate emotional flooding leads to greater tolerance for experiencing anxiety. Now no longer overwhelming, anxiety becomes a signal affect and does not lead to organismic panic. While experiencing anxiety, the patient begins to maintain an observing ego and soon indicates symbolically the presence of a new and healthier self-representation. This is a good sign, especially if the experience is accompanied by a sad affect representing a form of mourning for the loss of the adult psychotic self. When a sad affect follows the patient's revisitation of the terror, it indicates that the ties to the long-maintained adult psychotic self have been modified, and that a form of mourning process is under way. Genuine adult-type mourning will not appear in the repertoire of the schizophrenic until there is a healthy change in the infantile core.

Attis revisited his terror and experienced consequent temporary catatonia during one of his sessions. After tolerating it, he went to Philadelphia—the City of Brotherly Love—to see the Liberty Bell, demonstrating his liberation from the influence of his adult psychotic self. To him, this pilgrimage (Poland 1977) represented the taming of his aggression toward the brother (his mother's agent) who had accidentally mutilated his hand. Another patient, after tolerating a new terror experience in the therapeutic setting, dreamed of a flower opening, and still another feverishly rearranged the furniture in her home in a representation of the new arrangement she felt within herself.

PHASE THREE: AFTER THE PATIENT MODIFIES OR RELINQUISHES THE ADULT PSYCHOTIC SELF

An Overview

The drastic modification and/or removal of the adult psychotic self is a therapeutic turning point, but the patient is not fully cured as long as the infantile psychotic self has not been dissolved and replaced by a healthier core. The work on the adult psychotic self certainly modifies the infantile one, but it does not altogether get rid of it. After this turning point, some patients may reencapsulate the infantile psychotic core and seem to be well, but it is possible that they may become schizophrenic or develop a psychotic personality organization, or at least part of the healthier self's energy will be assigned to keep the infantile self dormant. A true cure would require the complete resolution of the infantile psychotic self. In order to accomplish this, the therapist directs attention to strengthening the healthier self-representation and slowly prepares the patient for still further therapeutic regression, in which the infantile core will be directly involved in a therapeutic story (Volkan

1984) related to the transference-countertransference. The patient lies on the couch after a healthier adult self-representation has been established. As I have become more experienced in treating schizophrenics, I have used the couch even before making drastic changes in their adult psychotic selves. I find that lying on the couch provides a degree of organization in the chaotic lives of such individuals and helps to replace the disorganized regressive state with one in which therapeutic regression dominates.

Different Types of Identification

After the patient has tolerated the terror, the therapist begins to experience increasingly more pleasant emotions in the sessions. The patient will not always maintain a forward movement, however. Progressions and regressions, as well as libidinal and aggressive relatedness, will alternate in both transference and countertransference. What is most observable, descriptively and functionally, are the patient's efforts to identify with the therapist's various representations and functions.

The patient's introjection of and identification with the therapist's representations differ in different phases of the treatment (Tähkä 1984a, Volkan 1976, 1994a, b). Attempts made in the initial phase are accompanied by incorporative fantasies referring to introjection in a gross, exaggerated way that features personified part-object images such as those of the therapist's penis, nipples, voice, or face. Once a new and healthier adult self evolves, gross cannibalistic fantasies start to disappear. In his efforts to assimilate certain representations of the therapist, the patient becomes involved in therapeutic stories that continue from session to session. It is in this phase that the patient can develop new ego formations that will enable him to deal with a specific area in his interaction with his mothering person(s) that was neglected. Thus, when we speak of identification with the therapist's representation as curative at this time, we refer to one or many different such representations that deal with one or many specific issues.

In this phase there is usually no fusion–defusion, but introjective-projective cycles continue, although more slowly and on a higher level. When the patient identifies with the therapist's representations, they still compete in his mind with archaic self- and object representations (Abse and Ewing 1960). The therapist should not prematurely encourage the patient to prefer his representation over the archaic ones but should acknowledge the competition as well as the patient's anxiety over losing the archaic representations with which he had been so long familiar (for clinical examples, see Chapter 14).

Neutralization of Aggression

As the patient identifies with the therapist's functions in this phase, aggression is further neutralized, and the need to fragment and split self- and object representations disappears. Tähkä (1984a, 1988, 1993) describes how the process takes place during normal child development, stating that with gradually greater ability to change passivity into activity (A. Freud 1936), the child starts to do for himself what his mother previously did for him. According to Tähkä (1988),

> As a function-specific frustration gives rise to a function-specific (functionally selected) identification, the result will be the emergence of a corresponding functional capacity in the self with corresponding changes in the representations of self and object. [p. 127]

The mother's failure in a particular function formerly led to frustration and the reactivation of aggression, but "After an established identification, failures of particular function no longer lead to frustrations since the arousal of the signal need will now activate the child's own newly acquired function" (p. 127). A similar process takes place during this phase of the psychoanalytic psychotherapy of an adult schizophrenic, and with it comes the lessening of frustration and aggression, which is usually referred to as the *neutralization of aggression* (Hartmann 1950). According to Tähkä (1988), "no changes in the energy itself are postulated here, while that which is energized has undergone a structural alteration" (p. 127).

Suitable Targets for Externalization

A phenomenon that has not had much attention in the psychoanalytic literature is the therapist's provision of suitable targets of externalization (Volkan 1986, 1988, 1990) for the schizophrenic patient so that he can maintain his internal world in a more cohesive way. Because this concept is rather new, I describe it here in some detail.

In treating schizophrenics, I have noted that in this phase of treatment they begin showing interest in social-political *us* and *them* designations: "We are Charlottesvillians from the East Coast; they are San Franciscans from the West Coast." Or "I [the patient] am American; you [the analyst] are Turkish. Can I be Turkish, too? Should I stay American?" At first I understood such observations solely from the standpoint of the patient's attempt at identification with me, and competition among his various identifications. Since the late 1970s, however, I have been involved in an interdisciplinary study of ethnicity and nationalism and in actual unofficial diplomacy dealing with ethnic and other large-group conflicts (Group for the Advancement of Psychiatry 1988, Volkan 1992c, Volkan et al. 1990, Volkan et al. 1991). Such activity gave me new insights about schizophrenics' distinguishing "us" from "them." In this treatment phase, schizophrenics function as though they have formed a borderline personality organization (Kernberg 1975, Volkan 1976, 1987) and behave like psychosis-prone borderline individuals (Boyer 1986, Gunderson, Carpenter, and Strauss 1975, Volkan 1987). They use more effective splitting and related defenses along with their relatively decelerated introjective-projective relatedness. Like borderline patients, schizophrenic patients in this phase of treatment see the world and themselves as black and white. The distinction between "us" and "them," however, as described here is not a simple expression of black and white splitting and needs further study.

A child between 6 and 36 months of age is expected to complete the mending of developmentally split self- and object representations. Developmental splitting in the child is due to his or her lack of effective integrative function. If it is not overcome, the patient becomes fixated in borderline personality organization. Then developmental splitting changes function, becoming defensive splitting. Even when this process takes its normal course, the task is never wholly completed; some unmended "good" and "bad" self- and object representations remain as a potential source of later object-relations conflict. In normal development the ego represses some of them (van der Walls 1952), or they are absorbed in the evolving superego and ego ideal (Kernberg 1976b); however, some are externalized under the guidance of the mothering person and important others within the child's own small and large groups, such as those composed of family or ethnic constellations. Because such targets are common to all members of the child's large group, they can effectively absorb his externalizations and projections and help to support his inner cohesion. Because of the attitude of the large group, such externalizations and projections are stable even if they are not realistic. Although the children in a large group have different personalities and intrapsychic problems, they share the suitable reservoirs that link them together as an invisible net. There are targets that absorb the children's positive unmended self- and object representations; they become the start of *we-ness*. Those that absorb the negative "bad" self- and object representations become the foundation of the "enemies"—usually neighboring ethnic groups.

> Think in terms of learning, from childhood on, to wear two layers of clothing. The first garment, which belongs just to the individual who is wearing it, fits him snugly. The second set of clothes, the ethnic layer, is a loose covering that protects him like a mother or caregiver. At the same time, because the garment is not form-fitting, it shelters many individuals under it as though it were one big canvas tent, so to speak. . . . As long as the tent remains stable and strong, the members of

> the group can go about their lives without paying much attention to it. If the tent is disturbed or shaken, however, this attracts more notice, and all the individuals under the tent collectively become preoccupied with trying to make the tent strong again. [Volkan 1992c, p. 8]

Because of her own or her child's difficulties, the mother of a child who will become schizophrenic characteristically fails to sponsor adequate targets of externalization for him. The child is kept from establishing developmentally necessary stable externalizations and/or projections to protect his sense of self and kept from investing positively in the second layer of protection he shares with his group. The schizophrenic patient is not ethnic in the usual sense, but he may be pathologically, exaggeratedly, and defensively *super-ethnic* because the second layer of clothing is unstable. Thus the patient may either show no interest in ethnic (or nationalistic) issues or exaggerate them in a delusional way. In this phase of treatment, the patient begins to use the therapist's representation to invest in suitable targets of externalization.

Toward the end of the third year of treatment of a young woman who sought analysis because "her middle core was missing," I rearranged the furniture in the office where we had our sessions. I considered this an entirely rational act; that it was a countertransference response escaped me at first.

> Above the couch I hung a new painting that showed the harbor of Kyrenia in Cyprus, which I consider one of the most beautiful spots on earth. Colorful and lively, the picture had been painted by my niece, from whom I obtained it on one of my visits to my homeland. When my patient began taking an interest in it, she showed uncanny perception by connecting it with my personal background. One day, when she asked me about the place in the painting, I found myself explaining, with some excitement in my voice, that it was the harbor of Kyrenia in Cyprus, and that it was a place I liked very much. Although she had been told when referred to me that I am Cypriot Turk, she had shown no interest in my accent or given any other acknowledgment of my being foreign until her attention was caught by the painting.

I must emphasize that I am not in the habit of making
disclosures about myself to any patient, whether neurotic,
borderline, or psychotic. It was most unusual for me to have
made the remark I did about the painting, with its disclosure
of my affection for the place. When the session was over, I
sought the meaning of this unusual happening. I believe that
at the deepest level the harbor picture represented my
"womb," and I might very well have wanted to show my
patient that I had a better womb in response to her absorption
in the insides of her mother's womb, in which she wanted to
stay in fantasy but where she feared she might drown.
[Volkan 1986, p. 127]

Dwelling on this incident, I began to realize that she needed
someone to provide suitable targets of externalization, and that
by changing the furniture in the office and hanging the picture
I was responding to her need, unconsciously at first.

This woman's parents were often absent during her childhood. Her mother was usually depressed and her father was a
hippie. They moved from place to place and provided her with
very few shared reservoirs. Although she considered herself a
Christian, she had had no religious instruction. A few months
before I changed the furniture, she spoke of a young Jewish
man she had been dating for about a year. When he began to
speak of marriage she had a dream in which, she said, "I saw a
little Oriental girl with her aunt and uncle, who wished to adopt
her. They were in a room where there was a piano. Some of the
notes—oh! I mean the *keys!*—were missing" (Volkan 1986, p.
128). She quickly identified herself with the little Oriental girl.
At that time she was reacting to my anticipated absence from
the office for a few days, and expressing a wish that I adopt her.
She had an aunt and uncle named Keyes, whose son was
happily married to an Asian woman. The Keyeses had accepted
into the family someone from another ethnic and racial group,
but my patient's dream showed condensation of an inadequacy
in that union, a wish for union, and fear that interracial
acceptance might be impossible. The dream of the missing keys
(Keyes) occurred just after a serious talk she had had about
marriage to her Jewish friend, whose family was stable and

traditional. He had urged that some Jewish observances be included in their wedding ceremony.

My patient had no conscious feelings of prejudice, and when her fiancé spoke so eagerly about his ethnic connections, she felt something missing in herself, although she did not know what. She telephoned her mother, telling her of the discussion about the wedding, and as she left the phone, her sense that something was missing increased. She then realized that she envied her fiancé's ethnic pride and traditions because she had so little of her own. I assumed that she had called her mother in the hope of uncovering her family's own ethic heritage, but her mother could offer her nothing. When she then dreamed of the missing keys, they represented the suitable targets of externalization that could strengthen her sense of self in her wedding. A few months after this, I unconsciously responded to her need by rearranging the furniture in my office and hanging up the painting of the harbor of Kyrenia.

Dreams

While the patient is floridly psychotic, his dreams, delusions, hallucinations, and bizarre symptoms merge, but now dreams can be taken seriously and interpretation becomes possible. As the patient advances further, interpreting his dreams begins to resemble interpreting those of a neurotic.

PHASE FOUR: COMING FACE-TO-FACE WITH THE INFANTILE PSYCHOTIC SELF

The Second Drastic Therapeutic Regression

Progress in treatment strengthens the patient's self-representation that replaces the adult psychotic self. The infantile psychotic self, now encapsulated, remains in the background. The patient becomes involved in another drastic therapeutic regression that allows the therapist to interact directly with the infantile psychotic self. The patient's introjective-projective relatedness, and sometimes even fusion-defusion, surfaces again with intensity, but the therapist senses that interaction with the patient is now in the service of replacing the fragile core with a solid one. After this experience the patient no longer "feels like a doughnut" missing a middle part, or a "bad seed" with a core full of "bad" affects. When the infantile psychotic self is dissolved, the patient will never again be schizophrenic.

Some patients resist further therapeutic regression after modifying the adult psychotic self; they get well with an encapsulated infantile psychotic self that is effectively repressed. I believe that because of the type of therapy he received, Attis never got rid of his infantile psychotic self, but over time, as the healthier self-representation he developed encapsulated his infantile psychotic core effectively, his new ego functions, including effective repression, precluded its coming alive again. He did not become schizophrenic after the modification of his adult psychotic self, but theoretically he might have. Other patients, with better treatment, visit their infantile psychotic selves in this phase of treatment. In the following chapter I describe one patient's experience of this phenomenon as *cosmic laughter*. Once the infantile psychotic self is replaced with a solid core, the previously schizophrenic patient is like a borderline patient with a typical borderline personality organization who travels, in treatment, through a developmental channel after experiencing a focalized psychosis (Volkan 1987) and becomes no longer prone to psychosis.

PHASE FIVE: UPWARD-EVOLVING TRANSFERENCE LEADING TO TRANSFERENCE NEUROSIS

During phase five, the patient seems involved again with the issues seen in phase three: neutralization of aggression, use of suitable targets of externalization, and identification with various functions of the therapist. These issues now appear on a more mature and sophisticated level, however, and the patient can observe them and grasp their meaning. Now, splitting is in the developmental channel and leads to *crucial junctures* (mending)—bringing about the formation of cohesive self- and object representations and crystallizing the patient's object constancy. Moreover, the patient begins to hear and to use interpretations more effectively and acknowledges the genetic aspects of the problems he has in facing his illness.

A more mature object relationship with the therapist will come about in a transference neurosis; introjective-projective relatedness will fall into the background of the relationship. The patient's transference neurosis is like a child's passage through the oedipal years. The patient was not altogether "normal" before his illness and as a schizophrenic had an undifferentiated, undeveloped sense of self. Thus his experiences of oedipal issues are new at this time because he faces them with a cohesive self-representation for the first time. Rather than analyzing away the oedipal conflict, the therapist pays attention to the psychological obstacles the patient may face in moving up the developmental ladder and interprets regressive moves and the reappearance of object relations conflicts. It is a good prognostic sign when stories about old object relations conflicts, and representations of old psychotic symptoms, appear in the patient's dreams without awakening him or causing anxiety. The patient now uses repression and other sophisticated defense mechanisms effectively in daily life.

Despite all these changes, the therapist should continue to monitor introjective-projective moves, however silent they may be. The therapist should use interpretation to help the patient move toward adaptive identifications and suitable targets of externalization. These efforts should bring about further differentiation and individuation of the patient's new sense of self.

Micro-identifications

The main focus in the analysis of a neurotic patient is on interpretation of unresolved mental structural conflicts as they relate to drive derivatives (and defenses against them) that appear in the transference neurosis. A continuous sense of micro-identifications (Rangell 1979) with the analyst's analyzing function can then be anticipated. The once-schizophrenic but now neurotic patient begins to use micro-identifications, although other more drastic and observable types of identifications persist.

Belonging to One's Own Group

In this phase, too, the patient uses the suitable targets of externalization that the therapist provides. The patient also differentiates between "us" and "them" in a more effective way. If the analyst does not belong to the patient's large ethnic group, the patient can move from an investment in the analyst's suitable target of externalization to the suitable targets of his own natural group. For example, one patient read extensively about Istanbul and played music that she thought of as Turkish on her piano, in reference to the analyst's suitable target of externalization. Then she began to collect Jewish folk songs and visited her first synagogue. This advance led her to explore wider horizons of culture and eventually of the world.

PHASE SIX: THE TERMINATION PHASE

I plan for this phase to take months, usually a longer phase than the termination phase of neurotic individuals. In coming to treatment, the schizophrenic patient has displayed great difficulty in object relations and used primitive, magical ways of dealing with separation. Even after treatment has given him some experience in adult-type grieving and letting go, he will need time and patience to deal with the highly significant separation from the therapist. In this phase the patient partly surrenders repression and other higher-level defensive and adaptive mechanisms and returns to old ways of controlling anxiety. Introjective-projective relatedness may reappear more clearly, but this does not make the experienced therapist anxious; the therapist's technique is to let the patient see that he or she is reacting to termination and to allow the patient to use his own insight to reorganize.

Searching for a Magical Object

In the termination phase a patient often activates some primitive magic as a bridge for the old psychotic self and/or a way of keeping the therapist as part of himself. The patient may, for example, plan to give the therapist a parting gift. Although it might be possible for such a gift to be an effective external receptacle for the patient's internal world, it might, on the other hand, keep the patient from truly owning his externalizations and projections. As I described earlier, I do not consider a gift given to the analyst a suitable target of externalization. I make it a policy not to accept a gift, although I analyze the psychological content of one that is offered. This is, of course, done tactfully, without rejecting the patient's genuine affection and gratitude.

Mourning

Because the core of a schizophrenic's self- and object representations is undifferentiated and he lacks stable object constancy, he is unable to mourn. The schizophrenic does experience a type of mourning—a sad affect—after surrendering the adult psychotic self, but to mourn effectively in an adult way, he must have a cohesive, stable self-representation that is differentiated from a similarly cohesive and stable object representation (Volkan 1981a, Volkan and Zintl 1993). Adult-type mourning requires the ability to examine the mental representation of the departed in a gradual way, both consciously and unconsciously, and to reach a *remembrance formation*. Tähkä (1984b) describes this as the mental process through which someone previously experienced as existing in the outer world becomes a remembrance of a lost object: "in this process the nature of the object representation alters, as an object belonging to the present and to the outside world changes into one belonging to the past and to the realm of memories" (pp. 17–18). It must also be remembered that in the mature mourning process the mourner once more selectively identifies with aspects of the one he has lost (Volkan 1981a, Volkan and Zintl 1993). Only in the termination phase is the formerly schizophrenic individual expected to mourn genuinely as an adult on leaving the analyst. The ability to mourn in this manner indicates the success of treatment and a positive prognosis that the patient will continue to be healthy. With most former schizophrenics, mourning continues silently for many years after treatment has been concluded and is a feature of learning how to function better in an adult world by assimilating and crystallizing many adult functions. The analyst will do well to prepare the patient for the possibility of a protracted period of mourning. The therapist should not deny his or her own grief at letting the patient go if the patient notices and comments on it. The patient's last important identification is with the representation of a therapist who is able to let go, grieve, and permit the true independence of an important other. In turn, the patient learns how to grieve while letting the analyst resume life without the person to whom he has devoted so considerable a period of his affective life.

COUNTERTRANSFERENCE

I was once criticized by a colleague who felt that although I had spent considerable time in my professional life treating schizophrenic, borderline, and narcissistic patients, I had written little about countertransference, which is an important consideration in dealing with the regressed. Although only two titles of my papers include the term *countertransference* (Volkan 1981b, 1993c), my colleague was not entirely accurate. I advocate that analysts give longitudinal accounts of cases, including particulars of the treatment process. In changing times, such reporting is necessary to justify psychoanalysis—to insurance companies as well as to those critical of this type of treatment. I have reported my share of total cases (Volkan 1982b, 1984, 1987, Volkan and Ast 1992, 1994) and have given more than the customary consideration to counter-response and countertransference feelings and their significance. In this book, references to and examples of countertransference are abundant. I agree, of course, with Boyer (1983) that countertransference problems pose perhaps the greatest threat to the psychoanalytic treatment of regressed patients, and that the analyst needs to use his countertransference feelings as a signal for exploration of the therapeutic process and its use as a therapeutic tool. We need only echo Ogden's (1994) remark that "in an analytic context, there is no such thing as an analyst apart from the relationship with the analysand" (p. 4).

The psychology of analysts and therapists undertaking intense work with schizophrenics needs consideration; for example, their ability "to regress in the service of the other" (Olinick 1980) is crucial. The necessity of tolerance and therapeutic use of countertransference in treating psychotic patients demands that the therapist meet the patient in his regressed state and, in a sense, validate it (Loewald 1982) without intruding into the therapeutic space. The patient must feel that he is not left alone in a strange place. This conduct helps change the patient's regression from chaotic to therapeutic.

Because of their own psychological make-up, certain therapists or analysts may be better equipped than others to use their personal responses to the patient's primitive activities. Training is also important; most psychoanalytic institutes do not provide the necessary training.

14

Jane

I call this patient Jane because, in mid-treatment, when she developed a borderline personality organization, she made abrupt shifts between investing self- and object representations with libido and aggression; this change reminded me of Tarzan swinging in great arcs through the jungle on a vine. When I recalled this scene, she replied, with her more integrated female self-image, "No! I am Jane!" In the past I have written about various aspects of her case (Volkan 1975, 1976, 1982a), but here I report her total case history for the first time.

When I first saw Jane in March 1964, she was 21, unmarried, and studying art at a college 100 miles or so from her home. Four months earlier, her college psychiatrist had diagnosed her with acute schizophrenia and eventually sent her to the hospital where I worked. He felt that she was terrified of something as she entered her last year at school. She reported seeing bizarre hallucinations in his office, such as wavy undulations of the walls and ceilings and changes in colors. She spent hours writing down her thoughts in the hope that the psychiatrist would read them, turning out page after page of loose associations and self-administered ink-blot tests, pseudophilosophical statements about life, and wishes that she might turn into a flower. When hallucinating she was especially preoccupied with machines and gave detailed descriptions of some balance scales, particularly one small machine that performed poorly. She wrote:

> Everyday people added more bits—every night the bigger machines asked more questions until the little balance could not even approximate her directions or her size. One night— well, it was nearly dawn—she decided. Before daybreak she tiptoed away, but one of the big machines awoke. "Where are you going?" "I must go into a vacuum to balance myself," she said. The others awoke in horror. "You are running away!" "Escape!" "You must face reality." "A vacuum is not living!" "Immature!" And she cried and crept away in spite of them. In the vacuum, in the dark away from bits and questions and answers, she measured herself in every direction, learning that she was bigger than she had thought and smaller than she had thought; and brighter and duller; prettier and uglier; more sensitive and less sensitive; more balanced and less balanced than she had thought. But all over she was one size bigger when she left the vacuum than when she sat in the corner—nearly untouched.

I believe that at the time she wrote about the machines she was sensing the fragmented self- and object representations within her, her break with reality, and her horror. The vacuum probably represented her adult psychotic self—a world where things fuse—where the big and the small, the pretty and the ugly, the sensitive and the insensitive are the same.

Many schizophrenics have *influencing machines,* a facet first studied by Victor Tausk in 1919. He suggested that machines such as those appearing in the dreams of "normal" people represent the dreamer's genitalia, and that their activity in hallucinations represents forbidden masturbation. I have had only one patient, a man, who had a classic influencing machine; there was evidence to suggest that the machine, which he believed was located in the CIA building in Langley, Virginia, represented his phallus. It was this machine that made him have forbidden sexual thoughts or engage in forbidden sexual activity. In other cases, machines have stood for representations of both body and psyche. In a case that Luttrell and I described (Volkan and Luttrell 1971), machines also represented reactivated transitional objects, indicating an attempt of the patient to keep a link between internal and external worlds. In view of Jane's childhood sexual history, I suspect that her machines also stood for genital activities. I feel that when she wrote about them, however, she was mainly describing her perception of her invaded part, the chaos and fragmentation of her self- and object representations, her wish to find a balance between aggressive and libidinally invested representational units, and a pull toward and a defense against further regression to a fused world.

PERSONAL HISTORY

Jane grew up on a Southern estate owned by a wealthy woman who divided her time between the estate's main house and her other homes in the United States and Europe. Jane's father was the manager of the estate, including a farm, and his family lived in the second largest house on the property. There were also smaller houses for workers. The relationship between the owner, the manager, the workers, and their respective families was conducted in accordance with Southern tradition. Jane's family could—and did—visit the owner's house, but the owner's family never called socially at the manager's house. The owner's granddaughter was Jane's age, and Jane was, in a way, her everyday but not favored playmate. Although the granddaughter was forbidden to go to Jane's house, Jane would be called to the owner's to keep her company. As an adult, Jane had some fond memories of her playmate, but she also recalled feeling a certain uneasiness—at times even humiliation and awkwardness—in the association. For example, when Jane ate with her playmate at the big house, she was faced with the unfamiliar custom of being presented with a finger bowl at the end of a meal.

What gave an unreal quality to life on the farm was the fact that the big house was empty for many months of the year, during which Jane's mother would preside over the estate, changing from the subsidiary role she played when the owner was in residence. There were tennis courts and a swimming pool, and Jane's family, especially her mother, made use of them. There were constant reminders, however, that the mother's aspirations of ownership were pretense; her family could not become members of the country club.

The history of Jane's family was relevant. Her paternal grandparents, who had not married until their late thirties, came from somewhat different backgrounds. As was not unusual in rural Virginia at the time, the husband worked in agriculture, moving from job to job rather often, while the wife, better educated than her husband, kept house and tried to make a place for herself and her family wherever they found themselves. Jane's grandparents were never hard-pressed to provide for their three children—two sons and a daughter. One son, who seemed to have been rather undependable, died young, but the only daughter gratified her mother's ambition by marrying well and then distancing herself somewhat from the family. The third child, Jane's father, became an agricultural worker, as was his father. During his developmental years, he competed with his sister, who was several years his senior, and always resented her, although Jane was later named after her. It seems likely that his unending and mostly conscious resentment and ambivalence toward his sister, and probably also his hatred toward his mother, were transferred to his daughter.

When the grandfather fell on hard times, he resorted to managing other people's property. Jane's father was 5 when the family moved to the estate that he would later manage after his father's death. He married a girl of 17 when he was in his late twenties and soon had 2 daughters and a son. When his father died, he moved his mother out of the parents' home and moved his own family in. His mother nevertheless was housed on the farm until she was overtaken by a "brain syndrome" (probably Alzheimer's disease) and was admitted to the state hospital, where she subsequently died before Jane reached puberty.

Jane's parents lost their first child, a girl who had a congenitally malformed lung and probably a heart defect. It was never expected that she would live long, and Jane was born 15 months after her sister, who died in her mother's arms on the way to the hospital. Jane had accompanied her parents on this sad journey. I wondered whether the mother unconsciously blamed Jane for the death because Jane required attention that might have gone to her ailing sister. Their pediatrician had outlined a rigid 4-hour feeding schedule for Jane, but according to the family story, her mother did not have enough milk, possibly owing to a breast infection, and gave up trying to nurse the baby after several months. Jane cried a lot, apparently without cause, and the family joked about how red she got around the eyebrows when she cried. It was said that the father once whacked her "to give her something to cry about," but she cried all the harder.

When Jane began to crawl she would go down stairs headfirst, and her caretakers did not try to show her a better way. On one of her precarious slides down the stairs, she bumped into a landing and broke a jardiniere that was highly prized by her mother, who often spoke later of how angry she had been over its destruction. It was unclear what symbolic meaning the jardiniere held; it is possible that it represented the frail child she had lost. Jane had a brother 4 years her junior whose emotional problems as a teenager caused the family to consult a psychiatrist. He was not schizophrenic—there is no schizophrenia in the family history—but occasionally Jane's father would say she reminded him of his "crazy" mother—the woman who had become senile and died in the state hospital.

One of Jane's childhood memories was of her mother resting in her bedroom because she had German measles. Jane realized that she had retained this memory because it showed her mother to be vulnerable. Even as a child Jane saw her mother as thoughtless and had begun having reservations about her judgment. During Jane's analysis I attributed her mother's inability to care adequately for her second child to her youth and unreadiness for children, the likelihood that she herself had less than adequate mothering from her mother (reportedly an intellectual), and her grieving over the loss of her first child.

Jane's father had become tubercular as an adolescent, and fearing that his life was in danger, he was sent away for 3 years to recuperate. He returned to the farm at 16 and remained healthy thereafter. Some years after his return, he became enamored with the pubescent girl who was to become his wife, and despite comments about robbing the cradle, he married her. She may have represented his lonely self in convalescent exile, or as the daughter of an educated woman, she may have been related to her husband's covert dependency on his own mother, whom he claimed to dislike. In many ways, Jane's parents reproduced the family pattern of her grandparents, with the mother making a social place for herself while her husband became engrossed in the management of the farm.

Jane had some good childhood memories, such as watching the trains go by, watching the animals in the fields, and playing among the flowers, but they were all shadowed by the secret she began sharing with her father. At a little older than 5, she found herself with her father in her parents' bedroom. They were both naked, and her father had an erection, which he explained as something that happened to boys when they were around girls. She felt no uneasiness at the time, but later she did. He had her touch and fondle his erect penis, and he kissed her genital area. No actual intercourse took place.

The incestuous relationship continued until Jane had her first menstrual period. Her mother was in the habit of expressing great excitement over any achievement of her child and celebrated her arrival at puberty. Soon thereafter her father came to her in her bedroom and kissed her breast so hard she screamed. He asked her if this act had not given her pleasure, but she cried "No" and wept. He never touched her sexually again. But for years when seated next to her father in their automobile, she would draw away from him, move as close as she could to the door on the passenger side, and refuse to talk to or look at him.

Jane did not know whether her mother was consciously aware of her father's sexual overtures. When she was in elementary school, she drew "dirty" pictures with a friend; they featured a woman bound, legs apart, surrounded by men with erections, who squirted semen (represented by a dotted line) into her vagina. She thought her mother knew about these pictures, and wondered why she never asked about them. Drawing later became a rather sublimating activity for Jane, whose childhood fantasy held that semen dripped from testicles and that erection of the penis occurred to get it out of the way. She seemed to confuse testicles with breasts.

As a teenager, influenced both consciously and unconsciously by her mother, Jane dreamed of growing up, making an advantageous marriage, and thus following in the footsteps of the farm's owner, who had met her wealthy husband while nursing him through an illness, living in luxury thereafter. Jane's mother encouraged her attempts at social climbing, but her daughter was not altogether successful in establishing herself in the set of the socially prominent. She was sent to a college patronized by girls of wealth, but she found herself waiting on tables there and was deeply resentful at having to work for financial reasons. Humiliated, she felt silent rage. At the start of her senior year she found herself going into the chapel, sitting on a stiff chair next to unlit candles, trying to talk to God, and feeling an aching emptiness.

When people began noticing her increasing aggressiveness, irritability, and brooding unhappiness, she was sent to the school psychiatrist, who gave her medication. She had somehow been told that the psychiatrist had large genitals, and tried to perceive their outline as she sat before him. I suspect that in her transference he represented her father, whose large genitals she had seen when they swam together naked before she entered puberty.

The psychiatrist did not investigate the transference, and her life began to be utterly chaotic. Her college room was a jumble of trash and books, and she spent most of her day masturbating and dreaming of drowning in oatmeal, something that reflected feeding experiences of her infancy. She started to hallucinate, and when her "acute schizophrenia," as the psychiatrist called it, became too much for him to handle, she was sent to the hospital.

THE TREATMENT

An Overview

Jane's treatment commenced in early March 1964 and terminated at the end of March 1970. She was admitted to the hospital 6 times during the first 16 months of treatment, initially for 2 months and later for intervals of from 7 to 10 days. A psychiatric resident was assigned to her during her periods of hospitalization; otherwise, she came to the hospital as a day patient. I saw her 4 times a week in my office, which was in the building where she was hospitalized; on a few occasions, when she was violent, we met in her hospital room.

When she became my patient, she had 6 months of college to complete in order to graduate. Because graduation was crucial for her self-esteem, she returned to school after 9 months of therapeutic work. During her final 6 months of college we continued working together; she returned each week to her family's home, which was not far from my office, and saw me twice on each visit, once during the afternoon and again on the following morning. We resumed the four-times-a-week schedule after she graduated. We worked face-to-face during the first year and a half; in early September of 1965 she began using the couch. The analysis ended 6 years and 1 month after our initial meeting. She was given no medication for her mental condition. For 18 years thereafter I was able to follow her progress; I have heard only occasional and indirect news about her since.

In describing this case I use as few theoretical and technical terms as possible. Jane's treatment was unlike that of Attis inasmuch as she was seen 4 times a week and eventually reached a classic psychoanalytic position.

The First Year and a Half

I first saw Jane on a beautiful day in early spring. She was a lovely young woman dressed like a typical college student; as she accompanied me to my office she walked with catlike steps against the wall, as though she were part of it. I did not know her story when we settled down in my office, and she gave no cohesive account of herself except to say that she had no identity and felt empty. Most of the time she lived in a dream-like, confused state in which light and color appeared in bright and wavy patterns.

We had four diagnostic interviews. I tended to agree with the diagnosis of her college psychiatrist, whom I knew to be a competent phenomenological diagnostician. I avoid lengthy diagnostic workups because if I were to refuse to take the patient, the possibility of his or her developing a complicated transference reaction to me would present problems not only for the patient but also for the therapist undertaking the case.

When I agreed to take Jane as a patient she found this satisfactory if "I never asked questions about sex." I explained that I would work with her only if she felt free to tell me anything—whatever and whenever it came into her mind—and also to speak about whatever physical sensations she might experience. I explained that my way of working was for both patient and analyst to be curious about the meaning of the former's thoughts, behavior, and bodily sensations. An understanding of these meanings might acquaint the patient with new ways of dealing with the self and the environment, and the new ways might provide comfort.

Jane agreed to be my patient and enter the hospital. Much later, she told me how much relief she had felt when I took her mental condition seriously and recommended the hospitalization. I soon learned that the quiet kitten could suddenly turn into a bloodthirsty tiger: she did physical harm to herself and others, hitting her nurses with a chair and breaking windows with it, and hitting herself on the head. Her psychiatric resident had to take appropriate measures, with the help of the nurses, to protect her and others.

I slowly realized that she lived in a terrifying inner world crowded with fragmented images of threatening animals—bulls or wolves, body parts such as eyes, faces, detached penises or nipples—and violent acts of mutilation and burning. For example, a fiery, diabolical face belonged to her father (Figure 14–1). A bull was also her father having intercourse with her, which she both desired and dreaded. Her disturbance seemed more marked when she related to me and to those nurses to whom she felt close. It was in intimate relationships that the greatest degree of disorganization in the personal realm appeared. Well into the third year of treatment, her hands were usually clenched. This reminded me of the way babies keep their hands in little fists.

Figure 14–1

Although splitting of self- and object images was evident even during the initial phase of treatment, it was not highly structured but appeared with quick fluctuations between "bad" and "good" images. She classified animate and inanimate objects alike as either benign or aggressive. She felt as though her world was full of poltergeists; inanimate objects were moved by mysterious, unseen powers. At first she demonstrated a fused identification with her "good" and "bad" fragmented object images rather than an organized, stable splitting of differentiated self- and object images. She behaved like the bloody bull but also like the purring kitten.

In her room and in occupational therapy she drew hundreds of pictures of frightened faces, detached penises, and sickly, wasted bodies (Figures 14–2 through 14–4). For a long time she made a practice of bringing them to therapy and trying to display them, offering associations that were very seldom sensible and often loose. I neither encouraged nor forbade this and was in fact fascinated by her productions, as she may have

Figure 14–2

Figure 14–3

surmised. As time went on, she made associations indicating that the drawings represented aspects of her childhood environment, among other things. Gradually I learned of the ailing sister who had died in infancy and with whom she was identifying through the wasted bodies of her fantasy. I learned that just before she exhibited acute schizophrenia, she had been fascinated by a weeping mulberry tree near her school; this obsession apparently represented an effort to control her disorganization by externalizing her developing psychotic self saturated with depressive (weeping) "bad" affects (Figure 14–5). I suspected that the tree also stood for the depressed and grieving young mother with whom she identified. It should be noted that her drawing of the tree, more realistic than the drawings she drew in the hospital, was made just before her schizophrenia became acute. The later pictures, however real they were to her, elicited affects of terror, sadness, and helplessness. She was afraid to take them back to her room or to her parents' house and asked me to keep them in my office. I told her that I would

Figure 14–4

keep them until our work enabled her to tolerate them, and she eventually took them back after working on the couch for a while. (After a year and a half together, she only infrequently showed me her drawings, but in the summer of 1969 she brought in drawings of herself and a boyfriend, male and female bodies done in considerable detail, indicating a close relationship. I felt that she offered them as evidence that she had changed.)

At the outset of our association she often found me very frightening and felt it necessary to protect herself from me. When somewhat organized, she would either attack me verbally or scoff at me, mocking the treatment process. At times she saw me as "good" and merged with me in a state of bliss, with a smile on her face that stayed as though painted on.

When planning to return to school, she made what I felt was a heroic effort to control her adult psychotic self. During her eighth month of treatment, her drawing altered, showing bright lights and organisms such as small plants; these gave way to

Figure 14—5

forests and then to fish that changed into monkeys. Then came dark, abstract drawings she claimed represented herself as a geisha girl; she could be a human girl but no more than a geisha (which she thought of as a prostitute). She had to hide this fact from others, concealing it in the abstract pictures. I verbalized for her the symbolic disclosure of her drawings, which indicated preparations to organize herself for the great effort to return to college without analyzing away how her father's incestuous advances had made her feel like a prostitute.

Introjective-projective relatedness was in full swing in the transference situation, coming into sharp focus when Jane returned to college after 9 months of treatment. She made a heroic effort to conceal her raging "craziness," and with the help of compassionate teachers, she did graduate, but not without difficulty. During this period I became aware of her need to use me as her auxiliary ego-superego. During our hours together she would ask me to look here and there, to move near or away from the light. She blinked her eyes as if they were photographic shutters. I did not follow her commands about posing for her but sat calmly and silently before her. One day, before returning to school, she showed me a snapshot of herself; this gave me a chance to tell her that I had been aware of her "taking my picture" as we worked together, and that it was not surprising that she wanted to reciprocate by showing me her picture. She understood and said that after taking my picture in a therapeutic hour she could return to school with the assurance that whenever she felt stress, she could go to a dark room and mentally develop the picture of me she had taken. This would let her sense my presence and use me as ego or superego and ease her anxiety. This process also defended against her aggression, and because she was not introjecting me but introjecting only my picture, I was safe from destruction by internalization.

When reviewing my notes on Jane's first year and a half of work, I realized that I could not fully recall the content of our exchange during that time. Most of the work was preverbal or nonverbal; there were many silent hours during which Jane fused with and/or introjected and projected my image. I could tell by her facial expression whether my representation was "good" or "bad." Sometimes she brought paper and scissors and cut a series of figures connected with one another. By emulating the crazy figures in the cartoons, I sensed that she was trying to form an identity, even if she had to settle for a caricature of one.

In our early years I did not perceive her as a sexually mature woman. I do not recall being bothered by negative and aggressive feelings toward her. There was, however, both open and indirect pressure on me to send her to the state hospital; the department head was not psychoanalytically inclined, and the hospital authorities disliked having a destructive patient like

Jane in their establishment. Because I was in psychoanalytic training at the time, I felt a conflict of loyalties but had opportunities and suitable targets to displace any anger I may have felt against Jane onto others. Having started in chaos, Jane's treatment continued in chaos, but I was able to provide her with a constant and stable object representation and a new object.

Jane slowly began to exhibit a more organized self when with me. She recalled temper tantrums in the years after her sister's death, during which her mother would laugh helplessly, unable to harness the child's rage. Jane even recalled childhood dreams in which she had seen herself in the center of a circle of chairs, every one empty except for the one in which her mother sat laughing while her child made convulsive gestures. These dreams reflected her actual experience with her mother, who had been helpless with her dying (convulsing) child. The convulsing girl represented the infantile psychotic self full of "bad" affects.

Starting to Use the Couch

After graduating from college, Jane lived at home, following her mother around like a shadow. The family seriously considered sending her to the state hospital; talk of this reminded her of her "crazy grandmother," who had been sent to the hospital to die, as Jane saw it. She was panic-stricken. I told her that she had had temper tantrums for 18 months in my office, and I had not laughed at her, but had instead tried to take them seriously as expressions of her tension and frustration. I also reminded her that she had once fantasized that I kept my couch for "better" patients but that I was willing to have her use it in the hope of giving more structure to therapy hours. Toward the close of her analysis, she confided that for over a month she had seen only two choices—go to the state hospital and experience a "crazy death," or undergo psychoanalysis—and had been terrified at the thought of either alternative. Although she began analysis on this basis, she worked at it with feverish zest, as though her life depended on it—as in truth it did.

She lay on the couch for the first time in early September of 1965 and offered this dream:

I went to the bathroom. There was a toilet for children and one for the big people. First I sat on the one for children, but I couldn't move my bowels. Then I sat on the one for adults, which was wrapped in cellophane as though it had not been used. But in my dream I had seen someone getting up from there, so apparently it had been used. Anyhow, I sat on the john for the big people.

I thought that, among other things, this dream disclosed her perception that the couch was for "better" (big) people; its main association came out in the course of analysis as she tried to "move her bowels" emotionally but defended against doing so. At times, "bad" self- and object images with their associated "bad" affects came out as a diarrheal stool that flooded her and made her fear that I might also be destroyed by flooding. It should be recalled that her sister had died when Jane was an anal child. It was significant that as time went on, she adopted the habit of spending 15 to 30 minutes in the restroom after each therapeutic session. I became aware of this later because the restroom was also used by the secretarial staff, and when Jane preempted its use for long intervals, the staff complained bitterly to the hospital administrator. He sent me an ultimatum about my patient's use of the facilities, but I declined to interfere. The administrator then wrote a letter to Jane on behalf of the hospital employees, limiting her use of the restroom. She brought the issue to her therapeutic sessions and was interested in my firmness in adhering to the analytic position in the face of such annoyance and in my continued curiosity about the meaning of all this commotion. The incident allowed her to see me more as a new object—a real person able to stay calm, to be curious, and to offer clarifications while refusing to manage her use of the bathroom.

Jane reacted to the couch with increased helplessness. Although at the time she was experiencing a break with reality, she was able to observe along with me, to some extent, the course and meaning of her irrational attitudes and behavior. For example, in her attempt to adjust to her first day on the couch, she looked intently at the ceiling and saw blood dripping from the perforations in the ceiling tiles. Because she had remarked earlier in the hour that she had just commenced her menstrual period, I was able to link her weird perception with this physical event. While reading one of Giovacchini's publications (1969), I realized that I had made what he called a *linking interpretation* (see Chapter 13). After this "interpretation," Jane was able to tell me about tensions she experienced in every body orifice. She had already referred to the rectal orifice in the toilet dream connected with her new experience on the couch. I identified the tension with her wish and fear that she and I might merge by flowing into one another's body through body openings.

During her first few months on the couch, she continued to see me as godlike and omnipotent. She felt that she was nailed onto the couch and floated in space on it. I was sometimes a "bad god" or a terrible Turk, and she had to kill me; she dreamed of a penis being torn to pieces—she expected me to attack her. She dreamed that her "penis"—a flesh-colored candle with which she habitually masturbated—was disintegrating. Then she would project the penises on the ceiling and see bits of macaroni ooze out of the holes in the ceiling tile. She had not yet begun to speak of incestuous activity with her father in an organized fashion. I knew little about this, but I sensed that I, as a terrible Turk, might be her father. What interested me was that she had fused with the "bad" father representation—owning a penis (the candle)—and that when her aggression was directed toward the father/analyst, not only his but also her penis disintegrated.

A month after she began using the couch, her childhood playmate, the daughter of the owner of her family's home, was crippled for life in an automobile accident. In a sense, this demonstrated to Jane the power of her aggression, and she internalized her as a representative of the crippled sister who had died in infancy. During her hours on the couch, Jane behaved symbolically as though being physically tortured and breathed as though strangling with asthma. I continued to link her behavior with the accident that had befallen her friend in the external world, although I felt that dealing with the couch and the accident together might be too much for her. I felt guilty about having put her on the couch; however, I soon realized that I might be experiencing the guilt her mother felt over the death of her first child and the consequent neglect of her second. This understanding made it possible for me to remain in the therapeutic position.

Jane was very much affected by the accident and experienced flooding on the couch with unnamable affects, which I tolerated. She wanted to leave home, but I said that in reality her "bad" feelings would not cripple me or her family, who continued living on the farm. I knew she would not survive living in an apartment by herself. She clowned in the transference situation, and at home, too, in the hope of being so entertaining that her mother/analyst would not let her leave.

One day she spontaneously asked her father about the particulars of her sister's death. She then reported that the baby had died in the arms of her mother, who had cried out, "I'm afraid she's gone!" After telling me this, Jane asked me to put her in the quiet room of the psychiatric ward and give her some clay. I suggested that her grief-stricken mother might have been unable to care for her and had not cleaned up her feces (clay), whereupon Jane turned on me, screaming, "I hate you!" Thus, in her own way she confirmed my interpretation, reacting toward me as toward the uncaring mother. In her experience, instead of allowing her to reenact her childhood inner world with me, I had given her a "cold" interpretation.

During her second month on the couch, I noticed that she was starting to use more effective splitting of self- and object images and representations. The first indication was an increase of references to the head nurse of her ward. (She was still a day patient when she first started using the couch.) She treated me as though I were split; my "good" and "bad" selves now were split between me and the head nurse. At the same time, further differentiation of her self- and object images occurred, with self-images becoming "good" and omnipotent or "bad" and helpless according to the characteristics of the split object to which they related.

While living at home she began to date a young transsexual she had met in the hospital. He was prone to psychosis, and she undertook to be his savior, often fusing with him. She centered her activities outside her analysis and her home around his problems, though she still had her own gender confusion.

She soon declared that she had discharged herself as a day patient in the hospital and began to look for a job, motivated by a conscious desire to obtain employment for its own sake and the need to help her family meet the cost of her continued treatment. She took the transsexual with her when applying for work, and because his appearance invited rejection in most business offices, she underwent one humiliating rebuff after another. She dealt with these rejections either by putting herself above any job that might have been within reach or by declaring that she was completely helpless. I explained the reality of the situation, stressing the unfavorable impression her companion made. She then went job-hunting on her own and was hired to work in a gift shop. However practical and indirect my interference had been, it sent an internal message to her. It took me some time to realize that she now experienced me internally as the mother who was concerned with her social standing.

She then met a boy from a good family who she thought might fulfill her mother's wish for her to marry well. Joe was well-to-do and self-assured, had ancestral portraits in his home, and belonged to the country club. Jane became his companion whenever he asked, but he often humiliated her, for example, turning her down at the last minute for a country club date because she was an outsider. His snubs led to discussions of how she perceived life at her home and her childhood humiliation at the big house. She understood why she felt so bitter about waiting on tables at college while well-to-do girls did not need to work. Yet she was unable to gain insight into this situation, and although she realized that she was attracted to Joe in the hope of "making it" through marriage to wealth, she was angered by the need to do so and was otherwise emotionally blind to her relationship with him. She idealized Joe and perceived herself as being empty. She brought to our therapy hours questions such as "Who am I?" and "Why is it important to be a virgin?" Concomitant emotional outbursts occurred.

Fusing with an object representation still continued. When her mother had a minor ear operation, Jane complained of an earache. She dreamed of cutting and curling her hair so that no one could tell her from her mother. Even when she could differentiate me from her mother, she tried to make me a replica of her representation—someone who would limit her activities. She asked me to be her "commanding officer" in her mother's stead—to tell her when to walk, when to talk, and so on. I told her that the comments I had made about her transsexual friend had been made in the service of acquainting her with the reality of the business world, but that I had not given an order. I tried to help differentiate my self-representation from the one that belonged to her mother. Her superego forerunners were in operation; after calling her mother a bitch during an angry outburst in a therapy hour, she bit her tongue. Her work made her feel humiliated because she felt herself to be above it, and her first job lasted only 2 months.

The head nurse, to whom Jane had been attached, resigned in December 1965. Jane had stopped visiting her once she ceased being a day patient, but she had kept up with her activities through a hospital acquaintance, and her departure filled our hours with crying spells. Jane returned to her mission to save the transsexual. In mid-January she screamed at me, "Why are you letting me masturbate?" She was afraid that her use of the candle was altering her labia. She brought to one session a red velvet handkerchief she had made, and I interpreted that the red velvet was her vagina that her father had touched and declared as soft as velvet. She spoke of recently seeing that her father was reading *Lolita*, and she turned her face toward me to see if I was also reading a book (obviously *Lolita*). She had not read it but thought that its heroine might be disposed to seducing older men. The notion that she might have played a part in the interaction between her father and herself lasted only fleetingly, and she continued to see herself as helpless against her father's approaches. Because of her experiences with him, she felt that she was not a virgin, although they had not had sexual intercourse.

A Physical Attack on the Analyst

While revisiting her incestuous childhood activities in my office, at home she angered her father to the point that he told her to get out of the house and get a job. She then saw him as Hitler and projected his image onto me. (Jane is not Jewish; I have noted [Volkan 1993d] how Hitler and Nazism have become universal symbols, at least in the unconscious of those in the Western world.) She became like a wild animal during her therapy hours and one day rose from the couch and tried to kick me and scratch my face. I protected myself and told her to stop. As she continued to attack me, I had to kick her away, and she fell on the floor, where she remained. When I caught my breath, I told her calmly that it would be good for both of us if she resumed her usual place on the couch. When she complied, I told her I had to stay calm to hear what she was saying and doing and to reflect on the meaning of her behavior. I told her that by her actions she was remembering what had happened with her father, and that she had wanted to be close to him but at the same time feared it. She had the same ambivalence about touching me, so that when she did touch me, it was in the form of an attack to overcome her fear and at the same time to conceal her wish. By now I knew that although her incestuous father frightened her, he was, in fact, a more stable and caring parent figure for her than her mother.

Attis also had attacked me before lapsing into temporary catatonia. I have described being attacked by yet another psychotic patient (Joseph) and the ideational and verbal understanding of infantile rage (and the defenses against it) that such patients exhibit (Volkan 1976). When a patient uses splitting excessively, physical attack on the therapist represents on one level the patient's attempt to bring together in action previously split opposing representations. Such aggressive contact is not, however, enough to work through the object-relations conflict or to achieve effective mending. It does not represent a true crucial juncture experience (Volkan 1993b). It is necessary to understand and verbalize the aggressive action and to add it to the routine analytic process.

Recalling and Reenacting the Incestuous Activities

After this incident, Jane returned to excessive masturbation, breaking her recent abstinence. The result was bloody; she would rub against tree trunks and bleed profusely. She recalled the story of a prisoner (herself) who had been in prison so long that he would go to bed with the picture of a naked girl—and was unable to have intercourse with real girls when released. Perhaps her childhood relationship with a depressed mother and an incestuous father would preclude normal sexual activity. When she gained more insight about this, she gave up rubbing against trees and went back to her candle. She reported masturbating fantasies filled with adults, children, and animals of both sexes performing sexual acts on each other and dreams of wars associated with rape. When sufficiently organized, she offered recollections of her childhood and present environment. For example, her parents and her brother had gone about the house naked, and her privacy had been invaded. She continued to have one of her recurring dreams in which, naked or half naked, she was held down by her father, gripped with paralysis. She offered to show me her breasts "so I could see how ugly they were," but I forbade this, saying that if she did, it would compromise my therapeutic position. I reminded her that at times she had felt nailed to the couch, and encouraged her to speak of her impulses and wishes instead, and she gave up the threat of opening her blouse and exposing her bosom.

At first I had a fantasy that Jane was a kitten, and cats were often mentioned during her treatment. Her cat at home—Miss Kitty—represented her symbiotic tie to her mother, and Jane used it as she might use a transitional object. Any attempt to move away from symbiotic relatedness to her mother made

Jane afraid that Miss Kitty would die. Her attempts at separateness and the thought of her surviving without her mother made her anxious.

That spring Jane secretly took and passed a typing test after I had suggested that she might be afraid to get a job and had been afraid to graduate because they meant separation from her mother. This induced a great deal of anxiety, and her search for the "good" mother, previously represented by the head nurse, intensified. Once again I became "all bad," and she consulted a "real physician" for a physical checkup. She dreamed that a house she was living in caught fire, and that she became anxiously preoccupied with deciding which treasures to rescue. The idea of physical separation from her mother meant intrapsychic separation from her mother's representation.

The couch became a swimming pool. On one level she fused with me in my "womb"; on another, the swimming pool had a progressive aspect. She had related to her father in the swimming pool in which they often swam naked, and the progressive move away from symbiotic relatedness to her mother also frightened her. My remarks about her dilemma ushered in further therapeutic regression and more total fusion with her mother/analyst's representation. According to Jane, her breasts felt as though she were about to nurse a baby, and her abdomen felt numb to the touch and had no boundaries. Fused with her mother, she herself feared death. I believe she was recapturing unconscious murderous wishes emanating from her mother very early in their interaction. She began to have oatmeal for breakfast, recalling dreams of choking on it. In a way, she was testing to see if she would be killed; at the same time, by feeding herself, she was developing a new ego function. Eating oatmeal had regressive and progressive aspects—the former when it represented her introjection of a "bad" mother, and the latter when it involved her new ability to feed herself.

While lying on the couch she often examined her hands, wondering if they were indeed hers and putting them in her mouth. I recalled Hoffer's (1949) paper "Mouth, Hand and Ego Integration." At home she stuck a pencil into one of her hands and felt relief when the consequent pain demonstrated that the hand did indeed belong to her.

Through these experiences she could, to a degree, retain an observing ego and respond to my curiosity about them. When she emerged from her regression, she felt that she was experiencing things for the first time. I felt that she was moving toward the formation of a borderline personality organization and slowly modifying and/or giving up her adult psychotic self. The head nurse continued to be "good," while her mother became the object most hated. Crystallized splitting was becoming obvious. At times, from the couch, she would scream like a wild animal at the "bad" mother/analyst.

Her relationship with her transsexual friend faded, and he moved away. Meanwhile, Jane secured a job in a business office. Defensively, she saw herself as omnipotent and superior to her fellow workers, and I wondered to myself how long she could keep a job. She let Joe kiss her vagina and touched his penis. In her next session she was flooded with anxiety and memories of her childhood experiences with her father. She feared being hurt by a large penis and felt numb between her legs as though there were nothing there. These preoccupations were transferred to her psychoanalytic hours. Her infantile curiosity increased; she wanted me to kiss her like a lover and teach her sexual behavior. But she was enraged when Joe ejaculated into her hand, and lapsed into a paranoid state, becoming acutely psychotic. In my office she would turn purple with fury. She protected us both by placing a cup of water next to the couch, symbolically putting out the fire of her anger. She became so frightened by my letter opener, which is in the shape of a Turkish sword, that once she could not continue her session. I told her it was her decision whether to tolerate the letter opener or remove it from its customary place. At her request I put it out of sight, and she continued our session. She did not object, however, when I eventually returned it to my desk.

I was pleased to learn that at such a highly critical point in her analysis she was offered a secretarial job in the office of a surgeon in our hospital. I sensed that she was now able to bring her commotions into analysis while at the same time being fairly comfortable in her daily life. The power she felt was condensed in an infantile wish to have her own powerful penis, and she dreamed of making one for herself out of a bottle. This notion was punctured, however, when her father asked if she had ever told her mother about their secret; when she said she had not, she decided that he would kill her to keep their secret. When her real father became "bad" in her eyes, I became "good"—a sponsor like Higgins in Shaw's *Pygmalion*.

In the early summer of 1966, she continued to have dreams about her father's approach. For example, she recalled one in which

> I was sitting in my bedroom preparing to go to sleep. I was combing my hair. I only had on my panties; otherwise I was naked. There were mosquito bites or hives on my breasts. I heard my father coming in, and I got up and put a towel around myself. My father came in the room. He looked like he was sleep-walking. He also looked horrible. He was wearing his pajamas. He held me around my hips and laid me down on the bed. I wanted him to let me go, but he kept holding me very tightly. I wanted to scream for help, but no voice came out. I could only whisper. Then I made a desperate attempt to scratch out his eyes. I was able to put my fingers under his eyelids, but he stopped me.

Reporting this dream, she whispered "Help!" but then was able to scream for help. I listened to her in silence, moved by her tragedy. Mosquito bites and hives reminded her of the numb feeling she recently had when Joe had touched her breasts and genitals. She could not remember whether her father's kisses had left marks on her breasts, but she knew that they had marked her neck. Calming down, she managed to tell me more about the dream—that, when under her father, she had not felt like fighting him off but wanted to join him. Then she quickly changed the subject. A week later it was obvious that I was the mother who did not help. The circle-of-chairs dream came again, but this time it was I rather than her mother who sat in one of the chairs.

Events in the Analyst's Life

Events that summer greatly influenced Jane's treatment. I told her that I planned a 3-week vacation in August, and the head nurse moved to a different city. Her response to such "abandonment" was to ask me silly questions so that she would have a memory of my voice during my absence. I told her that this recalled, in a sophisticated way, her preparation for my absence during our first year together.

She asked for medication, referring to it as spinach that would give her instant strength, as in the Popeye cartoons, but Jane later bravely suggested that drugs were only symbols and would not truly be part of me. Her brother was then in therapy with a psychiatrist who held group sessions, half-psychiatric and half-religious, in his home. Needing a substitute for me, she went to one of these meetings, which frightened her. In her mind I merged with the leader, and she saw all psychiatrists as dangerous. It was then, unfortunately, that we parted.

During my vacation, my two small children were in an automobile accident and I was called to the emergency room. I had not been informed of their condition until I arrived. It was a horrifying experience for me, though neither was critically injured. My daughter was treated by the surgeon for whom Jane worked, and my son was hospitalized with a broken leg. A few days afterward, while working on an emergency room report for her employer, Jane learned about the accident. Someone called her attention to a newspaper photo of the damaged car and a story about the accident that clearly indicated I had not been in the car when the crash occurred. When I returned to work, I was unaware that she knew what had happened to my children.

I found her extremely disorganized. She spoke openly of wanting to be in a womb, unborn. She was afraid of harming her brother, and I sensed that she was also reenacting the fantasy that she had killed her infant sister in a car. She said she was afraid of having children of her own lest she kill them. I assured her that I was comfortable enough to resume our work, but despite this, she managed to injure her leg slightly, and she consulted the surgeon who had treated my son's injury. She

came to her next session with her leg bandaged and associations that indicated feelings of guilt, because in her fantasy she
had caused the accident that my children were involved in. Her
leg injury allowed her to identify not only with the attacker but
also with the attacked.

Jane talked about bringing me peaches (good breasts) and
took some to my car in the parking lot but found it locked. This
greatly frustrated her, and she had a break with reality: the
parking lot pavement became as brittle as an eggshell, and she
hallucinated a huge insect devouring the world, the collapse of
the earth, and injury to her leg. I reminded her of her sister's
deformity and her own identification with the deformed child,
her own loss of good mothering, and other related issues. After
her sister died, her mother's breast (attention) was no longer
available to Jane. Thus, she felt a need to repeat her effort to
save the early-mother/analyst in order to repair her, to make her
well—and to receive care from her in turn. I doubted that she
heard my interpretation, so I changed my tactics and told her
she might be fearful because of my problems—that I might not
be a good analyst for her. I acknowledged feeling anxiety about
my children but assured her that they were no longer in danger
and that we had no choice but to work through the meaning of
the accident for both of us. I told her that I was sufficiently in
command of my feelings to listen to her, and I believe that it was
my calm manner of telling her this, rather than what I said, that
had a positive effect on her. As luck would have it, however,
another external event—a widely publicized earthquake in
Turkey—further taxed her ability to test reality. Not only was
she afraid of damaging the Turkish analyst, but she feared
having a shaky and undependable Turkish analyst resembling
her original undependable mother. Her fear that the earth
would collapse in the parking lot had come true! The only way
she could deal with all of this was to become deeply involved
with taking care of me (in fantasy) and her mother (in reality).
She made appointments for her mother to have a physical
checkup. I let things evolve because I could follow her therapeutic story and knew she would not respond to interpretations.

Toward the end of the summer she reported a dream in

which she was a salesgirl in a department store. The crowd waiting for attention was noisy, she reported, but then she began to stutter, and suddenly sat up on the couch and screamed "Shut up everybody!" I thought she was responding to an auditory hallucination—that she wanted to get rid of those who interfered with her efforts to repair a "good" mother–child representational unit. It seemed more important to me that she could now exhibit an ego function that made her cry "Enough is enough!"

Jane spent the fall of 1966 reorganizing herself at the level of a borderline personality. She began to heed my explanations of the interconnection between the external events of the past summer and her internal world and mine. She went to the medical library, hunting for pictures of cancerous breasts, which represented the infected and psychologically neglectful breasts of the mother of her infancy and her anxious analyst. As work on the cancerous breasts proceeded, she became once more involved with my representation, putting it into her introjective-projective cycle, now with improved ability to note this process. We were again back to the routine therapeutic track, and I felt that after both of us had tolerated the storm of the summer, she was getting ready to integrate our corresponding self-representations. As Jacobson (1964) stated, cathectic shifts and changes reflected in the mechanisms of introjection and projection are necessary and must occur until the child and/or regressed patient integrates self- and object representations and tolerates ambivalence.

Cosmic Laughter

Without conscious awareness that November 22 was the anniversary of John F. Kennedy's assassination, Jane announced, early in November, that her death would occur on that date. Kennedy had been assassinated in Jane's last year in college, after the onset of her acute schizophrenia. She had made an appointment with her college psychiatrist for November 22, 1963, but it was canceled because of the President's death. At the peak of her psychotic experience, she could not understand this and felt desperate and terrified.

I sensed that after the experience of the summer, and our ability to tolerate the crises, I had become an even firmer new object, and I wondered about the meaning of November 22; it might reflect both the fear that an internal father figure was dead and the wish that this were true. It might, on the other hand, reflect the death of her corresponding adult psychotic self. Beginning in November, she introjected and projected my representation in the therapeutic regression as a "good" or "bad" object, sometimes doing nothing else in a session. I was fragmented into various animals or little people. When I was projected outwardly, the animals or little people were on the floor next to the couch. When I was inside her, and "bad," she proposed writing to local radio stations asking for soothing music so that the "goodness" would combat the "badness." When November 22 came and we did not die, she acknowledged that it was the anniversary of Kennedy's death, and that what we had been doing was intrapsychic work and not something magical connected with a historic event. I was pleased with the therapeutic movement. It was then, however, that another event in the external world led her to experience what she called *cosmic laughter*.

I have examined Jane's cosmic laughter experience (Volkan 1975) in light of the Isakower phenomenon (Isakower 1938) and Lewin's dream screen (1948), both of which relate to derivatives of an infant's experience at the breast. Jane's experience with cosmic laughter was the result of an external event, but she was able to make it a turning point in her analysis. Ready or not, she began to examine the beginning of her infantile psychotic self.

I went away for a week in early December, in accordance with my announced plan. On my return I found her denying aspects of my absence and investing in the socially desirable Joe even more primitive idealization than before. Convinced that he would marry her, she was deeply shocked when in mid-December her mother told her of his marriage to another girl; she had no idea that he was planning anything of the kind, and the news gave her an inner hallucination of *cosmic laughter*. She managed to withdraw from the experience, only to have it develop fully as she lay on the couch the next day. I found it significant that she did not become fully disorganized at the moment she heard the news of the marriage, and that she had waited until the following day on the couch to respond to it. It was evident that she brought the event into the transference relationship and the analytic working through; her experience was in the service of observing, tolerating, and mastering this disappointment and what it represented at the deepest level. She began stuttering when she tried to tell me the news and shook her head in violent negation, as though she were using the first symbolic assertion (Spitz 1957, 1965) to arrest her overwhelming emotionality. She clenched her fists like a baby and tried to stop the shaking of her head by pressing it between her hands. Her body seemed in torment; she made crying sounds like an animal and no longer seemed human.

When she finally mobilized her early ferocious self- and object representations, she stopped herself by slapping her face and crying, "Shut up! Shut up!" It was interesting that she reported that part of her had been able to observe the experience—but what she observed was not the logical connection between her emotional storm and her rejection by Joe, or the rejection I had exemplified by my short leave from my office. She was experiencing herself at her mother's breast. I believe that what she observed was the symbolic representation of the earliest frustration during nursing as an infant—the sudden transformation of a "good" breast into a "bad" one, and that this was the earliest genetic (psychological) root of her cosmic laughter experience. She was revisiting the times when she had fused with her mother's breast and was filled with unbearable and unnamable "bad" affect; the fixation of this fused self-representation was her infantile psychotic core. Her experience of cosmic laughter on my couch was most dramatic.

On the following day she tried to explain what she had observed. The experience had been like a dream, but it was also real. It was difficult to follow her explanation, which had to be put in secondary process language. To clarify it she made a drawing (see Figure 14–6, a copy). (A) represents Jane as the observer and (C) the *cosmic plateau*, which she perceived as a puffy, oyster-colored cloud in which a window—(E)—appears. Over this window knelt an omnipotent person—(D)—mischievous and teasing, with whom, at times, Jane fused and became interchangeable. (B), a circle, also represented Jane made of a mouth (a *mouth-self*). During the experience, Jane had felt that the omnipotent person's relationship with her (the mouth-self) had ceased abruptly, and that when it ceased, the omnipotent person broke into cosmic laughter that echoed in Jane's mind long after it ceased. The past, the present, and the future converged in what was happening. To Jane the omnipotent person seemed to speak or laugh through other people at

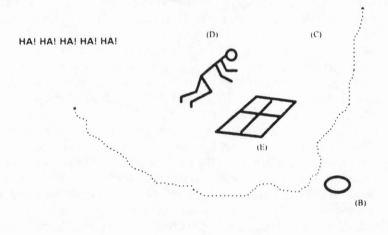

Figure 14–6   The cosmic laughter

times—through her analyst, for example. My representation was involved in this experience.

In telling about cosmic laughter, she recalled similar experiences in the first grade when the class performed rhythmic singing and she had swung abruptly from a happy mood into one of distress; another incident occurred while in church with her family. At the end of her therapy hour she remembered hearing of certain Indian tribes in which children were allowed to go hungry, given the breast briefly, and then deprived again in order to frustrate them and make certain that they would become fierce warriors.

As Jane and I talked about her experiences, we understood that the cosmic plateau (C) represented the mother's breast, (E) represented the nipple or the mother's face or eyes above the infant, and the circle (B) represented Jane's mouth-self. The omnipotent person (D) in all likelihood represented the omnipotent mother with whom the child sometimes fused. Her experience was related to her mother's nipple, the breast, and the mother—or at least the mother's reaction to nursing as revealed by her facial expression. The laughter came whenever the omnipotent person abruptly terminated the relationship, and the affective response was total humiliation.

Freud (1905) noted that the conditions for laughter depend on the rerouting of psychic energy previously employed in the cathexis of some paths so that the psychic energy can be freely discharged. Kris (1952) suggested that the word *suddenly* should be added to the formulation, explaining that the word was essential because it is the shock nature and abruptness of the discharge that is the specific precondition of laughter. Jane used the word *abruptly* in telling about her cosmic laughter experience and again in her associations.

It is quite possible that her mother may have laughed in an attempt to provide a symbolic and socially acceptable disguise for the sudden release of hostility associated with helplessness. I am certain that aspects of Jane's experience that she derived from the oral level were condensed with those from higher levels. The mother's laughter had been mentioned before in

connection with the circle-of-chairs dreams; it represented discharge of the helpless hostility that led her to leave Jane (during
her anal and phallic stages) to deal with her temper tantrums by
herself. Jane once told me that her mother seemed to be
ashamed of breast-feeding and recalled that when her brother
was born, her mother would take him into a room away from
everybody else to feed him. As for the mother's behavior with
baby Jane, I saw the possibility that because of her helpless
hostility and grief, as well as because of the reported infection of
the breast, she had been aggressive in feeding Jane, abruptly
removing her breast (and probably the bottle) from Jane's
mouth and then starting the feeding again.

It was impossible for Jane to organize the development of a
psychic structure with a solid child–mother core that was
infused with "good" affects and was stable. Had such an
organization existed, the core (fused) self-representation would
have been able to absorb and tame "bad" affect and eventually
evolve. I formulated that her psychic core instead remained
infused with "bad" affects and so was fixated, forming an
infantile psychotic self. After the difficulties of the previous
summer, however, we could now absorb and tame the "bad"
affect, so Jane allowed herself—perhaps prematurely, owing to
Joe's abrupt marriage—to have the traumatic nursing experiences in my office, sometimes substituting me for the entity (D).
This type of regression opened the progressive channels of the
original developmental path.

Because I stayed calm and maintained an analytic attitude,
her cosmic laughter experience on the couch was not a mere
reenactment of an event from the past. Much therapeutic work
had already taken place, and Jane surrendered her adult psychotic self and progressed to the level of borderline personality
organization. By identifying with the analytical attitude, being
curious, and finding with me meanings for her experience, her
ego was now able to tolerate the tensions and emotions associated with the experience. Reestablishment of a relationship to a
"different" nursing mother in the transference thus had a
corrective influence and allowed her to begin essential changes
in solidifying the previously fragile infantile core.

Moving out

At the beginning of the new year, 1967, the insurance Jane had taken out through her employment took effect, and some of her expenses in analysis were thereby covered. She could afford to pay the remainder herself, which was psychologically important because it made her financially responsible for her analysis and removed the image of parental financial support from our relationship.

Her parents went to a party given by Joe and met his new wife, reporting that they had a wonderful time. Jane thought this very insensitive of her mother, who knew of her hurt and disappointment over Joe's marriage. This reaction helped her to differentiate further between herself, her mother's representation, and the representation of her sensitive analyst. She dreamed of a woman (herself) who had an intestinal polyp and identified her mother as the polyp. She wanted more than ever to leave home and had a sense of being born again—a new core of the self.

I think Jane had many psychodynamic qualities characteristic of the female transsexual (see Chapter 8). She fantasized that the possession of a penis would differentiate her from her mother, whose depression she wanted to relieve. On one level, Miss Kitty, who stood for her mother, also represented a penis. Her desire for a penis was also related to identifying with the father to relieve the symbiotic pull and at the same time to protect her from his sexual approaches. Any fantasy or action may have many meanings, but it is best for the analyst to follow the interpretation that is "hot" and fits well with the therapeutic process in which the patient is involved at the time. Her wish for and her attempt at intrapsychic separation from her mother was "hot," and her open desire to have a penis became stronger and stronger.

She dreamed of her brother's penis and of it detaching itself from her brother's body and lodging between her legs like a small pink pig. Wanting more and more to leave home, she manifested transient conversion symptoms on the couch, such as thinking that her legs were paralyzed. I interpreted the meaning of such conversion reactions as condensation of the wish to get away from her mother with the wish to stay with her. I suggested that after her cosmic laughter experience, she better understood her relationship with the early mother, and hence with the present mother.

During the third week of January she reported that she had begun cooking her own breakfast. This small gesture of individuation released in her what she called *freed resentment* against her mother, and she took pride in her accomplishment. Her attitude toward me was one of open friendliness. When she offered me a ticket for a concert, I thanked her for thinking of me but did not accept it. She speculated as to whether her manner with boys put them off. It was true that a number of medical students had tried to make friends with her during their rotation through the surgical department where she worked, only to be met with an abrupt arrogance. At the end of January, her frustration over not being able to allow herself to date led her to buy a new flesh-colored candle (penis) to use for masturbation.

Jane felt that I was "driving her crazy" in the transference situation and remained stubbornly silent during some of her therapy hours toward the end of January and the beginning of February. She then called me at home at one o'clock in the morning to drive *me* crazy, to which Searles's (1959) formulation concerning one person driving another crazy and Heath's (1991) idea of making the therapist depressed were appropriate. Upon waking me up, I told her that I wished I knew how to do psychoanalysis on the phone, but because I did not, we would continue discussing driving each other crazy in our sessions. Then I hung up, and she did not call again.

She was preoccupied with some moles on her body and a premonition that they indicated melanoma. She wanted to get rid of them and also the intestinal polyp in her dream. She wanted to kill Miss Kitty, the cat she felt was her "root" into her mother—both the symbiotic link and her penis. On the couch she had temper tantrums and kicked the walls, but she did not physically attack me. The prospect of moving into an apartment of her own filled her with fears of being raped or involved in a fire. I gave no advice as to when to move.

At her job, Jane was often intolerant and had no social contact with her fellow secretaries. I believe that only the gentleness and tolerance of the man she worked for, and his genuine desire to give her a chance, made it possible for her to be employed during this phase. In turn she experienced the concept of loyalty and was careful and adept in her secretarial skills. For many months she was also hypochondriacal, preoccupied with her moles and with pictures of cancerous breasts. She spoke of being threatened by persons identified only as "them" and was flooded with anxiety during her therapy hours. Sometimes she identified herself with Helen Keller and identified me with Annie Sullivan, Keller's teacher and savior.

In early April 1967 she had her moles (the "badness") surgically removed. During this same period, she received another letter from the hospital administrator asking that she refrain from locking herself in the washroom for long periods of time. She organized herself sufficiently to reply, explaining that the sessions with me were highly emotional, and that she needed considerable time in the washroom to compose herself and to bathe her eyes, red from weeping, before returning to work. His reply was an order prohibiting her from using the common washroom for her recovery, but she did not bother to reply and ignored the administrator thereafter.

Jane also had a dream around this time in which she killed her father (also the administrator) by rubbing his penis. After she reported this, she provided another dream, one in which she seemed to find—or at least to want to find—a more benign father figure. In this dream, she faced a king from whom she asked permission to grow up and be eligible for marriage. The king cited old law books that kept him from complying, but when Jane insisted that "You are the king—you can change the laws," the old law books disappeared. After describing the dream, Jane wept.

To make sure symbolically that her newborn core could survive intrapsychic separation from her mother, Jane had another physical checkup and soon found an apartment and left her parents' home. Her father asked who would share her bathroom. Because she would be preparing her own meals, she asked me for Turkish recipes ("good" food), but instead of obliging her, I continued to offer to listen and provide clarifications and interpretations.

Miss Kitty

The move into her own apartment ushered in another meaningful therapeutic regression for Jane. She began having experiences with my representation in order to solidify her new psychic core. This therapeutic regression was followed by progress; she symbolically cut off her symbiotic tie to her mother.

During the first months of living alone, she talked monotonously in our sessions. I felt so sleepy that I could hardly keep my eyes open. Then I realized she was singing "lullabies" to me—I represented the infant patient, and she a caring mother. At home she spent hours cooking pastries for me, and her behavior in our four-times-a-week sessions reminded me of that of a conscientious mother nursing her baby on a schedule. She expressed a wish that we live together. She read about Turks and my homeland and began taking a more direct interest in me as a person, although she still occasionally identified me with intruding and hostile mother-father images and fantasized my being a member in a gang of conspirators seeking to drive her crazy. I slowly became more and more separated from her archaic mother representation. In our conversations, amid emotionally weighted bits of material, she shyly slipped in other topics, such as a concern with Vietnam and the trouble in the Middle East, as though I were not to notice her adult interests. She also slowly formed friendships with other young people in the apartment complex where she lived and with her associates at work. As late as mid-summer, however, as my 2-week holiday approached, she continued to have stormy reactions, demonstrating elements of temporary fusion between us, as though this would prevent the impending separation.

She wanted to give me a cat; working through the meaning of this wish, we associated it with her symbiotic relatedness to her mother and the cat's representation of Jane's genital area, which she wanted me to stroke and pet. She kept cycling between wanting to be close to me and fearing contact, and between seeing me as closely resembling the representations of her early parents and seeing me as a different person. The affective reactions associated with the swings of this cycle were very strong at times. In the meantime, she made attempts to be more in touch with the real world, reading newspapers and dating different men.

Early in the fall of 1967 she acquired a new friend, Tom, 2 years her junior, whom she "stole" from the brother whose penis she had previously wanted to "steal." They became much involved sexually, but she would not allow him to have intercourse with her. Meanwhile, her repeating dreams underwent significant change; in the version formerly reported, her father attacked her while her mother looked on silently with no display of emotion. She now reported,

> My father was lying in bed and my mother was in the room also. She was not saying anything or doing anything. A little girl came in. I was there, too. I was afraid that my father would attack the little girl. I began acting mean to the little girl to make her get away from the room in order to save her.

She was learning about the defensive aspect of her own aggression. After reporting this dream, Jane energetically tried to separate herself physically from her mother's representation. She took Miss Kitty to her apartment and then to a veterinarian, claiming that the cat was sick. She persuaded the veterinarian to give Miss Kitty a hysterectomy (symbolically getting rid of her mother's womb), although she knew the operation endangered the animal. The cat died very soon after the operation. Thus, the symbolic connection between Jane and her mother was literally killed. During Miss Kitty's last days, she was, in

Jane's association, little more than breast and nipples. Jane drew a picture of Miss Kitty lying on her back, with nipples as prominent as they had been during a pregnancy, and Jane's associations centered on them. At night, she lay in bed with the lights off, nestling with her new boyfriend Tom, touching only from the waist up. Then Jane confused this intimacy with her early relationships with both parents. As her father's representation, Tom was a dangerous phallus, although Jane connected him mostly with her early mother transference, kissing his chest. In bed, she would briefly confuse him with her mother. She recalled having nightmares as a child, crying loudly for her mother on awakening, wanting her to come to comfort her. When her mother responded, however, instead of being comforted, Jane could not bring herself to be close to her, possibly fearing actual fusion with a "bad" mother. She also recalled her rage at seeing her brother being breast-fed.

The day after Miss Kitty died, Jane sadly asked me, "Did you know that part of me wanted Miss Kitty to die?" I said "Yes." She explained that fundamentally until now her relationships with others came through osmosis, and this was no longer satisfactory. *Osmosis* was her word for "fusion."

Working through the Trauma of Incest

At the end of the year Jane reported two dreams, the first of which involved "Someone—feeding me. I was given more than I could chew, and I was choking." In the second, she reported, "I was at a dentist's office and the dentist was looking at my mouth, possibly taking measurements of my teeth, and I noticed that his hands were missing."

She declared with pride that she could analyze the dreams herself, without my help. She first suggested that she was too active in her recent attempts to grow up, that she was flooding herself; it also represented the way she was choked with "bad" feelings of the nursing mother. She suggested that in the second dream, the dentist represented me, and that she had bitten off my hands in her anger. She also became cognizant of her oral-aggressive tendencies when she had an impulse to bite off Tom's nipples or the head of his penis.

On her own initiative she asked a gynecologist to give her birth-control pills and took her first pill. This preparation for further intimacy—intercourse with Tom—increased her recollections of the conflicted intimacies of her childhood. Her fear of devouring Tom's nipples and penis increased. She began having intercourse with Tom—the first in her life—when I was away for a few days on Christmas vacation. Tom helped her get a new cat, which she tucked between them in bed, providing further evidence that she was repeating intimacy with the early mother.

More change came in her repeating dream of her father's advances.

> I was at home and my father came up to me, held me in his arms, and started touching my genital area. Even in my dream, the thought occurred to me that this dream would be like the previous ones and that I would not be able to move away from my father. But the dream was different this time. My father left me and went to Becky [a friend who is the same age as Jane]. Becky looked grown-up in the dream as she is in present life. She seemed to enjoy my father's attention. I thought that my mother might stop my father's behavior, and I said to my mother, "Stop this! Stop this!" However, my mother did not. She said that it was all right and my father would cry about it later on.

This dream had been precipitated by a visit to her parents' home on the previous day. She had found her parents loud, superficial, and competitive, reminding her of the old relationships she had had with them. She felt sorry for her father, a weak, degraded man who could not help what he had done. Nevertheless, he had to be stopped, and because her mother could not stop him, Jane might as an adult.

She spoke at length of love for her parents and of her father being a weak but sensitive man who had nurtured her interest in music and art. In a flood of tears, she started to talk about losing her "craziness," but she kept searching in the transference for an approving mother and an assertive father. She wanted me to teach her to say no. Spitz's (1957, 1965) findings concerning identification with the frustrator applied here (see also Volkan 1982b). She teased me by saying she had thoughts of getting up and walking out and fantasized that I would say no and stop her. I reminded her of the dream in which she had been mean to the little girl in order to save her from her father, and of the one in which she asked her mother to stop her father. I suggested that she could say no effectively herself, that she did not have to tease anyone else to say no, and, furthermore, that no could be said without meanness.

The spring of 1968 marked the completion of 4 years of work with Jane, who likened her relationship with Tom to her past relationship with the head nurse. It was too intense and had to end so that she could really be able to love. She was unable to reach climax in intercourse and continued masturbating when she wanted an orgasm. She continued to have intercourse with Tom, however; by now he was living in her apartment, eating her food, and getting her help with his schoolwork. This relationship repeated aspects of her mother's relationship with her father, because it was her mother who helped her father write letters.

In one of Jane's fantasies, she was having intercourse with Tom outside, as they had often done in reality. When a man who looked like a bear appeared, she climbed into a tree to hide. The man killed Tom and came after her; he was the "wild father" she had longed for as well as feared. That night she had a dream:

> You [Dr. Volkan] and I were staying at a lodge. The weather was bad outside so we had to stay together. I was wearing only a bra and my panties. I started to take off my bra, and you told me I looked much better than you had thought I would look. But you did not want me to take off my bra. I understood that you were not going to make love to me. Then your clothes disappeared. You were naked and had a very small penis.

We understood the dream to indicate her wish to find in me a father who could be excused, by reason of necessity, for being with her in a sexual setting. Moreover, she was in search of a father who at the appropriate time would stop them both from behaving sexually toward each other. Reversing her unacceptable wish for her father's love, however, she gave me only a small, insignificant penis. After all, she felt anger toward all men for what her father had done to her. She took her new cat—a male—to be castrated and was highly emotional, negativistic, and "bitchy" in her sessions.

Another External Event

In mid-spring, at the start of Jane's fifth year of work with me, I had a stone removed from a salivary gland and was out of the office for about 2 weeks. When I resumed our work I had a bandage on the right side of my neck. Although I told her that I had had a surgical procedure but was now all right and could give full attention to our work, she started another regression-progression loop; at first she was anxious about my having cancer and dying, and then she began to use splitting, making Tom a "good" object while I was all "bad." However, when Tom appeared at a concert inappropriately dressed, humiliating her, he became "bad" and I became "good."

Slowly regression set in. She would lie motionless on the couch, and when I asked what was going on she did not answer. One day she brought me two drawings (Figures 14–7 and 14–8) and said, "You have been wondering what has been happening to me. After I perceived you with an incurable disease, I had to go back to my plugging stage." She spoke of being "plugged into" another person in order to receive energy; an analyst would call this introjection and identification. The drawings showed her plugged into an energy source; the figures represented her as an angry, deprived, undeveloped oral baby at the analyst's breast. The baby's mouth was an electrical receptacle. "Now I know that you just had surgery but are still the same, I want my batteries charged by you now," she said.

While she had first feared a repetition of the nursing experience with a nonnurturing mother (an analyst with cancer), she now could get her batteries charged by a "good"

Figure 14–7

(healthy) analyst. She asked, "What is a woman?" and said that she wanted to experience womanness and freedom. She spoke of wanting a vacation in Europe but expressed fear of being raped there or of having her craziness return. One day, she unconsciously made unintelligible sounds on the couch that I realized represented the sounds of an airplane. In a sense, she first went to Europe on the couch!

The Black Penis

The idea of separating from her mother's representation and the notion of vacationing in Europe did nothing to quench her desire for a penis. She began fantasizing having a black one, especially for intercourse with Tom. She had become able to reach orgasm in intercourse but only after resorting to this fantasy—she was reaching orgasm with her own penis rather

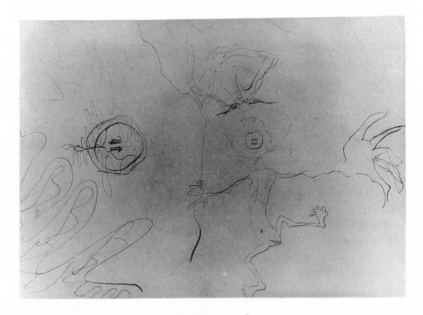

Figure 14–8

than Tom's. Her fantasy slowly changed to envisioning inter-course with an unknown black man. Before we could analyze the meaning of this fantasy, she took a 7-week summer break in her analysis, which postponed any such consideration. She and Tom had a satisfactory trip to Europe; she had enjoyed seeing new places and had used her relationship with Tom to exercise ambivalent relatedness. Tom had psoriasis, which later spread to his penis, and while she wondered whether her vaginal discharges were accountable, she believed that, in the long run, she would outstrip him in emotional development.

On the couch, her preoccupation with the black penis and/or a black man's penis returned. The black penis was everywhere—between the two of us, between her and Tom, between her and her mother. I slowly realized that she had created it and was playing with it. It was my work with her that initially taught me about what I later called *transitional fanta-sies* (Greer and Volkan 1991, Volkan 1973), which have a function similar to that of the transitional object (Winnicott

1953) of a normally developing infant. It is important to understand the function of this occurrence and to focus on it first rather than considering the content of such fantasies. Interpretation of the content comes later. When the patient has played with his transitional fantasy long enough without interference from the analyst, it relates more and more to the analyst's representation in the transference and ushers in more psychic development and more reality testing (Greenacre 1970, Greer and Volkan 1991, Modell 1970, Toplin 1972, Volkan 1973, 1976).

Gradually the black penis was involved in more formal fantasies, one of which related to the book *Exodus*, about Ben Gurion's establishment of a new Jewish nation. Jane was interested in the story of his early attachment to a gentile woman with whom he had been traveling. Their car broke down, which forced them to seek shelter in a cave. Her fantasy took over at this point: Ben Gurion turned into a black man with his penis occasionally out, and from time to time he played with Jane's nipples or clitoris; sometimes she confused the penis and the clitoris. She played with his penis and became excited until the images blurred, and she would fall asleep. The black penis she had first claimed for herself finally evolved to become a man's—a more appropriate perception. I interpreted its function, telling her that it was a new version—a mental one—of the function that Miss Kitty had provided: through its use she was learning to link herself to and unlink herself from others.

I went on later to analyze the function and the content of her fantasy. Ben Gurion represented me; she knew I was not Jewish, but my foreign origin made me similarly alien to her. She was the gentile woman in whom Ben Gurion had been interested, and a breakdown (in the dream, of a car) had regressed us into a cave (the mother's womb). She could get out of this regression and find reality by creating a transitional object (fantasy of the black penis) and by playing with it like a child, putting it between her mother and the external world in order to illuminate that world.

As this process evolved, the content of the black penis fantasy included more application of transference—it belonged to Othello. She had seen the film version of *Exodus*, which opens with an aerial view of my homeland, Cyprus, where Jews had gathered before sailing to Israel. Othello's Tower, which is in Cyprus, was shown, and I became the black Othello of Cyprus, while she became my Desdemona, whom I might love but whom I might also kill. She then saw me as the father of her childhood, exciting and sometimes helpful, but extremely dangerous, damaging, and murderous to her soul. When she thought of me as being like her incestuous father, she turned the black penis into a transitional object (and fetish) under her absolute control (as is a child's transitional object), and she would confuse it with her clitoris. She spent much time checking her genitals in a mirror to see if she actually had a penis.

A Loaded Gun

Progress became evident in Jane's analysis. One day she asked, "What happens to a young girl who is growing up?" The question was precipitated by the rape of a hospital employee, whom Jane identified with. But she answered her own question: She, a growing girl, would after all face the same fate she had experienced as a child. The father/analyst would rape her and her mind, and in the transference I became a black rapist. Settling down on the couch one day, she put her purse on her chest and told me that it contained a loaded gun to be used against the black rapist/analyst. I said one anxious person in the room was enough, and that I would be unable to do analytic work with her if I were anxious. I rose from my chair, opened my office door, and asked her to get rid of the gun and come back for analytic work. She seemed to be shocked at this but silently rose and left the room. I left the door open, and she came back 5 minutes before her time was over, without her gun, and lay on the couch. There was just enough time left for her to call me a bastard and other abusive names. I told her that she was putting her feelings into words, and that it was an expected and preferable way of understanding the meaning of the loaded gun.

I reinterpreted the meaning of her creation of the black penis and its evolution.

She soon underwent a drastic change, and I became the normal oedipal father she never had. She came to sessions with her hair hanging free in a way that greatly altered her appearance, and I perceived her as beautiful. Her hair had previously been tightly tied back from her face. She expressed open curiosity about me through associations and dreams. Tom's psoriasis had worsened, and she accepted a date with a doctor from Iran, which, she explained, is next to Turkey.

China Doll

In February 1969, I received a new chair for my office, and its color triggered memories of Jane's childhood. She remembered a doll of her mother's that had a china head, plastic hands, and a cloth body. We wondered if it had originally belonged to Jane's dead sister. When Jane was little it had been shown to her with the admonition not to play with it lest she break its fragile head. One day she dropped the doll and it broke. Her father tried to mend it, to no avail. I wondered if the meaning of the broken doll and the meaning of the shattered jardiniere were condensed or the same and if they represented her screen memory of the fantasy of destroying her sister.

Caught up in a flood of emotions, she re-experienced her early relationship with her grieving, depressed, and often bewildered and incompetent mother. It became clear that after losing her first child, her mother had cared for Jane as though she were the special doll—fragile and in danger of being broken, as her elder sister had been. Jane recalled her desire to have her mother touch her, her need to feel her warmth, and her dissatisfaction over its absence. She recalled identifying with her grieving mother and reflecting her as she played cautiously with her dolls, fearful that they would break. Further associations indicated that the broken, special doll was the crippled sister, Jane's depleted self-image and, later, her detached penis.

Jane began feeling better after pouring out these memories

and associations. She managed such adult tasks as negotiating a bank loan for the good stereo she wanted and visiting her college to see her old teachers, who were delighted with her. At the same time she began talking seriously of marrying Tom, even making out a list of wedding guests in her mind.

She obtained permission to be absent from work in order to attend classes that would enable her to become a teacher in an elementary school. In her dreams she alternated between being a little doll to being an adult woman, and from having a penis to trusting men. Dreaming of a man with an erect penis, she anticipated being raped, but "I was not, and I began to feel that I did not need to use weapons to protect myself!"

She had another dream:

> I had a gun between my legs and later it turned into a penis. I thought that I did not want a penis, and I wanted to be a girl. The dream took place at my home, and my parents and my brother were there. I saw that my brother did not have a penis. I gave mine, which was detachable, to him. It really belonged to him.

Getting out of the Forest

One day Jane's parents visited her apartment, bringing the owner of the estate with them, and this helped Jane see their interaction. She viewed her mother's interest in social advances as a wish to have a penis, and she saw her father being treated by his wife as if he were a small child. That night she caught herself trying to teach Tom proper table manners and realized that she was repeating the behavior of her mother, who similarly criticized her husband. Thus, separation of her image from her mother's widened.

She kept reviewing her relationship with Tom, sometimes deciding to break away but at other times deciding to marry him. She brought me some drawings of the two of them naked (Figures 14–9 through 14–11), and I kept them for a few days to have them photocopied. She realized that she wanted to have

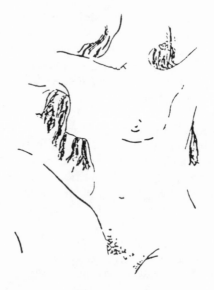

Figure 14–9

me compare her self-image in them as a grown woman with the self-image in the drawings she had made as she began treatment. Her review of her relationship with Tom climaxed in a dream reported in July.

> I was lost in a forest. I got out of the woods. I remember seeing Clark [a wealthy, single local man] with me. We were on the shore of a turbulent stream, and on the other side I saw this cool and nice place to live in. There was a gate to go through to this place. In order for me to reach the gate, I knew I had to swim in the turbulent water, and I did not know if I wanted to do this or not.

The wealthy man recalled her old fantasies of marrying money but reminded her also of Tom, who was also well connected. She recognized that Clark and Tom were both neurotic. The dream indicated to her that it was up to her to plunge into more analysis and work her way through to a more secure place.

Figure 14–10

Before having this dream she had asked if she might terminate her work with me and marry Tom. I told her that she was not ready for termination, and that one of the problems she must work on further was her fear of adult men. The dream reminded her that Tom was like a teenager, and that it was only when she herself felt like a teenager that they were compatible. Analysis offered a chance to move on into true womanhood.

She separated from Tom in the summer of 1969 and had a stormy grief reaction. Tom then moved away, and Jane was hired as a teacher in a county elementary school. In her grief over losing Tom, she had a series of dates with different "boys," jumping into bed with some of them to compare their smooth penises with Tom's, which was marked by psoriasis. By autumn she was able to realize that they were all younger than she, as Tom was, and that she had been repeating an old pattern. She began talking anxiously about wanting to know some mature men, and she again became interested in me, wondering about the women in my life and pondering what my

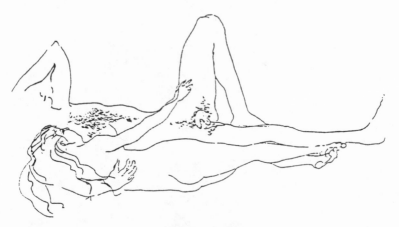

Figure 14–11

taste in women might be. She could now sustain friendly and witty participation in our analytic hours over longer periods of time. She spoke affectionately of my accent, particularly my pronunciation of the letter *v* as *w*. When she mocked my pronunciation of *vampire*, I told her that I was helping her to make something bloody and dangerous sound absurd and not frightening.

The Review Process

As a schoolteacher she felt confident and helpful to the children in her care, having considerable insight into their emotional problems. She took the initiative in getting psychiatric help for one troubled student and acknowledged ways in which her analysis had increased her ability as a teacher. Her identification with me was evident in many aspects of her work with her students. She especially liked a little boy named Philip and showed a great deal of tenderness toward him.

Now she wanted to have children with me and expressed disappointment and sadness when she realized that this was impossible. She fantasized walking with me near the hospital; I walked next to the building, while she accompanied me next to the street. Her association to this indicated that I stood by her but gave her freedom to explore the world around her. She felt tender toward me in making such associations but also said she was confused. I interpreted her confusion as arising from her denial of tender feelings, the danger of which she thought it necessary to defend herself against.

During her analysis she had two series of dreams that can be categorized as review dreams (Glover 1955). The first series came very early in her treatment, when she was acutely psychotic. She would report dreaming of a room without boundaries but that somehow accommodated electric outlets that seemed to suck energy gradually. This concept is reflected in Figures 14–7 and 14–8, in which electric outlets appear in the orifices of her body. As her ability to discriminate between self and nonself and among external objects developed, the dream room began to have walls, a floor, and a ceiling—transparent at first but eventually, as analysis progressed, solid and made of wood. Then came furniture in a variety of arrangements, and once Jane reported seeing a vacuum cleaner to clean up messes in the room.

The second series involved a stairway without walls on either side. It led into space, going nowhere. Throughout her treatment she dreamed of climbing this stairway. She would feel lost as she climbed and climbed, never reaching the top, although sometimes she would arrive at a plateau in space with no idea how to continue. Then the dreams about rooms and stairs became condensed; both the room and the stairs appeared in the same dream, as if they were integrated. In one memorable dream she climbed up to the plateau and wanted to jump into a furnished room across a gap.

> I ran on the plateau in order to make a long jump, but at the last minute I couldn't do it. Then I realized there might be another way. I went down several steps. There was a room there also. I was there with my student Philip. Then a black convict appeared; I was now faced with what had been

scaring me. The convict had an ice pick. I thought that he
might hurt Philip. I asked Philip if he were hurt, and he said
he was not. I thought I could walk on the structure of the gap
into the furnished room, looking the convict straight in the
eye.

Association to this dream and our understanding of it as a
condensation of her review dreams suggested that it was consistent with what she had been discussing during her analytic
hours—that she wanted to jump into the room (her enriched
self-representation) to finish her analysis without truly working
through the danger. The psychoanalytic work required another
regressive loop (going down the stairs). The black convict
represented the diffuse "them" of her former paranoid thinking, the dangerous phallic father-analyst, and her own aggression. The dream showed that she now wanted to face them
again, and that she was able to do so. Elsewhere (Volkan 1976)
I have described these review dreams in detail, focusing on
Jane's mending of her split self-representation, which was
evident in her creation of a structure in the gap between the
stairs and the furnished room.

Jane began to speak of termination soon after this, and I said
nothing at first. She analyzed her last neurotic links to her
father, one of which was keeping his car for her use. She revealed
a plan—which she subsequently carried out—of buying a car of
her own. The second link was her anxiety about being with men
in their thirties. Logic told her that men of that age would be the
most suitable for her, but her father had been in his thirties when
he had "played around" with her.

She gave a party in her apartment for men and women in
their thirties. She was extremely protective of her new role of
grown-up woman, which required responses not yet automatic
to her. For example, she worried lest her choice of Christmas
cards seem girlish, and she changed her hair style again,
dressing stylishly for our appointments, exhibiting self-con-
sciousness at having me see her so altered in appearance. In
early December she asked my age; what if I were in my thirties?

If so, this would be proof to her that men could be different from her father.

After an hour of discussion of her termination, she realized that she had been overreacting to our impending separation. I suggested that she talk freely about termination and take stock of what we had accomplished in her analysis. Such discussion made her feel "like a nervous cat," and she developed a temporary skin rash. She felt she was excreting something bad from every outlet of her body and wished psychology "would leave her body alone"; yet she commented that since this "purge," she felt silly about any attempt to be "bitchy."

During Christmas vacation, 1969, she spent a lot of time at her parents' home and returned with a list of observations she had made. She had taken stock! The observations noted her mother's panicky helplessness that brought others to her rescue and gave her power over them. After giving many examples of her mother's behavior, she had a mild temper tantrum, which I interpreted as a demonstration of what her mother had done to her. She stopped the tantrum herself and said sadly that she wished she could be given a model of how to be an adult. In the next analytic hour she talked about her father and his background and tried to understand why he was angry at women. The review of her objective perception of her parents was followed by a long period of silent weeping, which I found extremely moving.

When I arrived at my office for our first appointment in 1970, I found Jane looking at diplomas on the wall. She had taken advantage of her early arrival to satisfy her curiosity about my age and had learned from my diplomas that I was still in my thirties. Declaring that she wanted to work further on her relationship with "mature men," she read a number of books on sex, life, and being single and sought reassurance from me that she would find a strong man to marry. She was afraid that I would stop her analysis abruptly. I interpreted that the word "abruptly" had appeared in her cosmic laughter experience, indicating the loss of breast in a most frustrating way.

I noticed how she identified with me in dealing with her

students, even to the extent of using some of my phrases in speaking to them. She talked of her fantasy of being perfect, saying, "I want you to be God, to fix me so I can find a nice husband." Nevertheless, at home she unconsciously tried to puncture her fantasy of being perfect. While knitting a sweater, she made the collar inside out, but she recognized that she had performed an exercise in imperfection in order to be realistic.

She asked what I had learned from her, saying that while I had undoubtedly learned some new English words, she was more interested in finding out whether I had also learned that people can change. She then modified her statement, admitting that she realized I had known this before I met her, and that this knowledge was what she had learned from me. She spoke of having found a new self, to which she needed to become accustomed; it was "weird" to feel normal. It occurred to her that someone might want to marry her for her possessions, by which she meant at first such belongings as her stereo, but then considered that her possessions now included her newfound stability. She referred to the popular song that laments "Is that all there is?" and lapsed into a long spell of silent weeping and talk about her wishes for her future without me. She began asking directly about establishing a termination date.

TERMINATION

We decided to end our work in 3 months, and by the following day she was in full anticipatory grief reaction over the separation to come. She examined similarities between this reaction and the grief reaction she had experienced when she was separated from Tom. For example, she had found herself "jumping into bed" with men she knew only slightly, but then she stopped doing this. She spontaneously wanted to examine her former splitting of people. She found that in describing men with whom she had recently interacted, she classified them as "good" or "bad" and realized how, in the past, "good" and "bad" characteristics had seemed to be mutually exclusive.

She began writing hasty letters to friends and relatives,

sometimes as many as eight a day, as though she felt impelled to catch up with them and to complete something left unfinished. She dreamed about a doctor for whom she had worked on a temporary basis while employed by the surgeon. In the dream, he had died (evidence of her termination fantasy) while she was in the process of writing a letter to him, leaving loose ends in their transaction. I reminded her that *I* had not died, probably responding to my own anxiety that termination would mean "death" after such a strong relationship. Obviously, she knew that I was not dead! She wept and bewailed that we had not tied the loose ends together 6 months earlier so that we could simply have enjoyed the last months of our relationship.

She told of a blanket that she had begun making 6 years earlier while in the hospital. It was to be a baby blanket, fashioned of a number of squares stitched together to form a patchwork, but she had never finished it. She had recently turned to this work again and planned to complete it definitely before her analysis ended. The symbolism was clearly related to "putting things together" in psychoanalytic work. She fantasized giving it to me for my "next baby" (patient) but then thought of using it for a baby of her own.

She secured for herself an invitation to a relative's party in a nearby city, where she expected to meet some new young men, and she got a new coiffure for the occasion. She reported that her school principal had complimented her on her teaching and her initiative in the school, and that she had become active in the PTA and in campaigning for school improvements. At the close of this analytic hour, she pointed out that she had not used one Kleenex tissue during the hour and that this was probably the first session in 6 years in which she had been so tranquil.

Early in the spring of 1970, 6 years after we first met, Jane was still feverishly trying to put all the loose ends together. A visit to her parents' home reminded her that her mother might be rather helpless in the event of her father's death, so she decided to occupy herself with family affairs, prevailing upon her father to make a will and also making one herself, in which she made a small bequest to the local mental health association. She had death fantasies at home but was able to realize that the part of herself she saw dying was the part that was an extension of her mother. A week before the termination date she turned in her resignation, effective for the next school year. This left her free to determine her future course.

She talked of having seen the film *The African Queen*, which symbolized for her the psychoanalytic process. In it a man and woman go through trials and tribulations together, fight with a common enemy, and finally find safety as well as mutual knowledge that leads them to marriage. The couple in the film represented us; the enemy was her psychosis-neurosis. Although she recognized that we would not marry at the end of our work together, she knew that she would take and retain certain things from me (identifications). During her last hour, she talked about the difficulty those who lacked analytic experience must have in understanding what goes on in analysis and mourned that she would be all alone as she worked through and completed her grief. She had a dream the previous night but had forgotten it. Saying that she might as well make one up, she came up with a vision of a dead person thrown into a grave. She suggested that this was her neurosis that she was burying and wondered if it would return to haunt her. She acknowledged having wanted sometimes to cling to her illness in order to cling to me. I told her that this had been evident to me, and she cried.

Toward the end of the analytic hour, she recalled how she had talked about Alice in Wonderland, especially during the early part of her treatment, when she had been acutely schizophrenic. She spoke of the Cheshire cat who at times floated in the air. She recalled the cat's laughter and her own experience with cosmic laughter. I said it was interesting that she would refer to a cat at the end of her analysis because she had reminded me of a cat the first time I saw her. We talked about her killing Miss Kitty and how Miss Kitty had represented her early symbiotic attachment to her mother. As we finished these references to past events in her analysis, she said, "Well, that's the story of the cat, and this is the end." She rose, with tears in her eyes. I gave her a gentle hug; we said good-bye, and she left.

FOLLOW-UP

My first glimpse of Jane after her analysis terminated was in early autumn, when she unexpectedly appeared at my office. She said she had come to the hospital to see the surgeon she had worked for and to see me if I was available. She had come to say good-bye before leaving for a distant city, where she had secured a position as executive secretary to a university administrator. We had only a few minutes to talk, but she managed to say that she had a friend in that city who had shown her around a month earlier and who had helped her find an apartment. She talked with zest and excitement about the life she anticipated having there. We shook hands when she left, and I wished her happiness.

I heard nothing of her for a year but received a kind of progress report from her in the autumn of 1971. She wrote, "Mainly, I'm writing to let you know that I'm happy—at least as happy as I can allow myself to be." She wrote of a relationship with a young academician commenced the previous February and described him as strong and serene, adding that they were beginning to think of marriage.

> I know that I'm no longer afraid of age and am looking forward to my thirties. I still could not say this to you face-to-face (or top of my head to face) but I am fond of you. To this man I can express some of my positive feelings I never dared show you except in neurotic ways.
>
> Now I regard myself as having successfully completed analysis, although at the time of the termination it looked as though I had a long way to go, and even now I have to wrestle with my worst self. It helps that I love him and know my capacity for making him unhappy, but very much—because I love him—to make him happy. I'm glad I decided not to marry Tom—and instead to finish analysis. I wish you a happy life and I love you.

I sent her a postcard saying that I was glad to hear from her and to observe that she was working on her fear of marriage.

Late in the spring of 1972, writing of her plans to marry, she recalled her desire during her analysis for me to attend her wedding and explained that although she very much wanted me to meet her husband, the wedding they planned was to be limited to close relatives and friends, and that I might feel awkward among them, but I was nevertheless invited. The ceremony was to be held at the family farm, and she was to be given away by her father. She went on in some detail about her hopes for her future as a married woman and about plans for her life with her husband. I realized that, indeed, both of us might feel awkward were I to attend her wedding, and that I did not want to do anything to spoil her day, but I sent my wishes for her happiness. She telephoned me the day before the wedding, sounding happy. I again wished her the best of everything.

The young couple moved to the West, where she became the mother of four children and made a name for herself as a painter. Every few years or so, whenever she visited her parents, she would call me on the phone. Once she stopped by to show me pictures of children and her artistic productions. We had no formal interview, but it was clear that she had a very strong marriage and that she had become a caring mother.

The last time I saw her was 17 years after the termination of her work with me. She wanted to drop in with her husband, and when they came, it was clear that they were very close. Their visit was brief—no more than 5 or 10 minutes—and as they got up to leave, I walked with them to the door. Jane turned to me and exclaimed, "My God! I used to think you were so big! You're not that tall after all." I indicated to her that her perception was a good omen because it reflected her surrender of the last vestiges of the transference neurosis. She smiled. Many years have passed, and I have not since heard from her, but I have learned indirectly that Jane and family are all doing well.

Coda

While working on this book, I attended a psychiatric administrative meeting at the University of Virginia, where "old-style"
psychiatrists and psychoanalysts like myself were criticized for
not understanding the "new" psychiatry. I was told, for example, that research indicates that no patient needs to be seen
more than 6 times. Drastic changes in health care delivery
systems and insurance coverage are causing rationalizations
like this to be heard more often, the defense of which involves
considerable compromise of integrity. This book is my own
answer to such claims. I give details of the human drama and
human spirit that extend far beyond the specified 6 therapy
hours. Without taking into account the human aspect of mental
care we will, I fear, become robots.

Because of my age and my absorption with the study of the
application of psychoanalytic insights to international relationships—an activity that has increased considerably over the past
decade—I do not undertake the treatment of anyone who is
schizophrenic and/or has a psychotic core; my frequent absence

from my office will not allow me to commit myself again to the long-term work that is required in these cases. This book is a memorial of my grief over the loss of something dear to me—my psychoanalytic work with difficult patients.

Harold Searles (1961) has written about a therapist's identification with his or her predecessors. Knowing how those before us felt, and how they understood clinical phenomena, strengthens the new therapist's hand in effecting change. In scholarly fashion, Searles paid his respects to those before him who explored the inner world of very sick patients and likewise I want to recognize my predecessors, especially Harold Searles and Bryce Boyer. Although I never had the opportunity to develop a personal relationship with the former, I was able to observe his mind at work on occasions when I attended his lectures and when we were on the same panel discussion. This experience encouraged me to study and treat schizophrenia. Bryce Boyer has been like a caring big brother—always available with kind words of advice. This book was written to honor both of these good men.

References

Abse, D. W. (1955). Early phases of ego-structure adumbrated in the regressive ego states of schizophrenic psychosis, and elucidated in intensive psychotherapy. *Psychoanalytic Review* 42:228–238.

_____ (1987). *Hysteria and Related Mental Disorders: An Approach to Psychological Medicine.* Bristol, England: Wright.

Abse, D. W., and Ewing, J. (1960). Some problems in psychotherapy with schizophrenic patients. *American Journal of Psychotherapy* 14:505–519.

Abse, D. W., and Wegener, P. (1971). *Speech and Reason, Language Disorder in Mental Disease* (D. W. Abse) and *A Translation of the Life of Speech* (P. Wegener). Charlottesville: University Press of Virginia.

Ainsworth, M., Bell, S. M., and Stayton, D. (1974). Infant–mother attachment and social development: socialization as a product of reciprocal responsiveness to signals. In *The Integration of the Child into a Social World*, ed. M. Richards, pp. 99–135. Cambridge, England: Cambridge University Press.

Akhtar, S. (1992a). Tethers, orbits, and invisible fences: clinical, developmental, sociocultural, and technical aspects of optimal distance. In *When the Body Speaks: A Psychological Meaning in Kinetic Clues*, ed. S. Kramer and S. Akhtar, pp. 21–57. Northvale, NJ: Jason Aronson.

―――― (1992b). *Broken Structures: Severe Personality Disorders and Their Treatment*. Northvale, NJ: Jason Aronson.

Alanen, Y. O. (1993). *Skitsofrenia: Syyt Tarpeenmukainen Hoito (Schizophrenia: Need-adapted Treatment)*. Juva, Finland: WSOY.

Alanen, Y. O., Lehtinen, K., Räkköläinen, V., and Aaltonen, J. (1991). Need-adapted treatment of new schizophrenic patients: experience and results of the Turku Project. *Acta Psychiatrica Scandinavica* 83:363–372.

Apprey, M. (1984). Review of *Psychoanalysis and Infant Research* by J. D. Lichtenberg. *Review of Psychoanalytic Books* 3:451–457.

―――― (1993a). Dreams of urgent-voluntary errands and transgenerational haunting and transsexualism. In *Intersubjectivity, Projective Identification and Otherness*, ed. M. Apprey and H. F. Stein, pp. 102–128. Pittsburgh, PA: Duquesne University Press.

―――― (1993b). The African-American experience: forced immigration and transgenerational trauma. *Mind and Human Interaction* 4:70–75.

―――― (1994). The intersubjective constitution of the sense of disappearing in schizophrenia: a phenomenological description and a prefatory note. Paper presented at XIth International Symposium for the Psychotherapy of Schizophrenia, Washington, DC, June 12–16.

Arlow, J. A. (1963). Conflict, regression, and symptom formation. *International Journal of Psycho-Analysis* 44:12–22.

Arlow, J. A., and Brenner, C. (1964.) *Psychoanalytic Concepts and the Structural Theory*. New York: International Universities Press.

Bak, R. C. (1954). The schizophrenic defense against aggression. *International Journal of Psycho-Analysis* 35:129–134.

_____ (1968). The phallic woman: the ubiquitous fantasy in perversions. *The Psychoanalytic Study of the Child* 23:15–36. New York: International Universities Press.

Balint, M. (1955). Friendly expanses—horrid empty spaces. *International Journal of Psycho-Analysis* 36:225–241.

Bartfai, A., Wirsen, A., Levander S., and Schalling, D. (1989). Smooth pursuit eye tracking and neuro-psychological performance in healthy volunteers: exploring a possible genetic marker for vulnerability to schizophrenia. *Acta Psychiatrica Scandinavica* 80:479–489.

Bell, S. (1970). The development of the concept of object as related to infant–mother attachment. *Child Development* 41:219–311.

Beres, D. (1962). The unconscious fantasy. *Psychoanalytic Quarterly* 31:309–329.

Bion, W. R. (1957). Differentiation of the psychotic from the nonpsychotic personalities. *International Journal of Psycho-Analysis* 38:266–275.

Bleuler, E. (1911). *Dementia Praecox, or the Group of Schizophrenias*, trans. J. Zinkin. New York: International Universities Press, 1950.

Blos, P. (1979). *The Adolescent Passage*. New York: International Universities Press.

Bond, D. D. (1952). *The Love and Fear of Flying*. New York: International Universities Press.

Boyer, L. B. (1961). Provisional evaluation of psycho-analysis with few parameters in the treatment of schizophrenics. *International Journal of Psycho-Analysis* 42:389–403.

_____ (1967). Office treatment of schizophrenic patients: the use of psychoanalytic therapy with few parameters. In *Psychoanalytic Treatment of Characterological and Schizophrenic Disorders*, ed. L. B. Boyer and P. L. Giovacchini, pp. 143–188. New York: Science House.

_____ (1971). Psychoanalytic technique in the treatment of certain characterological and schizophrenic disorders. *International Journal of Psycho-Analysis* 52:67–85.

_____ (1983). *The Regressed Patient.* New York: Jason Aronson.

_____ (1986). Technical aspects of treating the regressed patient. *Contemporary Psychoanalysis* 22:25–44.

_____ (1990). Countertransference and technique. In *Master Clinicians on Treating the Regressed Patient,* ed. L. B. Boyer and P. Giovacchini, pp. 303–324. Northvale, NJ: Jason Aronson.

Brazelton, T., Koslowski, B., and Main, N. (1974). The origins of reciprocity: the early mother–infant interaction. In *The Effects of the Infant on its Caregiver,* ed. M. Lewis and L. Rosenblum, pp. 49–76. New York: John Wiley.

Bullard, D. M., ed. (1959). *Psychoanalysis and Psychotherapy: Selected Papers of Frieda Fromm-Reichmann.* Chicago: University of Chicago Press.

Burnham, D. L. (1969). Schizophrenia and object relations. In *Schizophrenia and the Need-Fear Dilemma,* ed. D. L. Burnham, A. I. Gladstone, and R. W. Gibson, pp. 15–41. New York: International Universities Press.

_____ (1970). Varieties of reality restructuring in schizophrenia. In *The Schizophrenic Reactions: A Critique of the Concept, Hospital Treatment, and Current Research,* ed. R. Cancro, pp. 197–215. New York: Brunner/Mazel.

Burnham, D. L., Gladstone, A.I., and Gibson, R. W. (1969). *Schizophrenia and the Need-Fear Dilemma.* New York: International Universities Press.

Cambor, C. G. (1969). Preoedipal factors in superego development: the influence of multiple mothers. *Psychoanalytic Quarterly* 38:81–96.

Cameron, N. (1961). Introjection, reprojection, and hallucination in the interaction between schizophrenic patients and the therapist. *International Journal of Psycho-Analysis* 42:86–96.

Cancro, R. (1986). General considerations relating to theory in the schizophrenic disorders. In *Towards a Comprehensive Model for Schizophrenic Disorders,* ed. D. B. Finesilver, pp. 97–107. New York: Analytic Press.

Charlesworth, W. R. (1969). The role of surprize in cognitive development. In *Studies in Cognitive Development: Essays in Honor of Jean Piaget*, ed. E. Elkind and J. H. Flavell, pp. 257–314. London: Oxford University Press.

Cortes, L. (1978). *Un Enigma Salmantino: La Rana Universitaria*. Salamanca, Spain.

Crow, T. J., and Done, D. J. (1992) Prenatal exposure to influenza does not cause schizophrenia. *British Journal of Psychiatry* 161:390–393.

Dalen, P. (1990). Does age incidence explain all season-of-birth effects in the literature? *Schizophrenia Bulletin* 16:11–12.

Davis, K. L., Kahn, R. S., Ko, G., and Davidson, M. (1991). Dopamine in schizophrenia: a review and reconceptualization. *The American Journal of Psychiatry* 48:1474–1486.

Deutsch, H. (1942). Some forms of emotional disturbance and their relationship to schizophrenia. *Psychoanalytic Quarterly* 11:301–321.

Dorpat, T. L. (1976). Structural conflict and object relations conflict. *Journal of the American Psychoanalytic Association* 24:855–874.

Eagles, J. M. (1991). The relationship between schizophrenia and immigration. *British Journal of Psychiatry* 159: 783–789.

Eissler, K. R. (1954). Notes upon defects of ego structure in schizophrenia. *International Journal of Psycho-Analysis* 35:141–146.

Emde, R. (1988a). Development terminable and interminable. I. Innate and motivational factors from infancy. *International Journal of Psycho-Analysis* 69:23–41.

_____ (1988b). Development terminable and interminable. II. Recent psychoanalytic theory and therapeutic considerations. *International Journal of Psycho-Analysis* 69:283–296.

Erhat, A. (1972). *Mitoloji Sözlüğü (Dictionary of Mythology)*. Istanbul: Remzi Kitabevi.

Escalona, S. (1968). *The Roots of Individuality*. Chicago: Aldine.

Federn, P. (1952). *Ego Psychology and the Psychosis*. New York: Basic Books.

Feinsilver, D. B. (1980). Transitional relatedness and containment in the treatment of a chronic schizophrenic patient. *International Review of Psycho-Analysis* 7:309–318.

Fenichel, O. (1945). *The Psychoanalytic Theory of Neurosis*. New York: Norton.

Franzek E., and Beckmann, H. (1992). Season-of-birth effect reveals the existence of etiologically different groups of schizophrenia. *Biological Psychiatry* 32:375–378.

Freeman, T. (1983). Reexamining schizophrenia. *Psychoanalytic Inquiry* 3:71–89.

Freud, A. (1936). The ego and the mechanisms of defense. In *The Writings of Anna Freud, vol. 2*. New York: International Universities Press, 1966.

——— (1954). The widening scope of indications for psychoanalysis. In *The Writings of Anna Freud, vol. 4*, pp. 356–376. New York: International Universities Press, 1968.

Freud, S. (1900). The interpretation of dreams. *Standard Edition*. 4 & 5.

——— (1905). Jokes and their relations to the unconscious. *Standard Edition*, vol. 8.

——— (1911). Psychoanalytic notes on an autobiographical account of a case of paranoia. *Standard Edition* 12:3–84.

——— (1914a). On the history of the psycho-analytic movement. *Standard Edition* 14:7–71.

——— (1914b). On narcissism: an introduction. *Standard Edition* 14:67–104.

——— (1917). Mourning and melancholia. *Standard Edition* 14:237–260.

——— (1923). The ego and the id. *Standard Edition* 19:3–68.

——— (1924a). Neurosis and psychosis. *Standard Edition* 19:149–156.

——— (1924b). The loss of reality in neurosis and psychosis. *Standard Edition* 19:183–190.

——— (1926). Inhibitions, symptoms, and anxiety. *Standard Edition* 20:77–175.

——— (1938). Constructions in analysis. *Standard Edition* 27:265–266.

——— (1940). An outline of psychoanalysis. *Standard Edition* 23:141–208.

Frosch, J. (1983). *The Psychotic Process*. New York: International Universities Press.

Gedo, J. E. (1979). *Beyond Interpretation*. New York: International Universities Press.

Gedo, J. E. and Goldberg, A. (1973). *Models of Mind*. Chicago: University of Chicago Press.

Gillespie, W. H. (1971). Aggression and instinct theory. *International Journal of Psycho-Analysis* 52:155–160.

Giovacchini, P. L. (1967). Psychoanalytic treatment of character disorders. In *Psychoanalytic Treatment of Characterological and Schizophrenic Disorders*, ed. L. B. Boyer and P. L. Giovacchini, pp. 208–234. New York: Science House.

—— (1969). The influence of interpretation upon schizophrenic patients. *International Journal of Psycho-Analysis* 50:179–186.

—— (1972). Interpretation and definition of the analytic setting. In *Tactics and Techniques in Psychoanalytic Therapy*, ed. P. L. Giovacchini, pp. 291–304. New York: Science House.

—— (1983). The persistent psychosis-schizophrenia: with special reference to *Schizophrenic Disorders* by P-N. Pao. *Psychoanalytic Inquiry* 3:9–36.

Glass, J. M. (1985). *Delusion: Internal Dimensions of Political Life*. Chicago: University of Chicago Press.

—— (1989). *Private Terror/Public Life: Psychosis and the Politics of Community*. Ithaca, New York: Cornell University Press.

Glover, E. (1955). *Technique of Psychoanalysis*. New York: International Universities Press.

Goldstein, W. N. (1991). Classification of projective identification. *American Journal of Psychiatry* 148:153–161.

Gottesman, I., and Shields, J. (1972). *Schizophrenia and Genetics: A Twin Study Vantage Point*. New York: Academic Press.

Greenacre, P. (1970). The transitional object and the fetish: with special reference to the role of illusion. *International Journal of Psycho-Analysis* 51:447–456.

Greenspan, S. I. (1977). The oedipal–pre-oedipal dilemma: a

reformulation according to object relations theory. *International Review of Psycho-Analysis* 4:381–391.

———— (1989). *The Development of the Ego: Implications for Personality Theory, Psychopathology and the Psychotherapeutic Process.* Madison, CT: International Universities Press.

Greer, W. F., and Volkan, V. D. (1991). Transitional phenomena and anal narcissism controlling the relationship with the representations of the mother and father: the transference in a case of latent homosexuality. In *The Homosexualities and the Therapeutic Process*, ed. C. W. Socarides and V. D. Volkan, pp. 109–141. Madison, CT: International Universities Press.

Grotstein, J. (1983). Deciphering the schizophrenic experience. *Psychoanalytic Inquiry* 3:37–70.

Grotstein, J. (1986). Schizophrenic personality disorder: ". . . And if I should die before I wake." In *Towards a Comprehensive Model for Schizophrenic Disorders*, ed. D.B. Feinsilver, pp. 29–71. Hillsdale, NJ: Analytic Press.

Group for the Advancement of Psychiatry. (1988). *Us and Them: The Psychology of Ethno-centrism.* New York: Brunner/Mazel.

Gunderson, J. T., Carpenter, W. T., and Strauss, J.S. (1975). Borderline and schizophrenic patients: a comparative study. *American Journal of Psychiatry* 132:1259–1264.

Harrison, G. (1990). Searching for the causes of schizophrenia: the role of migrant studies. *Schizophrenia Bulletin* 16:663–671.

Hartmann, H. (1939). *Ego Psychology and the Problems of Adaptation.* New York: International Universities Press, 1958.

———— (1950). Comments on the psychoanalytic theory of the ego. In *Essays on Ego Psychology*, pp. 113–141. New York: International Universities Press, 1964.

———— (1952). The mutual influences in the development of ego and id. In *Essays on Ego Psychology*, pp. 155–182. New York: International Universities Press, 1964.

———— (1953). Contributions to the metapsychology of schizophrenia. In *Essays on Ego Psychology*, pp. 182–206. New York: International Universities Press, 1964.

Hawkins, D. R. (1985). Sleep and depression. In *Depressive States and Their Treatment*, ed. V. D. Volkan, pp. 359–379. Northvale, NJ: Jason Aronson.

Heath, S. (1991). *Dealing with the Therapist's Vulnerability to Depression*. Northvale, NJ: Jason Aronson.

Hoffer, W. (1949). Mouth, hand and ego-integration. *The Psychoanalytic Study of the Child* 3(4):49–56. New York: International Universities Press.

Isakower, O. (1938). A contribution to the patho-psychology of phenomena associated with falling asleep. *International Journal of Psycho-Analysis* 19:331–345.

Jackson, D. (1960). *The Etiology of Schizophrenia*. New York: Basic Books.

Jacobson, E. (1964). *The Self and the Object World*. New York: International Universities Press.

Kafka, J. S. (1969). The body as transitional object: a psychoanalytic study of a self-mutilating patient. *British Journal of Medical Psychology* 43:207–212.

Katan, M. (1954). The importance of the non-psychotic part of the personality in schizophrenia. *International Journal of Psycho-Analysis* 35:119–128.

Kendell, R. E. (1989). Maternal influenza in the etiology of schizophrenia. *Archives of General Psychiatry* 46:878–882.

Kendler, K. S. (1983). Overview: a current perspective on twin studies of schizophrenia. *American Journal of Psychiatry* 140:1413–1425.

Kerényi, C. (1960). *The Gods of the Greeks*. New York: Grove Press.

Kernberg, O. F. (1966). Structural derivatives of object relationships. *International Journal of Psycho-Analysis* 47:236–253.

_____ (1970). A psychoanalytic classification of character pathology. *Journal of the American Psychoanalytic Association* 18:800–822.

_____ (1972). Early ego integration and object relations. *Annals of the New York Academy of Science* 193:233–247.

———— (1975). *Borderline Conditions and Pathological Narcissism*. New York: Jason Aronson.

———— (1976a). Foreword. In *Primitive Internalized Object Relations* by V. D. Volkan, pp. xiii–xvii. New York: International Universities Press.

———— (1976b). *Object Relations Theory and Clinical Psychoanalysis*. New York: Jason Aronson.

———— (1984). *Severe Personality Disorders: Psychotherapeutic Strategies*. New Haven: Yale University Press.

———— (1992). Foreword. In *The Psychotic: Aspects of the Personality* by D. Rosenfeld, pp. vii–xiii. London: Karnac Books.

Klaus, M., and Kennell, J. (1976). *Maternal-Infant Bonding: The Impact of Early Separation or Loss on Family Development*. St. Louis: C. V. Mosby.

Klein, M. (1946). Notes on some schizoid mechanisms. *International Journal of Psycho-Analysis* 27:99–110.

Klein, S. (1980). Autistic phenomenon in neurotic patients. *International Journal of Psycho-Analysis* 61:395–402.

Kohut, H. (1971). *The Analysis of the Self: A Systematic Approach to the Psychoanalytic Treatment of Narcissistic Personality Disorders*. New York: International Universities Press.

Kramer, P. (1955). On discovering one's identity. *The Psychoanalytic Study of the Child* 10:47–74. New York: International Universities Press.

Kramer, S. (1986). Identification and its vicissitudes as observed in children: a developmental approach. *International Journal of Psycho-Analysis* 67:161–172.

Kris, E. (1952). *Psychoanalytic Exploration in Art*. New York: International Universities Press.

Lehtonen, J. (1991). The body ego from the point of view of psychophysical fusion. *Psychotherapy and Psychosomatics* 87:487–489.

Lewin, B. D. (1948). Inferences from the dream screen. *International Journal of Psycho-Analysis* 29:224–231.

Lichtenberg, J. D. (1983). *Psychoanalysis and Infant Research*. Hillside, NJ: Analytic Press.

Lichtenberg, J. D., and Pao, P-N. (1974). Delusion, fantasy and desire. *International Journal of Psycho-Analysis* 55: 273–281.

Lidz, T. (1973). *Origin and Treatment of Schizophrenic Disorders*. New York: Basic Books.

Lipsitt, L. (1966). Learning processes of newborns. *Merrill-Palmer Quarterly* 12:45–71.

Loewald, H. W. (1960). On the therapeutic action of psychoanalysis. *International Journal of Psycho-Analysis* 41:16–33.

_____ (1982). Regression: some general considerations. In *Technical Factors in the Treatment of the Severely Disturbed Patient*, ed. P. L. Giovacchini and L. B. Boyer, pp. 107–130. New York: Jason Aronson.

London, N. J. (1973a). An essay on psychoanalytic theory: two theories of schizophrenia. Part I: Review and critical assessment of the development of the two theories. *International Journal of Psycho-Analysis* 54:169–178.

_____ (1973b). An essay on psychoanalytic theory: two theories of schizophrenia. Part II: Discussion and restatement of the specific theory of schizophrenia. *International Journal of Psycho-Analysis* 54:179–193.

Mahler, M. S. (1952). On child psychosis and schizophrenia: autistic and symbiotic infantile psychosis. *The Psychoanalytic Study of the Child* 7:286–305. New York: International Universities Press.

_____ (1968). *On Human Symbiosis and the Vicissitudes of Individuation*. New York: International Universities Press.

Mahler, M. S., and Furer, M. (1966). Development of symbiosis, symbiotic psychosis, and the nature of separation anxiety. *International Journal of Psycho-Analysis* 47:559–560.

Mahler, M. S., and Gosliner, B. J. (1955). On symbiotic child psychosis: genetic, dynamic and restitutive aspects. *The Psychoanalytic Study of the Child* 10:195–224. New York: International Universities Press.

Mahler, M. S., and La Perriere, K. (1965). Mother–child interaction during separation-individuation. *Psychoanalytic Quarterly* 34:483–498.

Marcus, E. R. (1992). *Psychosis and Near Psychosis: Ego Function, Symbol Structure, Treatment.* New York: Springer-Verlag.

Meltzoff, A., and Moore, K. (1977). Imitation of facial and manual gestures by human neonates. *Science* 198:75–78.

Mitchell, S. A. and Greenberg, J. R. (1983). *Object Relations in Psychoanalytic Theory.* Cambridge, MA: Harvard University Press.

Modell, A. H. (1963). Primitive object relationships and the predisposition to schizophrenia. *International Journal of Psycho-Analysis* 44:282–292.

—— (1968). *Object Love and Reality: An Introduction to a Psychoanalytic Theory of Object Relations.* New York: International Universities Press.

—— (1970). The transitional objects and the creative art. *Psychoanalytic Quarterly* 39:240–250.

—— (1990). *Other Times, Other Realities.* Cambridge, MA: Harvard University Press.

Moore, B. E., and Fine, B. D. (1990). *Psychoanalytic Terms and Concepts.* New Haven: Yale University Press.

Mueser, K. T., and Berenbaum, H. (1990). Psychodynamic treatment of schizophrenia: Is there a future? *Psychological Medicine* 20:253–262.

Niederland, W. G. (1956). Clinical observations on the "little man" phenomenon. *The Psychoanalytic Study of the Child* 11:381–395. New York: International Universities Press.

—— (1974). *The Schreber Case: Psychoanalytic Profile of a Paranoid Personality.* New York: Quadrangle/The New York Times Book.

Novick, J., and Kelly, K. (1970). Projection and externalization. *The Psychoanalytic Study of the Child* 25:69–95.

O'Callaghan, E. (1991). Season of birth in schizophrenia: evidence for confinement of an excess of winter births to patients without a family history of mental disorder. *British Journal of Psychiatry* 158:764–767.

O'Callaghan, E., Sham, P., Takei, N., et al. (1991). Schizophrenia after prenatal exposure to 1957 A2 influenza epidemic. *Lancet* 337:1248–1250.

Ogden, T. H. (1994). *Subjects of Analysis.* Northvale, NJ: Jason Aronson.

Olinick, S. L. (1969). On empathy and regression in the service of the other. *British Journal of Medical Psychology* 42:41–49.

——— (1980). *The Psychotherapeutic Instrument.* New York: Jason Aronson.

Olinick, S. L., Poland, W. S., Grigg, K. A., and Granatir, W. L. (1973). The psycho-analytic work ego: process and interpretation. *International Journal of Psycho-Analysis* 54: 147–151.

Pao, P-N. (1973). Notes on Freud's theory of schizophrenia. *International Journal of Psycho-Analysis* 54:459–476.

——— (1977). On the formation of schizophrenic symptoms. *International Journal of Psycho-Analysis* 58:389–401.

——— (1979). *Schizophrenic Disorders: Theory and Treatment from a Psychodynamic Point of View.* New York: International Universities Press.

Peto, A. (1968). On affect control. *International Journal of Psycho-Analysis* 42:341–361.

Piaget, J. (1962). The stages of the intellectual development of the child. In *Childhood Pathology,* ed. S. Harrison and J. McDermott, pp. 157–166. New York: International Universities Press.

Poland, W. S. (1977). Pilgrimage: Action and tradition in self-analysis. *Journal of the American Psychoanalytic Association* 25:319–416.

Pollock, G. (1989). *The Mourning-Liberation Process,* 2 vols. Madison, CT: International Universities Press.

Pulver, A. E. (1990). Age-incidence artifacts do not account for the season-of-birth effects in schizophrenia. *Schizophrenia Bulletin* 16:13–15.

Pulver, A. E., Liang, K. Y., Brown, C. H., et al. (1992). Risk factors in schizophrenia: season of birth, gender, and familial risk. *British Journal of Psychiatry* 160:65–71.

Rangell, L. (1979). Countertransference issues in the theory of therapy. *Journal of the American Psychoanalytic Association* 27(Suppl.):81–112.

Rogers, R. R. (1979). Intergenerational exchange: transference attitudes down the generations. In *Modern Perspectives in the Psychiatry of Infancy*, ed. J. Howells, pp. 339–349. New York: Brunner/Mazel.

Rosenfeld, D. (1992). *The Psychotic: Aspects of the Personality*. London: Karnac Books.

Rosenfeld, H. A. (1965). *Psychotic States: A Psychoanalytic Approach*. London: Hogarth Press.

_____ (1985). Psychosomatic symptoms and latent psychotic states. In *The Yearbook of Psychoanalysis and Psychotherapy*, vol. 1, ed. R. Langs, pp. 381–398. Emerson, NJ: New Concept Press.

Sacchetti, E., Calzeroni, A., Vita, A., et al. (1992). The brain damage hypothesis of the seasonality of birth in schizophrenia and major affective disorders: evidence from computerized tomography. *British Journal of Psychiatry* 160:390–397.

Salonen, S. (1979). On the metapsychology of schizophrenia. *International Journal of Psycho-Analysis* 60:73–81.

Sandler, J. (1960). The background of safety. *International Journal of Psycho-Analysis* 41:352–356.

Sandler, J., and Joffe, W. G. (1969). Towards a basic psychoanalytic model. *International Journal of Psycho-Analysis* 50:79–90.

Schulz, C. G. (1975). An individualized psychotherapeutic approach with the schizophrenic patient. *Schizophrenia Bulletin* 13(Summer):46–69.

Schulz, C., and Kilgalen, R. K. (1969). *Case Studies in Schizophrenia*. New York: Basic Books.

Searles, H. F. (1951). Data concerning certain manifestations of incorporation. *Psychiatry* 14:397–413.

_____ (1959). The effort to drive the other person crazy: an element in the aetiology and psychotherapy of schizo-phrenia. In *Collected Papers on Schizophrenia and Related Subjects*, pp. 254–283. New York: International Universities Press, 1965.

_____ (1960). *The Nonhuman Environment in Normal Development and in Schizophrenia.* New York: International Universities Press.

_____ (1961). Phases of patient–therapist interaction in the psychotherapy of chronic schizophrenia. In *Collected Papers on Schizophrenia and Related Subjects*, pp. 521–559. New York: International Universities Press, 1965.

_____ (1965). *Collected Papers on Schizophrenia and Related Subjects.* New York: International Universities Press.

_____ (1979). *Countertransference and Related Subjects.* New York: International Universities Press.

_____ (1986). *My Work with Borderline Patients.* New York: Jason Aronson.

Segal, H. (1973). *Introduction to the Work of Melanie Klein.* New York: Basic Books.

Shapiro, E. R., Shapiro, R. L., Zinner, J., and Berkowitz, D. A. (1977). The borderline ego and the working alliance: indications for family and individual treatment in adolescence. *International Journal of Psycho-Analysis* 58:77–87.

Shengold, L. (1988). *Halo in the Sky: Observations on Anality as a Defence.* New York: Guilford.

Socarides, C. W. (1970). A psychoanalytic study of the desire for sexual transformation ("transsexualism"): the Plaster-of-Paris man. *International Journal of Psycho-Analysis* 51:341–349.

_____ (1988). *The Preoedipal Origin and Psychoanalytic Therapy of Sexual Perversions.* Madison, CT: International Universities Press.

Spitz, R. A. (1957). *No and Yes: On the Beginning of Human Communication.* New York: International Universities Press.

_____ (1965). *The First Year of Life: A Psychoanalytic Study of Normal and Deviant Development of Object Relations.* New York: International Universities Press.

Sroufe, L. A., and Waters, E. (1977). Attachment as an organi-
zational construct. *Child Development* 48:1184–1199.

Stern, D. N. (1985) *The Interpersonal World of the Infant.* New
York: Basic Books.

Stoeri, J. (1992). The interplay of symbolic and nonsymbolic
modes of representation, self-definition, and early object
ties: a case illustration. Paper presented at a conference on
Emptiness: Theoretical and Clinical Aspects, at New York
University.

Sullivan, H. S. (1962). *Schizophrenia as a Human Process.*
New York: Norton.

Suslick, A. (1963). Pathology of identity as related to the
borderline ego. *Archives of General Psychiatry* 8:252:262.

Tähkä, V. (1984a). Psychoanalytic treatment as a developmental continuum: consideration on disturbed structurali-
zation and its phase-specific encounter. *Scandinavian Psychoanalytic Review* 7:133–159.

_____ (1984b). Dealing with object loss. *Scandinavian Psychoanalytic Review* 7:13–33.

_____ (1988). On the early formation of the mind. II: From
differentation to self and object constancy. *Psychoanalytic
Study of the Child* 43:101–134. New Haven, CT: Yale
University Press.

_____ (1993). *Mind and its Treatment: A Psychoanalytic Approach.* Madison, CT: International Universities Press.

Tausk, V. (1919). On the origin of the "influencing machine" in
schizophrenia. *Psychoanalytic Quarterly* 2:519–556,
1933.

Tienari, P. (1991). Interaction between genetic vulnerability
and family environment: the Finnish adoptive family study
of schizophrenia. *Acta Psychiatrica Scandinavica* 84:
460–465.

Tienari, P., Sorri, A., Lahti, I., et al. (1985). The Finnish
adoptive family study of schizophrenia. *The Yale Journal
of Biology and Medicine* 58:227–237.

Tolpin, M. (1972). On the beginning of a cohesive self: an
application of the concept of transmuting internalization to
the study of the transitional object and separation anxiety.

The Psychoanalytic Study of the Child 26:316–353. New Haven, CT: Yale University Press.

Torrey, E. F., and Bowler, A. E. (1990). The seasonality of schizophrenic births. *Schizophrenia Bulletin* 16:1–3.

Tuczek, K. (1921). Analyze einer Katatonikensprache. *Zeitschrift für die gesamte Neurologie und Psychiatrie* 113. Berlin.

Tustin, F. (1986). *Autistic Barriers in Neurotic Patients.* London: Karnac Books.

van der Waals, H. G. (1952). Discussion of "The mutual influences in the development of ego and id." *The Psychoanalytic Study of the Child* 7:66–68. New York: International Universities Press.

Volkan, V. D. (1964). The observation and topographic study of the changing ego states of a schizophrenic patient. *British Journal of Medical Psychology* 37:239–255.

——— (1965). The observation of the "little man" phenomenon in a case of anorexia nervosa. *British Journal of Medical Psychology* 38:299–311.

——— (1968). The introjection of and identification with the therapist as an ego-building aspect in the treatment of schizophrenia. *British Journal of Medical Psychology* 41:369–380.

——— (1973). Transitional fantasies in the analysis of a narcissistic personality. *Journal of the American Psychoanalytic Association* 21:351–376.

——— (1974). A cautionary psychiatric insight: a clinical report. In *Marital and Sexual Counseling in Medical Practice*, ed. D. W. Abse, M. M. Nash, and L. M. R. Louden, pp. 393–404. Hagerstown, MD: Harper and Row.

——— (1975). Cosmic laughter: a study of primitive splitting. In *Tactics and Techniques in Psychoanalytic Psychotherapy*, vol. 2, ed. P. L. Giovacchini, A. Flarsheim, and L. B. Boyer, pp. 425–440. New York: Jason Aronson.

——— (1976). *Primitive Internalized Object Relations: A Clinical Study of Schizophrenic, Borderline and Narcissistic Patients.* New York: International Universities Press.

——— (1980). Transsexualism as examined from the viewpoint

of internalized object relations. In *On Sexuality: Psychoan-analytic Observations*, ed. T. B. Karasu and C. W. Socarides, pp. 199–221. New York: International Universities Press.

―――― (1981a). *Linking Objects and Linking Phenomena*. New York: International Universities Press.

―――― (1981b). Transference and countertransference: an examination from the point of view of internalized object relations. In *Object and Self: A Developmental Approach*, ed. S. Tuttman, C. Kaye, and M. Zimmerman, pp. 429–451. New York: International Universities Press.

―――― (1982a). Identification and related psychic events: their appearance in therapy and their curative values. In *Curative Factors in Dynamic Psychotherapy*, ed. S. Slipp, pp. 153–170. New York: McGraw-Hill.

―――― (1982b). A young woman's inability to say no to needy people and her identification with the frustrator in the analytic situation. In *Technical Factors in the Treatment of the Severely Disturbed Patient*, ed. P. L. Giovacchini and L. B. Boyer, pp. 439–465. New York: Jason Aronson.

―――― (1986). Suitable targets of externalization and schizophrenia. In *Towards a Comprehensive Model for Schizophrenic Disorders*, ed. D. B. Feinsilver, pp. 125–153. New York: Analytic Press.

―――― (1990). The psychoanalytic psychotherapy of schizophrenia. In *Master Clinicians on Treating the Regressed Patient*, ed. L. Bryce Boyer and P. L. Giovacchini, pp. 245–270. Northvale, NJ: Jason Aronson.

―――― (1992a). The inner world of the schizophrenic patient. In *Psychotherapy of Schizophrenia: Facilitating and Obstructive Factors*, ed. A. Werbart and J. Cullberg, pp. 28–36. Oslo: Scandinavian University Press.

―――― (1992b). Nesne ilişkileri kuramı ve psikosomatik hastalıklar (Object relations theory and psychosomatic illnesses). In *Birinci Psikosomatik Sempozyumu Bilimsel Yayınları* (Scientific Papers on the First Psychosomatic Symposium), ed. A. Çevik, pp. 1–42. Antalya, Turkey: Roche.

―――― (1992c) Ethnonationalistic rituals: an introduction. *Mind and Human Interaction* 4:3–19.

_____ (1993a). Immigrants and refugees: a psychodynamic perspective. *Mind and Human Interaction* 4:63–69.

_____ (1993b). The intrapsychic story of integration in a borderline patient. In *Master Clinicians on Treating the Regressed Patient*, ed. L. B. Boyer and P. L. Giovacchini, pp. 279–297. Northvale, NJ: Jason Aronson.

_____ (1993c). Countertransference reactions commonly present in the treatment of patients with borderline personality organization. In *Countertransference: Theory, Technique, Teaching*, ed. A. Alexandris and G. Vaslamatzis, pp. 147–163. London: Karnac Books.

_____ (1993d). What the Holocaust means to a non-Jewish psychoanalyst. In *Persistent Shadows of the Holocaust: The Meaning to Those Not Directly Affected*, ed. R. Moses, pp. 81–117. Madison, CT: International Universities Press.

_____ (1994a). Psychodynamic formulations for psychotherapy of schizophrenic patients. *Directions in Psychiatry* (Special Report), vol. 14, March 9.

_____ (1994b). Identification with the therapist functions and ego-building in the treatment of schizophrenia. *British Journal of Psychiatry* 23(Suppl.):77–82.

Volkan, V. D., and Akhtar, S. (1979). The symptoms of schizophrenia. In *Integrating Ego Psychology and Object Relations Theory*, ed. L. Saretsky, G. D. Goldman, and D. S. Milman, pp. 270–285. Dubuque, Iowa: Kendall/Hunt.

Volkan, V. D., and Ast, G. (1992). *Eine Borderline Therapie*. Göttingen: Vandenhoeck & Ruprecht.

_____ (1994). *Spektrum des Narzißmus*. Göttingen: Vandenhoeck & Ruprecht.

Volkan, V.D., and Berent, S. (1976). Psychiatric aspects of surgical treatment for problems of sexual identification (transsexualism). In *Modern Perspectives in the Psychiatric Aspects of Surgery*, ed. J. G. Howells, pp. 447–467. New York: Brunner/Mazel.

Volkan, V. D., and Corney, R. T. (1968). Some considerations of satellite states and satellite dreams. *British Journal of Medical Psychology* 41:283–290.

Volkan, V. D., and Greer, W. F. (1995). True transsexualism. In

Sexual Deviations, ed. I. Rosen, 3rd ed. London: Oxford University Press.

Volkan, V. D. and Itzkowitz, N. (1980). *The Immortal Atatürk: A Psychobiography.* Chicago: University of Chicago Press.

Volkan, V. D., Julius, D. A., and Montville, J. V., eds. (1990). *The Psychodynamics of International Relationships, Vol. 1: Concepts and Theories.* Lexington, MA: Lexington Books.

Volkan, V. D., and Kavanaugh, J. G. (1978). The cat people. In *Between Fantasy and Reality: Transitional Phenomena and Objects*, ed. S. Grolnick and L. Barkin, pp. 291–303. New York: Quadrangle Press.

Volkan, V. D., and Luttrell, A. S. (1971). Aspects of the object relationships and developing skills of a "mechanical boy." *British Journal of Medical Psychology* 44:101–116.

Volkan, V. D., and Masri, A. (1989). The development of female transsexualism. *American Journal of Psychotherapy* 43:92–107.

Volkan, V. D., Montville, J. V., and Julius, D. A., eds. (1991). *The Psychodynamics of International Relationships, Vol. 2: Unofficial Diplomacy at Work.* Lexington, MA: Lexington Books.

Volkan, V. D., and Zintl, E. (1993). *Life after Loss: The Lessons of Grief.* New York: Scribner's Sons.

von Domarus, E. (1944). The specific laws of logic in schizophrenia. In *Language and Thought in Schizophrenia*, ed, J. S. Kasanin, pp. 104–114. Berkeley, CA: University of California Press.

Watson, C. G. (1990). Schizophrenia birth seasonality and age-incidence artifact. *Schizophrenia Bulletin* 16:5–10.

Weigert, E. (1938). The cult and mythology of the magna mater from the standpoint of psychoanalysis. *Psychiatry* 1:347–378.

Weinberger, D. R. (1987). Implications of normal brain development for the pathogenesis of schizophrenia. *Archives of General Psychiatry* 44:660–669.

Werner, H. (1948). *Comparative Psychology of Mental Development.* New York: International Universities Press.

Werner, H., and Kaplan, B. (1963). *Symbol Formation.* New York: John Wiley.

Winnicott, D. W. (1953). Transitional objects and transitional phenomena. *International Journal of Psycho-Analysis* 34:89–97.

_____ (1960). Ego distortion in terms of true and false. In *The Maturational Process and the Facilitating Environment*, pp. 140–152. New York: International Universities Press, 1965.

Wynne, L., Matthysse, S., and Cromwell, R. (1978). *The Nature of Schizophrenia: New Approaches to Research and Treatment.* New York: John Wiley.

Index

Mahler, M. S., 5, 22, 26, 27,
28, 30, 42, 67, 69, 98,
146, 148, 208
Malignant experience. *See*
Trauma
Marcus, E. R., 207
Masri, A., 100, 106
Matthysse, S., 69
Meltzoff, A., 43
Microidentifications,
schizophrenia treatment,
233–234
Mind, nature/nurture issue,
69–71
Mitchell, S. A., 27
Modell, A. H., 7, 25, 26, 41,
222, 284
Moore, B. E., 25
Moore, K., 43
Mother and Baby
Observations Congress
(Toulouse, France), x
Mother–child relationship
channel metaphor and, x,
2, 66–67
neonate negative response
in, 68
schizophrenia, 45
transsexuals and, 102–103,
105
Mueser, K. T., 10

Narcissistic personality,
object relations conflicts,
29
Nature/nurture issue, 63–71.
See also Genetic factors
generally, 63–69

mind and, theory, 69–71
Need-fear dilemma,
schizophrenia, object
relations and, 39–40
Niederland, W. G., 17, 85
Nonencapsulation, infantile
psychotic self, adult
consequences of, 89
Nonhuman objects,
schizophrenia, object
relations and, 40–41
Novick, J., 34

Object attachment, object
relations, schizophrenia
and, 26–28
Object relations
conflict, 2–3, 28–30
schizophrenia and, 25–44.
See also Schizophrenia:
object relations and
trauma and, x
O'Callaghan, E., 64
Oedipus complex
Attis case example,
120–121
schizophrenia and, 52, 53
Ogden, T. H., 237
Olinick, S. L., 169, 206, 214,
237
Organismic panic/distress, 5,
22, 53

Panic. *See* Terror
Pao, P.-N., 5, 7, 13, 18, 22,
23, 24, 37, 51, 52, 58,
59, 80, 222